Allen Leonard Brent is Senior Lecturer in
History, James Cook University of North
Queensland, Townsville, Australia. Publica-
tions: various articles on theological and
philosophical subjects.

CULTURAL EPISCOPACY
AND ECUMENISM

STUDIES IN CHRISTIAN MISSION

VOLUME 6

CULTURAL EPISCOPACY AND ECUMENISM

*Representative Ministry in Church History from the
Age of Ignatius of Antioch to the Reformation
With Special Reference to Contemporary Ecumenism*

BY

ALLEN BRENT

E.J. BRILL
LEIDEN • NEW YORK • KÖLN
1992

This series offers a forum for scholarship on the history of Christian missionary movements world-wide, the dynamics of Christian witness and service in new surrounds, the transition from movements to churches, and the areas of cultural initiative or involvement of Christian bodies and individuals, such as education, health, community development, press, literature and art. Special attention is given to local initiative and leadership and to Christian missions from the Third World. Studies in the theories and paradigms of mission in their respective contexts and contributions to missiology as a theological discipline is a second focus of the series. Occasionally volumes will contain selected papers from outstanding missiologists and proceedings of significant conferences related to the themes of the series.

Enquiries regarding the submission of works for publication in the series may be directed to Professor Marc R. Spindler, IIMO, University of Leiden, Rapenburg 61, 2311 GJ Leiden, The Netherlands.

The paper in this book meets the guidelines for permanence and durability of the Committee on Production Guidelines for Book Longevity of the Council on Library Resources.

Library of Congress Cataloging-in-Publication Data

Brent, Allen.
    Cultural episcopacy and ecumenism: representative ministry in church history from the Age of Ignatius of Antioch to the Reformation, with special reference to contemporary ecumenism / by Allen Brent.
        p.   cm.—(Studies in Christian mission, ISSN 0924-9389; v. 6)
    Includes bibliographical references and indexes.
    ISBN 9004094326
    1. Indigenous church administration—History of doctrines.
2. Church polity—History of doctrines.   3. Bishops—Appointment, call, and election—History.   4. Anglican Communion—Missions.
5. Episcopacy and Christian union.   6. Christianity and culture.
I. Title.   II. Series.
BV2082.I5B74   1992
262'.12'09—dc20   92-190
                                                                    CIP

ISSN   0924-9389
ISBN   90 04 09432 6

For our Right Revd. Father in God,
Arthur Malcom,
First Bishop of the Aboriginal Peoples of Australia

CONTENTS

CHAPTER FOUR

CHAPTER FIVE

CHAPTER SIX

INTRODUCTION AND ACKNOWLEDGEMENTS

This monograph originated in what might seem at first sight as a parochial, Australasian problem. It began as a paper on ethnic ministries in the Anglican Diocese of North Queensland, and the theological justification for setting up cultural bishops for the Aboriginal and Torres Straits Islander peoples of Australia. As, however, the concept proceeded to unravel, it soon became clear to me that my discussion was concerned with an issue of far wider moment. The question of a *cultural* rather than a *territorial* episcopate forms part of a set of quite wider considerations, involving the enculturalization of liturgy, concerning which there is great concern amongst black, catholic communities in North America. The question also strikes at the very roots of traditional forms of episcopal church government, emanating from undivided, late medieval Christendom, which defined a bishop's authority in terms of *territorial* jurisdiction. In other words, it soon became clear to me that any proposal to alter our concept of *episcope* in one area could not fail to have some quite universal implications, particularly for relations between episcopal and non-episcopal churches which divided from each other at the Reformation.

I regard theological method as arising from the ground rules of a creative and developing tradition of theological inquiry. In the witness of the Fathers and Councils in particular, and in the general history of the faith, life, and practice of Christian communities, theological inquiry finds the raw data for its analysis and reflection. Theology is a form of discourse which, while it should not be enslaved dogmatically by tradition, must nevertheless, if it is to be creative, enter into a critical though earnest and genuine dialogue with the tradition. Thus my study begins with Ignatius of Antioch and earlier strands in the development of the Christian ministry that preceded him in New Testament times. I then examine the first sea change in reflection on church Order and the Apostolic Tradition, to which Irenaeus and his contemporaries bear witness. The continuing developments, evidenced by the *Didascalia Apostolorum* and the age of Tertullian, Cyprian, and Augustine, are then traced. Finally we end with Gregory VII and what we shall argue to be the second sea change in theological reflection on church Order and the

Tradition, which has left a firm though not immediately obvious legacy for classical Anglicanism, as well as for the churches of the continental Reformation in Europe.

Although my study is rooted in patristics and historical analysis of the development of a theology of Order and Tradition, I enlist some sociological and epistemological insights into the development and distortions of that tradition, derived principally from Durkheim, the later Wittgenstein, and the cultural theories of Lévi-Strauss. As a result, I have, I believe, been able to introduce some valid parallels between the development of the three-fold Order in the second and third centuries, and the progress and problems of modern ecumenical dialogue. How successful I have been I look to my readers and reviewers to establish or to deny.

My work was completed, during my sabbatical year from James Cook University, at Cambridge University in the Divinity Department. I am particularly grateful to Professor Stead and the Patristics Seminar, and to Dr Ernst Bammel and Dr Caroline Bammel, for scholarly conversation and encouragement. I should also thank Professor Nicholas Lash and Professor Stephen Sykes, not only for their senior seminars, but also for their critical comments on the paper with which I initiated this project. I must also thank Mr. Gerald Bonner of Durham University, Dr John Coulson of Bristol University, and Professor Hugo Meynell of Calgary University, who also commented on the first draft of that paper. What I have made of their critiques, however inadequately, remain of course my own responsibility. My thanks also go to my College at Cambridge, Emmanuel, for their customary and generous hospitality during my sabbatical year.

Finally I would like to thank Mr J.G. Deahl and my publisher E.J. Brill, and particularly their Academic Readers, for persevering with me through the first draft of my earlier attempt, and for the magnificent, word processed format of the outcome.

Department of History,   Allen Brent
James Cook University of North Queensland,
April 1991.

ABBREVIATIONS

AHAW	Abhandlungen der Heidelberger Akademie der Wissenschaften, philosophisch–historische Klasse
ATANT	Abhandlungen zur Theologie des Alten und Neuen Testaments
ArFil	Archivio di Filosofia
AThR	Anglican Theological Review
Aug	Augustinianum
EThL	Ephemerides Theologicae Lovanienses
BR	Biblical Research
BRev	Biblical Review
BThAM	Bulletin de Théologie Ancienne et Médiévale
BZHT	Beiträge zur Historischen Theologie
ChH	Church History
CSLE	Corpus Scriptorum Latinorum Ecclesiasticorum
DR	Downside Review
EThL	Ephemerides Theologicae Lovanienses
FRLANT	Forschungen zur Religion und Literatur des Alten und Neuen Testaments
FZPhTh	Freiburger Zeitschrift für Philosophie und Theologie
HThR	Harvard Theological Review
HA	Handbuch der Altertumswissenschaft
JbAC	Jahrbuch für Antike und Christentum
JBL	Journal of Biblical Literature
JEH	Journal of Ecclesiastical History
JES	Journal of Ecumenical Studies
JSNT.S	Journal for the Study of the New Testament: Supplementary Series
JThS	Journal of Theological Studies
LeDiv	Lectio Divina
MGH	Monumenta Germaniae Historica. *Libelli de Lite.*
MSR	Mélanges de Science Religieuse
NA	Neutestamentliche Abhandlungen
NT	Novum Testamentum
NTS	New Testament Studies
RAC	Reallexikon für Antike und Christentum
RecSciRel	Recherches de Science Religieuse
RelStRev	Religious Studies Review
RevHPhR	Revue d'Histoire et de Philosophie Religieuses
RSR	Revue des Sciences Religieuses.
RivAC	Rivista Archeologia Cristiana
SecCent	The Second Century
SGK	Schriften der Königsberger Gelehrten Gesellschaft, Gewissenschaftliche Klasse.

SC	Sources Chrétiennes, (Paris: Les Éditions du Cerf 1942-)
SciEsprit	Science et Esprit
SPAW	Sitzungsberichte der Preussischen Akademie der Wissenschaften: philosophisch- historische Klasse
StTh	Studia Theologica
StudPatr	Studia Patristica
ThG	Theologie und Glaube
ThQ	Theologische Quartalschrift
ThR	Theologische Rundschau
ThS	Theological Studies
ThZ	Theologische Zeitschrift
Theoph	Beiträge zur Religions- und Kirchengeschichte des Altertums
TU	Texte und Untersuchungen zur Geschichte der altchristlichen Literatur
TWNT	Theologisches Wörterbuch zum Neuen Testament
VC	Verbum Caro
VCh	Vigiliae Christianae
WMANT	Wissenschaftliche Monographien zum Alten und Neuen Testament
WUNT	Wissenschaftliche Untersuchungen zum Neuen Testament
ZKG	Zeitschrift für Kirchengeschichte
ZKTh	Zeitschrift für Katholische Theologie
ZNW	Zeitschrift für die neutestamentliche Wissenschaft und die Kunde der älteren Kirche
ZRGG	Zeitschrift für Religion- und Geistesgeschichte
ZThK	Zeitschrift für Theologie und Kirche.

CHAPTER ONE

CHALLENGES TO TERRITORIAL JURISDICTION

Historical challenges to traditional episcopacy

The Anglican, Roman Catholic, and Orthodox communions function predominantly in terms of the traditional concept of episcopacy which achieved its final articulation in the eleventh century, in the reforms of Gregory VII. That concept of episcopacy presupposes basically that the office of the bishop is defined in terms of jurisdiction over all souls living in a definable territorial domain called a diocese, for whose care he takes measures either directly himself, or through presbyteral delegates who are normally parish priests. Such parishes too are geographically defined and financially self sufficient, and to their individual priests the bishop gives his authority by due canonical process. The justification of the bishop's office is, therefore, that of a grant of geographical jurisdiction over the cure of souls, and the right to maintain the apostolic tradition amongst those over whom he has received that jurisdiction. We shall argue that such a theory of territorial, episcopal jurisdiction mirrored the nascent secular and political concept of sovereignty and the nation state in the late medieval period. (Chapter 5) This monograph is written in the conviction that this traditional understanding and justification of episcopacy, the final flower of the late medieval understanding of Order, whether in its "catholic" ("Roman" or "Orthodox") or "reformed" ("Anglican") form, is being challenged by three contemporary developments.

The first development is the clearly expressed desire of ethnic groups such as the Aboriginal and Torres Straits Islander peoples of Australia, the Maoris of New Zealand, North American Indians, and groups in the African sub-continent, for bishops who will reflect their own cultural and historical traditions, regardless of the canonical and territorial jurisdiction of the particular See in which they are living. It is this desire that the then

Primate of the Anglican Church of Australia, Archbishop John
Grindrod, sought to realize in the Province of Queensland, as we
shall mention in Chapter 6. As such, the indigenous peoples of
Australia are following in the steps of their Maori neighbours
who have achieved their own cultural episcopate in territories co-
extensive with the Anglican, New Zealand dioceses. Their cultural bishop, the bishop of Aotearoa, bears the Maori name for
all New Zealand.

The second is the desire of non-episcopal, mainline churches to
seek ecumenical re-union with episcopal churches on the basis of
the consecrations as bishops of representative ministers within
their communions, as the guarantors that what they would regard
as certain, essential features of their traditional faith and worship
will be both safeguarded and accepted by those with whom they
are re-uniting. The Methodist Church in England, for example,
has frequently affirmed its desire "to receive episcopacy into its
system" in both the ill-fated re-union scheme in 1970, and the
equally unsuccessful covenant proposals of 1980. Moreover, at
the Lambeth Conference of 1988, the (Anglican) Church of
Wales was most exercised in its submission to the Conference's
ecumenical section regarding its proper relationship with the proposed Covenant between various churches in Wales.

The third challenge comes from what Vatican II had to say
about the Church as the extension of the incarnation, and the demand for "enculturalization" being felt in the Roman Catholic
communion, particularly in view of the failure of the Western
mission to make significant impressions on the cultures of Asia
and the far East. Indeed, "enculturalization" has become a live issue in North America where the demand for a cultural liturgy, in
an extreme form, has been met by the suspension of a priest.
This question, too, was prominent at the 1988 Lambeth
Conference as the agenda reading for that Conference shows.
The question that ever becomes more demanding regarding the
"indigenization" of liturgy, we shall argue, cannot fail to be
asked too of Order that both celebrates and is celebrated by that
liturgy. A further question which will inevitably follow is: what
has Rome's experience with her own, Eastern Rite patriarchs to
say on this question?

All three developments, we shall argue, are challenges for the
traditional episcopal communions to take a fresh look at episco-

pacy in terms of the bishop as the representative, in a sacramental sense, of a cultural community with a historical tradition in process of redemption. All three developments are interrelated in the demands they are making for a new theological solution common to all three. Accordingly we shall be seeking such representational strands in the biblical and patristic concepts of church Order in order to lay the proper, theological foundations for justifying such a doctrinal development. We shall discover that the territorial and jurisdictional concept, at all events in its final form, is late medieval and obscures important theological and sacramental features of Order in the earlier Fathers, notably with Ignatius of Antioch in contrast with the later *Didascalia Apostolorum*. (Chapters 3 & 4) In such an investigation, moreover, we shall find that both our Western episcopal traditions, whether Roman or Anglican, must inevitably face the conflict between the classical, post Irenaean and Gregorian jurisdictional and geographical paradigms of *episcope,* and certain practical demands leading to provisions which square ill with those paradigms. (Chapter 5) It will now be my intention to outline in this chapter, in more detail, the character of this conflict of paradigms and the new, practical situations represented by our three challenges. We shall take the theoretical problem of the Anglican communion first, not simply because the proposed cultural concept of episcopacy is more self-consciously in process of realization in that communion, in the persons of bishops actually consecrated apparently with such a role, however poorly conceived in theological terms that role may be. Rather we take the Anglican model first because, in a paradoxical way which has become all too generally familiar in such matters, Anglican approaches to episcopacy are far more intractably tied to the later medieval and Gregorian model than Rome's appear in fact to be.

1. *Cultural episcope: the Anglican dilemma*

The development of a theology of non-territorial, cultural *episcope*, for which I will be contending in this monograph, originated initially as a response to the practical demands for indigenous Australasian bishops. But I believe it is profoundly related to the means to ecumenical reunion too. Both the ecumenical situation and the indigenous cultural demands must inevitably

challenge the classical, Anglican *modus vivendi* on the nature of
that church's commitment to the principle of episcopacy. That
modus vivendi, I suppose, could be expressed as follows.
Though many Anglicans may regard the episcopate as the *esse* of
the church with the result that a church that lacks and episcopate,
no less than a presbyterate or diaconate, is in some sense sacramentally defective, it is not necessary for all Anglicans to so believe. It is possible for an Anglican to reject this stronger claim
that the episcopate as the source of Order is, to use a very traditional way of expressing matter, the *esse* (the "very being") of
the church, and to substitute for it a far weaker one, namely that
episcopacy is rather the *bene esse* (the "well-being") of the
church. Though a priest could ordain another priest or even, so a
more extravagant version of this claim would suggest, a group
of laymen ordain one of their number, nevertheless it is for the
church's well-being (*bene esse*) that one presbyter amongst
many is authorized to ordain on behalf of all. The church's unity
is more likely to be preserved from schism and heresy by having
a bishop providing the centrifugal force derived from canon law
in order to perform the ministry of ordination, or so the argument runs.

We shall be arguing that such a jurisdictional view of *episcope*,
the subject of so many a seminarian's examination papers, was
characteristic of the distortions of the late medieval period whose
legacy left its debilitating impress on the post-Reformation controversies. Historical precedents supposedly supportive of this
view were hotly disputed in the late-nineteenth and early twentieth century by Anglican historians representing our divergent
traditions on episcopacy still vigorously debated at that time. For
example, Whitgift, archbishop of Canterbury in Elizabeth's de-
clining years, and bishop Overall in the next reign, appear ready
to distinguish between men like Travers who had deliberately
gone overseas to receive presbyteral ordination, and men like
deLaune who had been originally overseas where they had no
opportunity to be episcopally ordained.[1] Why, therefore, it may
be asked, should a perfectly sensible, English compromise now

---

[1] B. Hamilton Thompson, "The Post Reformation Episcopate in
England," in K.E. Kirk (ed.) *The Apostolic Ministry*, (London: Hodder and
Stoughton 1946), p. 387-432.

be called into question by claiming more strongly that *episcope* is the essential form of Church government? After all, the weaker claim allows that greater comprehensiveness, so beloved by Anglicans that though episcopacy is not essential, it nevertheless constitutes the best for any church. And surely in such "comprehensiveness" is the best ecumenical basis for the re-union of episcopal with non-episcopal communions?

The answer to this question is that the essential meaning of episcopacy on what may be described as the "comprehensivist" view must be a purely jurisdictional meaning in a territorial sense. A bishop's prerogative in ordaining on this view does not arise from the sacramental nature of his office but simply from the need to have things done decently and in order, to preserve the church from schism to which the church would be prone were every presbyter or every group of lay people to possess the authority to ordain sacred ministers. Thus such a view enables episcopacy to be defined purely in terms of jurisdiction given by canon law to a bishop over those who live within a given territorial boundary. Such a view may have served well those Erastian elements in the church of the Elizabethan, and Jacobean periods along with the Victorian church, however much the Carolines may have assailed its inadequacy given their sacral-political philosophy, and the Tractarians protested the indispensability of the apostolic succession. Such a view had certainly served well the medieval Papacy from Gregory VII onwards, as we shall argue latter in this work. (Chapter 5) But, in the mid to late twentieth century, the cultural and ecumenical demands that I have mentioned above are revealing the dated and constricting character of such a view of episcopacy.

Yet the jurisdictional view as central to the bishop's office survives in the twentieth century as may be seen represented recently by Halliburton and the 1988 pre-Lambeth conference literature and subsequent Conference statements. Halliburton, who was a consultant to the Anglican-Catholic International Commission (*ARCIC*) no less, has, in his interesting, recent study of episcopacy, a chapter on bishops and non-episcopal churches.[2] Here he laments that "one of the fundamental weak-

---

[2] Ibid. p.53.

nesses in all unity schemes since the end of the Second World War has been an evident disjunction between the task of reconciling *churches* and reconciling *ministers*."[3]

Halliburton correctly sees that the bishop's office is meaningless without the church by and to which he was ordained, and of which "he is also in a real sense the embodiment...In himself he represents its beliefs and convictions and is its foremost representative in the relation of that church to other churches."[4] But rather than seeing how the office of a free-church minister, consecrated as bishop as a representative of a Christian, cultural or sub-cultural tradition (terms that we shall be defining in Chapter 2), can be a dynamic and integrative force for mutual recognition and inter communion, as the result of his acceptance by other bishops in virtue of his representing that tradition, Halliburton now ignores the insights of his previous position and treats the ecumenical reconciliation of ministers as if it were purely a jurisdictional problem. In his own words:

> Whatever happens, each diocese should have no more than one bishop... But where Free Church superintendents or presiding ministers serve an area which either overlaps with or is coterminous with an existing diocese, three possibilities arise. Either they should be made bishop of that diocese, and the existing Anglican bishop translated to another See, or they themselves should be moved to another diocese. Or for a time, two chief pastors should remain responsible for the one diocese, one of them acting as coadjutor with right of succession should the other move, resign, or die.[5]

Thus it is not, after all, the newly consecrated, Free Church bishop who as such is to be allowed to remain the embodiment of his community, and his recognition and acceptance the sign of the recognition and acceptance his community. No sooner has the sign been acknowledged but it must be eradicated. He is to be moved to another diocese so that the embodiment and sign of another tradition may preside in his stead. Or his character as a sign is to be ignored and he is to preside over two separate traditions, as though ecclesial unity can be externally imposed by a

---

[3] J. Halliburton, *The Authority of a Bishop*, (London: S.P.C.K. 1987), p. 52-62.

[4] Ibid. p. 54.

[5] Ibid. p. 55.

purely jurisdictional entity, and his character as a distinctive sign of his community was irrelevant. We shall examine in Chapter 3 the Ignatian insights on the bishop as the sign of a redeemed community.

The unity of the church is, of course, vital, but clearly we are being confronted with two kinds of unity. The first is a unity imposed externally by means of the imposition of an external ecclesiastical head. The second is an internal unity born of the mutual recognition by the two representative ministers of each other, and thereby of the community that each incorporates as a sign. We shall be contrasting the two kinds of unity in Chapters 2 and 5 of this monograph in terms of what the sociologist Durkheim described as "mechanical solidarity" in contrast with "organic solidarity." In such a unity in the latter sense Halliburton's lamented disjunction between reconciliation of churches and recognition of ministers will be, we shall argue, dissolved. And, furthermore, their Orders will have meaning as remaining Orders of the church to which and by which they were ordained.

If we turn, in concluding this section, to the 1988 Lambeth Conference, at first sight we might think that we would be exploring ground in which the cultural dimension to the ordained ministry would be acknowledged and developed. The theme of the enculturalization of the Gospel was well explored in the pre-conference literature.[6] Subsequently, Lambeth 88, in the section on Dogmatic and Pastoral Concerns, concluded under the heading of "Christ and Culture":

> It is right and proper that the one faith and *discipline* of the Church should be "incarnate" in a number of cultural forms; as was said earlier, the Gospel of Jesus does not come to people in the abstract but to specific men and women... But if we imagine that we have discovered a way of being Christian quite independent of culture, or if we fail to notice that what we think is distinctively Christian is

---

[6] A Report of the Inter-Anglican Theological and Doctrinal Commission, *For the Sake of the Kingdom*, (London: Anglican Consultative Council 1986).

actually cultural, we are liable to put serious obstacles in the way of preaching the Gospel.[7]

If both *discipline* (my italics) as well as faith were to be incarnated in a culture, then one would have thought that some attention would then have been given to the question of the ordained ministry in such a cultural context.

When however the Conference came to consider the report of its section on *Ecumenical Relations,* the perspective changed. Faced with the development of cultural episcopates in different parts of the world, in particular those of Australasia, documentation for which were before *Ecumenical Relations*, the Conference affirmed on the one hand:

> In recent times.. movements of population have lead to people of different races, cultures, and languages settling down side by side.... In these circumstances the Church has to find ways of ministering to people in a particular situation or in their diversity, while retaining the fundamental unity of the whole people of God in that place. Cultural, ethnic or non-territorial bishoprics are being developed in Australia, New Zealand, Southern Africa, and the United States of America in order to try to achieve this. In these experiments bishops are appointed to look after particular cultural, ethnic or racial groupings, and they work across the boundaries of existing territorial bishops.
>
> (Section 41)

On the other hand, the Conference was to say:

> Within his diocese, the bishop is the focus of unity. The ideal for Anglicans as for many other Christians is that there should be one bishop in each place... There has, traditionally, been a dislike of "parallel" or "overlapping" episcopates.
>
> (Section 40)

In support of this continuing Anglican position, the assembled bishops mentioned that the Lambeth Conference in 1908 had affirmed "the principle of one bishop for one area... as the best means of securing the unity of all races and nations in the Holy

---

[7] The Lambeth Conference 1988, *The Truth Shall Make You Free. The Reports, Resolutions, & Pastoral Letters from the Bishops*, (London: Anglican Consultative Council 1988), Dogmatic and Pastoral Concerns, sects 23 and 24.

Catholic Church." There was unfortunately no consideration of the critical question here as to why the "one area" or "diocese" has to be defined geographically and territorially. Though debate within the confines of a universe of discourse set by pre- First World War imperialism may have used the term "race" rather than "culture," even in that situation "race" was not co-terminus with "nation." Some nations consisted of a number of what were called "races" in tension, and it could hardly be maintained that every such national grouping was the ideal recipe for "the unity of all nations and races."

It was at this juncture in the Report of Lambeth 88 that the words "heretical or schismatic" were used, as far as I am able to ascertain, solely and uniquely in all the Report, including surprisingly that on the ordination of women. It could therefore be argued that, in the following passage, Lambeth's emphasis on one territorial bishop had been in the interests of maintaining the apostolic faith against disintegration with which a cultural episcopate might otherwise threaten that faith. As *Ecumenical Relations* expresses the point:

(a) The Gospel and the Church may be radically distorted by adaptation to a particular culture, so that the Church in that place becomes heretical or schismatic, and no longer witnesses to the truth of the reconciliation of all people to God in Christ. (b) Though faithful to Scripture and tradition, the Church in different places may take on such different forms that it is hard to find and express a substantial unity with the Churches in other cultural contexts; and so it is unable to witness effectively to the unity of all people in the world.

Regarding objection (a), the further question as to how one can determine what is heresy and indeed what is schism is never answered, so vital in a communion which is now facing what is described as "impaired communion" over the ordination of women, in which some bishops will not recognize the acts or putative acts of ordination of others. (*Missions and Ministry* 132-150; *Resolutions* 1) The only response that the Report can make is that meetings of bishops in dialogues in which they "take their dioceses with them" will foster mutual recognition of life and doctrine, and mutual recognition of errors, but that is to beg the question as to how territorial rather than cultural *episcope* will better realize that end.

Within a communion with a concept of dispersed authority, as the Orthodox Ecumenical Patriarch was thoroughly justified in pointing out to the Conference, no one diocese, province, or group of provinces can act alone in determining the common faith. Within such an authority structure, the only method of determining the common faith is one of "debating the issues for as long as it is necessary to reach unanimity or at least common consensus."[8] Our present concept of jurisdictional and territorial *episcope* is hardly serving the Anglican communion well, as exhibited by the crisis in authority over the ordination of women, in terms of witnessing "effectively to the unity of all people in the world." My argument will be that a concept of cultural *episcope* will enable the real conflicts in faith and life of whole communities to be brought out and given adequate representation in inter-diocesan dialogue. Territorial *episcope* merely leads to their jurisdictional suppression. We shall examine this process in the context of Durkheim's sociology of "organic" and "mechanical" principles of social solidarity. (Chapters 5 & 6) Certainly objection (b) mirrors, as I have already argued, our contemporary ecumenical situation, whose divisions our concept of territorial *episcope* exacerbates rather than resolves, as we saw was Halliburton's lament.

Thus Lambeth 88 acknowledged only grudgingly the principle of cultural *episcope* in restricted pastoral areas, whist insisting on one geographical and jurisdictional bishop per area in accordance with Halliburton's norm. Clearly the ghost of what we shall argue (Chapter 5) to be late-medieval territorial, episcopacy still haunts the Anglican mind and threatens to defeat other, deeper insights that might otherwise replace it.

---

[8] Response by the Most Revd. John D. Zizioulas, Metropolitan of Pergamos, (Ecumenical Patriarch) ibid. APPENDIX 32, p. 285. Cf. G. White, Collegiality and Conciliarity in the Anglican Communion, in S.W. Sykes (Ed.), *Authority in the Anglican Communion*, (Toronto: Anglican Book Centre 1987), p. 202- 220, where both Ratzinger's and Meyendorff's challenges to the loss of centralized organs of church government are discussed. See also S.W. Sykes, *The Integrity of Anglicanism*, (London: Mowbrays 1978) where he argues to the contrary that "a dispersed authority implies recognition of the probability of conflict."

But let us turn to Rome's historical experience and see whether this will take us further in our quest for a new concept of cultural episcopacy. If we now turn to Rome's mainly post-Gregorian experience, we shall find some interesting and important exceptions to the territorial view which, we shall argue, show that territorial jurisdiction cannot be integral to a catholic concept of episcopacy. In addition, such a consideration will give some important clues as to how an articulated concept of cultural episcopacy might be developed from patristic and New Testament sources, but rooted in concretely existing, ecclesial structures outside of what otherwise might be thought to be the historical vacuum of the early patristic period centred on Ignatius of Antioch. (Chapters 3 & 4)

2. *Cultural episcope and catholic churches of the Eastern Rite*

In one sense current Roman catholic practice in certain confined areas represent a *de-facto* acceptance of some concept of *episcope* as essentially linked with culture. If we look at the forms of episcopacy that have emerged in the Roman communion, we find that the late medieval requirements of territorial jurisdiction have never always been satisfied. Moreover, the failure to satisfy such requirements have quite a long history. There are two basic exceptions to the territorial rule which Rome recognizes.

Firstly, there are some 2000 titular Sees of, as they were called before Leo XIII's decree in 1882, *episcopi in partibus infidelium*.[9] The titles of such Sees are found in various places in Asia Minor, North Africa, the Balkans, and Greece. Their origin appears to have been in the eighth and ninth centuries when bishops displaced from their Sees by the Islamic invasions appeared at the papal court in Rome. In order to ordain (canonically) or confirm they must have authorization from a diocesan or be his suffragan or auxiliary. Consequently they are found at Rome, manning as officials principally the papal administration, but acting liturgically for the pope as bishop of Rome, as occasion demands. That there is some essential connection

---

[9] J.A. Hardon (Ed.), *A New Catholic Dictionary*, (New York: Doubleday 1980), article "Titular Sees."

between such bishops and the titles of the Sees that they possess is a canonical fiction, though that they have such titles betrays the medieval unease about the notion of a bishop without territorial jurisdiction. On the other hand, such bishops hardly have any cultural element in their episcopal office.

However, the second example is, for our purpose, more telling. There are a number of so-called "uniate" patriarchs, although the title is to be avoided as considered offensive by those patriarchs themselves, amongst Christians of the eastern Mediterranean who are in communion with Rome but whose territories overlap with each other. The Maronite church in Syria, separating from eastern Orthodoxy in A.D. 680 and united with Rome at the time of the crusades (A.D. 1182 and 1216), was allowed to retain its own patriarch of Antioch as head of its national, Syrian rite. Latin using western congregations had their own western, catholic bishop who was destined to be expelled with the crusaders. With the Maronites, were joined the Melchites at the great schism in A.D. 1054 as those desiring to continue in union with the pope, and whose patriarch, likewise, has jurisdiction over "Antioch and all the East," with which in his case are also joined Alexandria and Jerusalem.[10] One important symbol of such a patriarchal principle today, in the form of the beautiful church of Santa Maria in Cosmedine in Rome, stands on the Lungotevere Aventino. The basilica is a composite monument, transformed through the centuries, but still housing the Greek-speaking rites which began there in the eighth century, as the bequest of Pope Hadrian I to the orientals who fled to Rome from persecution in the eastern empire.

Rome, therefore, does recognize several catholic, eastern, patriarchs, occupying the same geographical Sees as their western counterparts, but distinguished by different linguistically and culturally based rites. Moreover, when the Ukraine fell to the Lithuanians in the fourteenth century, the Russians (Ukrainians) retained at first cultural leadership and it was the Lithuanians that joined the Orthodox Church. But when the rulers of the nation thus formed needed a dynastic alliance with Poland, Grand Duke Jagiello was required to convert to Rome (A.D. 1386), but re-

---

[10] C.G. Herbermann et. al. (Ed.), *The Catholic Encyclopaedia*, (New York: Encyclopedia Press 1912), article "Bishops," sect. 15.

CHALLENGES TO TERRITORIAL JURISDICTION 13

frained from forcible conversion of his predominantly Orthodox people to Catholicism.

However, in A.D. 1569 a closer union was formed in terms of which Kiev and part of the Ukraine was handed over to Poland. The Jesuits were then invited in so as to combat both Orthodoxy and Calvinism. But in faith and language the Ukrainians and Lithuanians remained firm. The offer was now made to allow the Orthodox to retain the liturgy and faith of their culture intact if their bishops were to submit to the pope, to which the majority of their bishops agreed, to the chagrin of the majority of clergy and laity, at the Orthodox Council of Brest Litovsk.[11] Thus in the Ukrainian church of the Eastern Rite we see yet another example of Rome recognizing in practice that territorial jurisdiction is not of the *esse* of episcopal Order, but rather the representation of the cultural and historical expression of the liturgical life of the local gathered church. There is here a practical acknowledgement of a far older notion, namely that the bishop presides over distinct liturgy, so that a different liturgy requires a different oversight regardless of territorial jurisdiction. For Clement of Rome, after all, to be "expelled from office" was the equivalent of being expelled from one's liturgical function (ἀποβάλλεσθαι τῆς λειτουργίας). (*Cor.* 44, 1, 4, 6)

The force of this objection is not furthermore diminished by the fact that, as a result of events not of Rome's choosing, the Eastern Rite churches of the Ukraine (in 1946) and of Rumania (in 1948) were separated forcibly from Rome, and joined by their communist government to the Russian and Rumanian Orthodox churches.[12] Historically nearly every one of the Orthodox churches, with their patriarchs owning allegiance to the Byzantine rite, has a Greek catholic equivalent owning a version of that rite. The catholic Byzantine rite claims the allegiance of a diverse collection of Greek speaking peoples including Bulgarians, Russians, Serbians, Ruthenians, Africans (Ugandans) and Italo-Albanians in Southern Italy. In some areas

---

[11] N. Zernov, *Eastern Christendom: A Study in the Origin and Development of the Eastern Orthodox Church*, (London: Weidenfeld and Nicolson 1963), p. 146-148.

[12] L. Cross (Ed.), *The Oxford Dictionary of the Christian Church*, (London: Oxford University Press 1957), article "Uniate Churches."

adherents of the Latin rite are directly under the Apostolic See with no local bishop, but in, for example, Yugoslavia and Hungary there are two distinct groups subject to Latin bishops. Moreover, the Byzantine rite jurisdiction clearly overlaps with Latin jurisdiction in the same geographical areas in south Italy. In the United States and Canada, despite the Ukrainian suppression already mentioned, there are seven Ukrainian eparchies (dioceses) and two Ruthenian, originally formed through emigration from persecution, and now in consequence territorially co-terminus with Latin dioceses.[13]

There remain today four further eastern rites, in addition to the Byzantine maintained by churches in communion with Rome, who have achieved that status at different times over the past one thousand years: the Alexandrian of the Copts (1741) and Ethiopians (1839), the Antiochene of the West Syrians (1930), the Maronites (1182) and the Malanarese (1900), the Chaldean of the Syro-Chaldeans (1551) and Malabarites (1599), and the Armenian (1198-1291 and 1741). There are six patriarchs with episcopal jurisdiction (eparchies) over these rites, namely the Coptic, Syrian, Maronite, Melchite, and Armenian patriarchs. Obvious ritual differences with the Latin rite are baptism by total immersion and, before Vatican II, communion in both kinds, as well as the marriage of the clergy in the sphere of ecclesiastical discipline.[14]

It is of course possible to attack these examples in the particular political context from which they arose on the grounds that they were cunning manipulations of the Christian congregations concerned into submission to Rome. Certainly in the Ukrainian example, the Eastern Rite clergy did not historically achieve their promised seats in the Senate by which Poland was governed as did their Latin-rite counterparts.[15] Moreover, before the mid-twentieth century, Rome undoubtedly "looked on the Christian East as inferior and degraded, to be redeemed only by absorp-

---

[13] F.W.M. Abbott, *The Documents of Vatican II*, (Baltimore: The American Press 1966), p. 375 note 8.
[14] K. Rahner (Ed.), *Encyclopedia of Theology*, (London: Burns Oates 1975), article "Eastern Churches".
[15] Zernov op. cit. p. 149.

tion."[16] But the acceptance of such bishops into Rome's communion does imply that there can be no absolute theological bar to cultural bishops on the part of Rome on the grounds of the absence of territorial jurisdiction alone. If there can be only "one bishop one diocese," two or more bishops in a diocese implies that the "one diocese" is not necessarily definable geographically. A "diocese" can therefore refer to a culture over which there is ἐπισκοπή. Territorial jurisdiction cannot in that case be of the *esse* of the Order of the church.

Furthermore, the principle of jurisdiction in terms of rite cutting across the principle of territorial jurisdiction is not merely a survival from the missionary compromises of the past. It is a principle that the Fathers of Vatican II positively affirmed in terms of a proper catholic diversity. A quite separate decree (*Orientalium Ecclesiarum*) was issued on the Eastern Churches in communion with Rome, as distinct from the Eastern Orthodox Communion dealt with in the decree on ecumenism (*Unitatis Redintegratio*). *Orientalium Ecclesiarum* "holds in high esteem... their liturgical rites, ecclesiastical traditions, and Christian way of life" (art.1). The "Mystical Body of Christ is made up of the faithful... who, combining together into various groups held together by a hierarchy, form *separate churches or rites*." Thus it appears at this point that it is "rite" that defines the church as a diocese and not a geographical area. Unity is not harmed by such diversity but rather "it is the mind of the Catholic Church that *each individual Church or rite* retain its traditions entire whilst adjusting its way of life to the needs of time and place." (art. 2 my italics)

As if in sorrow for past wrongs, the decree goes on to affirm the absolute equality and dignity of such rites with the Latin (art.3). Thus the extension in North America of Eastern patriarchies and rites is commended:

> Therefore, attention should everywhere be given to the preservation and growth of each individual Church. For this purpose, parishes and a special hierarchy should be established for each where the spiritual good of the faithful so demands. The Ordinaries of the various individual Churches which have jurisdiction in the same

---

[16] Ibid. p. 171.

territory should, by taking common counsel at regular meetings, strive to promote unity of action.

(art. 4)

Thus multiple bishops as well as multiple churches within the same geographical territories are thus acknowledged, with their *episcope* exercised over "rite" and not territory. The authority of patriarchs and their bishops goes beyond the territories which they occupy alongside others for: "Whenever an Ordinary of any rite is appointed outside the territorial bounds of its patriarch, he remains attached to the hierarchy of the patriarch of that rite in accordance with the norm of law." (art. 7) It is, furthermore, to be emphasized that we are not here concerned with principles derived purely from *ad hoc* concessions and arrangement special cases. What has been said of patriarchs "applies equally well to major archbishops who preside over the whole of some individual Church or rite." (art. 10)

Nor are the general ecumenical implications of such arrangements ignored or glossed over by restricting the generality of the principles only to the specific "Eastern" situation and history. The decree continues:

> Finally each and every Catholic, *as also the baptized member of every non-Catholic Church or community who enters into the fulness of Catholic communion*, should every where retain his proper rite, cherish it, and observe it to the best of his ability.
>
> (art. 4, my italics)

At first sight the words that I have italicized in the preceding quotation might appear to license the ecumenical dimension to cultural *episcope* to which I am drawing attention. Surely this implies that whole Christian communities, even those created by the Reformation, could by means of a consecration of a patriarch, achieve union with Rome whilst retaining their own rites? And by extension could not the same principle apply to North American, African, Far-Eastern and Australasian indigenous cultures?

Before, however, we assume prematurely that the concept of cultural episcopacy for which we are seeking already exists in the Roman communion in a fully-fledged form, we must sound a cautionary note. It may be thought first of all that the decrees of Vatican II use "rite" almost in a cultural sense in so far as this term is used in a more general sense than simply "liturgical practice." "Rite," like other terms, must be read in terms of the decree *Unitatis Redintegratio* which, regarding Eastern Orthodoxy itself:

> ..solemnly declares that the Churches of the East, whilst keeping in mind the necessary unity of the whole Church, have power to govern themselves according to their own disciplines, since these are better suited to the temperament of their faithful and better adapted to foster the good of souls.
>
> (art. 16)

"Temperament of their faithful," as expressed by their rites, clearly goes beyond ritual minutiae to cultural characteristics, which are further praised in the case of the Eastern Rite congregations who are "already living in full communion with their brethren who follow the tradition of the West." Their "rites" embody "an entire heritage of spirituality and liturgy, of discipline and theology in their various traditions" which belong to "the full catholic and apostolic character of the Church." (art. 17),

But the cautionary note that we must now sound is that it is unclear whether Vatican II is emphasizing culture as the real justification for difference, as mention of "temperament" suggests, or whether this is simply an after thought in this context and that the emphasis is really on the apostolic foundation of a community's tradition. *Orientalium Ecclesiarum* implies the latter at many points. Does the diversity of permitted rites and patriarchs really derive its validity from the fact that "they are bright with the tradition handed down from the apostles to the Fathers, and which forms part of the divinely revealed and undivided heritage of the universal Church" (art.1)? Are each of the Eastern Rite churches to "do so according to its proper and individual procedures, *inasmuch as practices sanctioned by a noble antiquity harmonize better with the customs of the faithful.*" (art. 5, my italics)? Is in other words the right to a separate rite conditional upon the apostolic foundation traditionally attributed to the five patriarchies of Eastern Christendom, Jerusalem (James), Constantinople and Ephesus (John)), Alexandria (Mark), Antioch and Rome (Peter), rather than any intrinsic value in their cultural expression of the gospel or the sacraments? Certainly the former is emphasized in *Unitatis Redintegratio* where of the

Eastern Churches it is said that "among them the Patriarchal Churches hold first place; and of these, many glory in taking their origins from the apostles themselves." (art.1) To them before the Great Schism is attributed the Ecumenical Councils defining the Trinity and Mary's role in the Incarnation. (art.1) Is such an historical apostolicity the essential pre-condition of the unalterability of their liturgical life "except by an appropriate organic development" (*Orientalium Ecclesiarum* art. 6)? Certainly *Lumen Gentium* implies such to be the case in the following passage:

> By Divine Providence it has come about that various churches established in diverse places by the apostles and their successors have in the course of time coalesced into several groups, organically united, which, preserving the unity of faith and the unique divine constitution of the universal Church, enjoy their own discipline, their own liturgical usage, and their own theological and spiritual heritage. Some of these churches, notably the ancient patriarchal churches, are parent-stocks of the faith, so to speak, have begotten others as daughter churches.
>
> (art. 23)

It is clearly not possible, therefore, without further argument and discussion, to use the examples of the Eastern Rite churches as models for cultural episcopates without territorial boundaries in new, former missionary situations of the Western, Roman (or for that matter Anglican) Church. Such former missionary situations clearly cannot claim a traditional apostolic origin separate from the See of Peter, but derive their validity from the existing Eastern or Western tradition, if validity is to be conceived in terms of apostolic foundation in this way.

The question therefore clearly remains open in the documents of Vatican II whether churches such as these can have the episcopal or patriarchal power autonomously to redefine that received liturgical and theological tradition in terms of their own cultures. Nor will we be able in consequence, without further clarification and development of certain key concepts, be able to use the decrees of Vatican II to license a model of ecumenical reconciliation in terms of a diversity of ecclesiastical cultures as being validly analogous with a diversity of patriarchal rites. As we shall see, part of the obstacle is, on the one hand, the failure of Vatican II to provide any clear, satisfactory definition of "culture," for on this hinges the right of a Christian community to diverge from its apostolic "parent-stock" whilst, as it were, preserving a true, filial image. On the other hand, Vatican II also failed to spell out what it means to bear the apostolic tradition or be of apostolic foundation, given the weight of historical and theological evidence that both these concepts have undergone post-Irenaean distortions, as we shall be arguing in detail later in this monograph (Chapters 3 & 4). Both these concepts stand in need of clarification, and, in the case of "apostolicity," careful reformulation, given the problematic nature of the development of the apostolic tradition and ministry in the first two centuries.

Regarding a definition of culture, the relevant passages in *Gaudium et Spes* which applaud human culture and commend the Church's mission in terms of entering "into communion with various cultural modes" are vitiated by a failure to distinguish "culture" in an anthropological and "culture" in an educative sense (arts. 53-62). "Culture" is here understood wholly in terms of "refined taste" or "education." We shall return to more detailed consideration of this problem in Chapter 2. We have seen, therefore, how the traditional Anglican model of episcopacy must fail to be able to come to terms either with the enculturalization implied by the demands for cultural episcopates in the Australasian context. We have implied, though we must argue further for such a position, that similarly discussion for ecumenical reconciliation founder on inadequacies of the Anglican model that are closely related to the the changes implied by a cultural model for *episcope*. We have examined with interest the insights of the Roman Eastern Rite model and what these might imply. But we have noted the problem of drawing in detail such implications without an adequate concept of culture, and a proper theological delineation of the ecclesiology of Order in the light of such a concept and in relation to questions of historical continuity with Christian tradition. It will be our task to outline in this book a tentative delineation of the concept of cultural episcopacy in such terms as these. But let us briefly sketch at this point an outline of the case that this monograph will seek to make out in more detailed substance in subsequent chapters, as we proceed.

3. *The case for cultural episcope*

The preceding sections will have made clear that my search for a concept of cultural episcopacy has radical implications for our contemporary understanding of ecclesial Order. But I must emphasize from the outset that the theological argument that I seek to construct is not founded upon the assumptions made by those usually regarded as radical theologians. Whilst open to contemporary philosophical and anthropological concepts, theories, and methodologies, I wish to use these in illumination of the sources of Scripture and Tradition rather than as their replacements. My argument will be one that seeks essential continuity with the Church's historical theology and tradition.

My thesis is, therefore, not a response to radical political pressure that reflects the fads and phantasies of the impoverished secularism of the late twentieth century. Indeed we shall show in the course of the next chapter that cultural relativism, even in a highly nuanced and qualified form, hardly commands a general consensus either in epistemology or in anthropology, despite what is too frequently assumed. Rather I am advocating the concept of cultural *episcope* because it reflects the representative character of the episcopal Order which I will be arguing to be derivable from biblical and historical expressions of that Order. In other words, the indigenous peoples of Australia, or of any other area of christian mission, are justified in their aspirations for Order that reflects their cultural heritage because it draws our attention to forgotten aspects of the traditional Christian theology of the sacrament of Order. What I shall therefore emphasize throughout is that the representative character of *episcope*, as part of the sacrament of Order, is a character deeply rooted in the church's understanding of that sacrament from its origins in the Upper Room as recorded by John and throughout history, however controverted the interest of that evangelist in ecclesial Order may be.

The second misunderstanding which I would anticipate is one that would dismiss the proposal from the outset on the grounds that there are so many indigenous tribes and so many immigrant groups with the consequential *reductio ad absurdum* that we would end up requiring a thousand bishops to represent all of them. Such an objection, at all events, is blind to the absurdity of the present situation with territorial *episcope*. Bishops in the threefold Order are claimed to be essential, on one influential ecclesiology, to the sacramental nature and existence of the church. But how do we determine when and where to have them. Geographical dioceses come in all shapes and sizes, with a great variation in size of church population. The existing, territorial model of *episcope* is likewise arbitrary, and seems to rest on little else than the availability of resources to found a diocesan registry and employ the staff for the burocracy. An *episcope* that constitutes the essential nature of the church can hardly be said credibly to rest on such arbitrary and contingent foundations. As Rahner says:

> It is impossible to divide up the Church *exclusively* on a territorial basis... The territorial principle is *one* important natural and permanent structural principle... But it is not the only structural principle.[17]

Nevertheless, there is a real problem here regarding definition of culture, and one which our study will be shown to share with the general anthropological problems about obtaining a scientific definition of culture which can be generally agreed on, whether it is useful to talk about "sub-cultures" within cultures, whether there is not a general, human culture of which individual cultures are variations, how to locate a culture's existence in time and space, etc.

But the concept in anthropology, or in terms of missiology, or political argument cannot for that reason be dismissed. "Culture" in terms of shared understandings and values is something which people find of vital importance regarding what they believe, what they claim the right to, and about what they claim consideration in both national and international contexts. That we have not yet succeeded in articulating precisely, in a generally agreed way, what it is that has this importance cannot therefore be allowed to prohibit our serious consideration of it, however limited that consideration in consequence may be. And, as we saw earlier in this chapter (sect. 2), the Roman Catholic Church

---

[17] K. Rahner, *Theological Investigations* Vol. VI, trans. D. Bourke, (New York: Herder 1971), p. 328. See also his discussion on what a diocese is, idem p. 333-337 ff.

does take the rights of cultures seriously in its provision for the Eastern Rite patriarchies, however obscure its grounds for so doing may be to date.

Our argument will be that a person's cultural identity rests neither upon definitions about race in biological terms nor historical origins that the second misunderstanding assumed. A person's culture is not determined like the colour of his skin or the place of his birth. It is not a prison that confines him and from which he has insufficient autonomy to find release. Rather a culture is an instrument which can be chosen in terms of which the world can be both understood and valued. A person's culture is therefore a feature of a person's consciousness. To locate a person's culture is therefore to describe the kind of consciousness that he has, and that he shares with others in his cultural group, rather than to trace biological or historical ancestry.[18] We are therefore looking at shared and distinctive social constructions of reality that are a definitive part of the consciousness of their participants.

In consequence of such an argument, our perspective on what it is to be human is necessarily changed. What it is to be human is no longer defined exclusively in terms of individual biology or history. The new perspective on what it is to be human is derived both from the individual's biological and historical endowment and from his collective, social roots. It is in *both* a biological *and* a social matrix that the formation of the human person takes place. In consequence we experience change in our perspective of the human in Jesus taken by the Word made flesh in the incarnation.

---

[18] See such contemporary phenomenological perspectives in the social sciences such as those heralded some two decades ago by P. Berger and T. Luckman, *The Social Construction of Reality*, (London: Penguin 1967). I remain unimpressed by the relativist epistemology to which these gave rise. See both P. Berger's subsequent *Rumor of Angels*, (London: Penguin 1972), and my own *Philosophical Foundations for the Curriculum*, (London: Allen and Unwin 1978) chapter 4, and *Philosophy and Education Foundations*, (London: Allen and Unwin 1983), chpts 7-9.

4. *Incarnational theology, culture, and liturgy*

Turning from sociology to theology, my argument will rest upon the theological principle articulated by Thomas Aquinas that grace completes nature but does not destroy it. A human culture as a shared consciousness— a social construction of reality— is as much God's providential gift as our individual physical and mental endowments. It is the instrument that God has given us, diverse though our human cultures may be, through which our understanding reaches out to grasp ultimate truths and values. The grace of God, operative through the Church and its tradition, completes our varied cultural inheritances given to us in our natural condition and situation. It is about how grace completes or perfects nature in terms of our cultural endowments that my discussion makes contact with the concept of "incarnation in a culture."

If we are talking about how grace completes or perfects nature, we are necessarily involved with the theology of the incarnation which is about the taking and perfecting of our nature through the entry of God in Christ into human life. I believe therefore that a synthesis between concepts already widely used by theologians such as "incarnation in a culture" and "the Church as the extension of the Incarnation," when applied to our understanding of Order, will yield a new insight into the nature of *episcope* as being essentially representative and cultural. My argument for a cultural episcopate in consequence has little relation with any modern, secularist, and relativistic system of thought which would rule out the historical continuance of catholic and apostolic Order in doctrine and sacred ministry.

In seeking to discuss the concept of incarnation in a culture particularly in terms of Order, my argument can be regarded as arising in, and taking its point of departure from, the current discussion within the Roman Catholic Church regarding the indigenization of liturgy. The focus of the discussion of "incarnation in a culture" in the post Vatican II situation has undoubtedly been primarily on the theme of "indigenization of liturgy." As Seasoltz has written:

..expedience is not the primary reason for the indigenization of liturgy... The mystery of the incarnation provides the theological foundation for indigenization. In becoming man, the Word of God

bound himself to human nature, and in so doing he committed himself to be bound up inextricably with the history, culture, and traditions of human beings ...he became a Jew... This lineage, however,
did not limit the sphere of the incarnation... If the Church is called
to be the body of Christ and to incarnate his Spirit in all times and
places, it will be faithful to that mission to the extent that it incarnates itself in the various races and cultures of the world..[19]

But liturgy not only celebrates the incarnation but also the sacrament of Order as part of the ongoing testimony to the Church as
the "extension of the incarnation."

In consequence, my objective in this monograph will be to relate the concept of "incarnation in a culture," already understood
and deployed fruitfully by liturgical scholars in the area of the
indigenization of liturgy, to the implications that it has for a theology of the sacrament of Order in general, and of cultural *episcope* in particular. Liturgy, after all, celebrates sacred Order. In
forging this link, I will be helped considerably by another concept familiar to New Testament scholars from recent though by
now classical research into the Johannine literature, and that is
the concept of the Church as "the extension of the Incarnation."
The qualities and gifts focused in the three sacred Orders of
bishops priests and deacons are the qualities and gifts of the
whole body of Christ which they represent.

Let us summarize where this introductory chapter has so far
taken us.

5. *Towards a concept of cultural episcope*

It should by now be clear that this work is not simply a justification for a restricted set of episcopal arrangements to placate
political movements from the indigenous peoples of the former
British Colonies of Australia and New Zealand. The consecration of bishops for cultures in Australasia, and the issue of theological justification, is simply one example of a Western (or
Eastern) Mediterranean paradigm of *episcope* under stress. As an

---

[19] R.K. Seasoltz, *New Liturgy, New Laws*, (Liturgical Press 1980), p.
187-188. Seasoltz acknowledges his indebtedness to A.J. Chupungco,
Towards a Philipino Liturgy, (Manila 1976). He also quotes Vatican II, Ad
gentes. no.10: AAS 58(1966) 959, and no. 22: AAS58(1966).

example it must take its place alongside the broader question of enculturalization of the gospel in the Christian mission of the late twentieth century amongst peoples whose cultural homes and history cannot be located in the Mediterranean civilization where the historical incarnation took place, and the first Christian churches grew. Here we have the missiological thrust of this present work. Moreover, as a more general thesis, cultural *episcope* in an Australasian context must also take its place also alongside the quest for a suitable model of *episcope* that can play an active and dynamic role in ecumenical reconciliation in a way in which territorial *episcope* clearly cannot. The strongly evidenced desire of the indigenous peoples of Australia for bishops representative of their distinctive cultures, now beginning to be realized, is therefore a particular instance of a far broader development.

We can of course dismiss such movements as reflecting ephemeral political fads without theological justification and doing injury to our proper, Anglican or Catholic, territorial model. But if we are prepared to listen seriously to what is being asked and for what reason, I believe that we shall find the questions that illuminate our historical and theological traditions of what episcopacy is about. My argument, in summary, has been that our cultural is inseparable from our individual experience and consciousness of the world and of human life within it. The bishop as the sacred representative of a culture becomes the sacramental instrument of the redemption of a culture, and thereby of the individual within it, as he offers and represents his culture to the redeeming activity of God in Christ. But we have noted how such an expression of the indigenous desire for a cultural episcopate, once we recognize the justifiability of such a claim, begins to challenge the territorial concept ingrained in most current understandings of episcopacy.

Since many different cultural inheritances are to be found within the area of a single diocese, it becomes impossible for the one territorial bishop to represent all of the many varied cultures which exist side by side in a pluralistic society, whether in the U.S.A., Australasia, or the United Kingdom, yet the persistence of the territorial concept makes the achievement of a distinctive cultural and episcopal representative of any one of them impossible to attain. But this is a case which presents a not dissimilar parallel, as we have seen, with tensions between formally episcopal and non-episcopal Christian communions in the Western, Northern Hemisphere. Our missiology must clearly be sufficiently general to encompass all that the Church represents, whether interdenominationally, to our own societies, or to the traditional "mission field."

We see, therefore, that at this point tensions over the cultural concept represent quite general tensions with the territorial one quite apart from any particular application to indigenous peoples. At a sociological level we shall see that the tension is between what Durkheim called mechanical solidarity and organic solidarity which will help us explain why the representative concept, which we will argue to have been latent in Christian tradition, could only achieve explicit expression in modern societies. Preindustrial societies could only hold together by means of conformity to fixed and exhaustively defined patterns of behaviour and articles of belief with the smallest deviation thus threatening social cohesion. Such cohesion was therefore purely mechanical. Post industrial societies find by contrast their principle of social cohesion in the division of labour, in other words by people functioning differently rather than identically. Such ecumenical slogans as "unity in diversity" we shall see (Chapters 2 and 5) to be explicated sociologically in what Durkheim described as "organic solidarity."

The mention of this ecumenical slogan brings us back to the second group whose claims are rendering problematic the territorial and jurisdictional concept of episcopacy, namely non-episcopal churches seeking reunion. The recent proposal of the "covenanting" churches in the United Kingdom failed, as is common knowledge, over the failure to achieve consensus on the sacramental requirements of reunion at a presbyteral level. But had the problem of the proposed means of reconciliation in terms of what was unkindly called "ordination through the post" been resolved, the mechanism through which reunion would have been achieved would have been as follows. Such ministerial representatives as Presidents of Methodist Conferences and Moderators of United Reformed Churches would have received episcopal consecration. As bishops they would then have been in a position to ordain every new priest (and, deacons for that matter) according to a liturgical form that would have been recognized as valid by all churches participating in such a covenant.

But at this point we find that inevitably our territorial definition of episcopacy would be rendered highly ambiguous. The dioceses of the new, free-church bishops initially and at least for the foreseeable future, would overlap with different groups of clergy sharing the same communion and mutually recognized as sacred ministers of the church of God, but owing canonical obedience to different ordaining bishops as the source of their Orders. If the essential justification of episcopacy is to be located solely in good order and territorial jurisdiction arising from canon law, then such a concept is severely challenged by such ecumenical developments.

We can at such a juncture either deny the logic of the ecumenical developments or seek to refashion the concept. If we deny the logic of the developments as we saw Halliburton, explicitly, and Lambeth 88 implicitly, to have done, we must simply revert to the policy of seeking not ecumenical reconciliation but simply the submission of non-episcopal communicants, however discretely veiled that submission may be. Such a policy would have, after all, much in common with simply requiring the submission of members of indigenous Australasian cultures to a church whose gospel and Order has a Mediterranean, cultural form, and requiring the eradication of the indigenous culture as "pagan." Unless, therefore, we are prepared (as I and the majority of Christendom is not) to reject any form of episcopacy as anachronistic, we must seek to construct on the basis of catholic tradition a new concept that will reform the territorial one, compelled by our conviction that the ecumenical movement is the work of God in Christ, as are also indigenous Christian movements. Our conceptualization of missiological *and* ecumenical concerns are thus systematically and even organically related.

The justification for the new, free church bishops, I will suggest, is little different from the justification for an Aboriginal or Islander cultural episcopate. Cultural experience being inseparable from individual experience, the new bishops are representatives of cultures which, like all human cultures, are in process of being redeemed. Reconciliation is part of redemption so that, in the mutual recognition of bishops, the faith and life of their distinctive communities are also being recognized as part of the Catholic Faith. And at this point Anglican "comprehensiveness" will have become a sacramental rather than a jurisdictional one. A sacrament, according to the classical definition, is, after all that which "effects what it symbolizes and symbolizes what it effects." The ecumenical movement, in this form, is part of human salvation history, and the representative bishop becomes the sacramental instrument through which God in Christ is redeeming mankind. Such at least, *prima facie*, I would suggest is a far more effective concept than a territorial one which, in an ecumenical context, must become increasingly irrelevant. Moreover, it will assist both new indigenous and new free church bishops to understand their ministry and consecration in theological terms. Thus they will have a proper justification for accepting episcopacy into their systems rather than a shallow political compromise in order to placate Anglican, Orthodox, and Catholic susceptibilities with which they may otherwise have little real sympathy.

Having traced in bare outline both the theoretical and the practical importance of a concept of episcopacy which emphasizes the bishop as a representative, in a sacramental sense, of a redeemed culture, let us now proceed with our argument in justification. This argument will be partly theological, and partly historical and sociological, as we seek to define "culture" and "sacrament," and their interrelationship with Order in the context of the historical but developing catholic tradition.

CHAPTER TWO

CULTURE AND ECUMENISM

The relation between cultural theory and ecumenical dialogue

The argument with which my our previous Chapter concluded was that, since the essence of *episcope*, as of all sacred ministry, is to represent sacramentally the gifts and the calling of the total people of God, there is a strong case where those gifts and calling have a distinctive cultural incarnation for there to be a bishop of that culture representing them. It will our task in this chapter to set out a theory of society, culture, and language in terms of which terms such as "culture" and "sub-culture" may be better understood. This task has become additionally pressing because of our additional, parallel claim to that for ethnic episcopates namely that, in so far as the concept of "culture" or "sub-culture" can be extended to denominational Christian communities, there is a like argument for them to have bishops regardless of territorial notions of jurisdiction. But so far we have been using the terms "culture" and "subculture" as though their referents were clear and obvious. We must now look at each of these terms more carefully in order to define more clearly the sense in which we are using them.

Let us now delineate more carefully, in anthropological terms, what we mean by "culture."

1. *Anthropological definitions of culture*

In seeking a definition of "culture," we face the real problem of a lack of any agreed, "scientific" definition amongst anthropologists. Kroeber and Kluckhohn listed "about 175 separate definitions."[1] Furthermore the problem is compounded by the lack of definite criteria by which the boundaries between one culture and another can be fixed. Are, for example, the nations of Western Europe to be understood as different cultures, French, German, British, and Italian, or should we speak of a common European culture of which these "national" cultures are "subcultures"? How indeed fixed is culture, and how fluid as a concept, as different cultures meet and experience mutual influence? Moreover, would it be preferable to dispense with the concept of "sub-culture" entirely, and consider different systems by means of which different groups identify themselves as such as cultures, whether such a group be "East-End London culture," Jamaican culture" or "Aboriginal culture"? Indeed, the current debate in Australia over the concept of multi-culturalism would appear to assume such a view of the unit of culture existing at a sub-national level.[2]

Despite the problem of agreed definition, "culture" is far too vital an issue simply ignore. Groups at a national and international level are making claims bound up with their self-identity, and political rights associated with that self-identity. Furthermore, at a theological level, we have seen Vatican II making claims about patriarchs and their liturgical customs and religious traditions that imply far more about culture and identity than what we saw to be the otherwise glib association by that Council of the word with "education" or "refined taste."(Chapter 1) And so we must seek tentatively to arrive at some working definition of this term for the purposes of our current discussion.

If we compare the concept of "society" with that of "culture" it will soon become clear that we are talking about identical sets of phenomena from different perspectives. In social theory, basically, we are looking at how human societies, those characteristic creations of the human animal, are similar to each other. When we study kinship systems, patterns of power and authority, political and religious systems etc. in terms of *social* theory, we assume that all human societies have institutions that can be

---

[1] Quoted in F.R. Vivelo, *Cultural Anthropology Handbook*, (New York: McGraw Hill 1978), from A.L. Kroeber and C. Kluckhorn, *Culture: A Critical Review of Concepts and Definitions*, (Cambridge Mass.: Harvard University Press 1952).

studied in terms of these concepts and as such are formally comparable. When, however, we regard these societies in terms of *cultural* theory, we are contrasting them in terms of their distinctive differences. We are focusing upon the particular form that the exercise of power and authority, matrimonial and family relations, religious observances and rites, economic life etc assume in the particular society under examination. As one of the founding fathers of anthropology, Sir Edward Tylor, said in his famous statement which has gained a certain notoriety:

> Culture is that complex whole which includes knowledge, belief, art, morals, law, custom and any other capabilities and habits acquired by man as a member of society.[3]

One respect in which Tylor's definition was deficient was its failure to delineate the relation between bodies of knowledge, belief, etc. and the cultural products such as tools and artifacts, in which they achieve their concrete expression. But as soon as we sharpen the focus of such a definition of culture in such terms, we are confronted by the danger of the reification of the naive realist. The danger is that we shall regard culture by analogy with a material possession that we receive, adopt, pass on or give away.

But there is never a purely contingent relation between the cultural clothes of a society and its fundamental social organization such that government, authority, the economy, and the maintenance of moral consensus, etc. could proceed regardless of any one cultural form in which it was expressed. And perhaps we have made a similar mistake in the sociology and anthropology at the foundations of our theologies of church Order. Historically the ecumenical argument has been in terms of a form of social organization, episcopalianism, as opposed to, say, presbyterianism or *vice-versa* as the proper and invariant societal form of the "true" church in contrast with the accidental cultural accretions of time and place. In other words, the debate has been about what makes Christian communities identifiably different in their authority and governmental structures, that is to say the de-

---

[2] D. Kaplan, and R.A. Manners, *Culture Theory*, (New Jersey: Prentice Hall 1972), p. 3-4.

[3] E.B. Tylor, *Primitive Culture*, (London: John Murray 1871), p. 1.

bate has been about cultural and not social organization. But no society acquires a culture in this contingent way.

Do we for example simply acquire a culture by collecting carved heads of totems or cave paintings and placing them on our bookshelves for decoration? Do we simply acquire catholic Order by wearing chasubles, stoles, and the other classical and traditional appertances of liturgical worship? Indeed we do not, since we may have transported the artifacts outside of the inter-personal conceptual scheme of the society from which they are derived, as a backcloth to which they derive their meaning and significance as cultural objects. Indeed, to say that the conceptual scheme expressed in a shared language is the backcloth, is in some way, a misleading way of making the point. Rather the cultural objects themselves are part of the conceptual scheme, for they are related as symbolic forms of expression and meaning to both words and patterns of activity which are part of an interrelated whole. It was this aspect of culture and its definition, in which Tylor's work was defective, that was to be unraveled by Durkheim and his functionalist and structuralist successors.

2. *Durkheim's phenomenology of culture*

It was Durkheim who first emphasized the necessity of understanding culture in terms of a sociology of knowledge. Durkheim described the central value system of a society as its "collective consciousness" which he defined as "the set of beliefs and sentiments common to the average members of a single society which forms a determinate system that has its own life." However, the expression "that has its own life" should not be taken as a metaphysical assertion that societies have collective souls or essences, but rather Durkheim's way of saying that social facts are *sui generis*. The collective consciousness, without being therefore some metaphysical group mind, was not able to be reduced to any one particular mind, nor indeed the sum total of particular minds. Particular minds can impose individualist or partisan group interpretations on the products of consensual meanings that can depart from or break particular consensuses.[4] A motor-bike gang can call itself the "Renegades" without conforming to the general expectations and understandings of the term "renegade." A policeman's helmet can be used as a flower-vase and occasion delight that it is so used when one's friends come round for coffee. Yet in neither case do individual or collections of individual consciousness change the general, shared meanings of the concept of a renegade or the symbolic value of the policeman's helmet.

Furthermore, in some circumstances the attempt to change the general conceptual scheme shared by members of a social group may fail, irrespective of the particular wills of the living members of that group. But at other times they may succeed. When x and y originally met each other, the feeling that they had of some relationship in which they both shared was originally purely subjective and no part of society's collective consciousness or shared value system. But when x vocalized this relationship by means of the hitherto meaningless collection of letters and sounds that constitute the word "cousin," and thus labeled their lineal relationship through father's or mother's brothers or sisters to one another, they objectified a relationship that their deaths could not annul. Others than x and y were constrained to acknowledge a like relationship which the now meaningful term described between themselves and the children of their maternal or paternal siblings. So too with the patterns of behaviour now morally required towards such relatives. The objectified relationship thus has a facticity that it is difficult to ignore even on the part of those who do not wish to acknowledge their cousins. A similar phenomenon is also observable in the way that 16th Century Reformation polemic, like that of certain fundamentalist religious groups today, defines a protestant theological position with constant reference to the Roman Catholic doctrines (or assumed doctrines) that are being rejected. The rejected doctrines have a facticity for them which cannot be simply be ignored, since such doctrines tell them what they consider that they are

---

[4] E. Durkheim, *The Division of Labor in Society*, (Trans. G. Simpson) (New York: MacMillan 1933), p. 4 quoted in S. Lukes, *Emile Durkheim, His Life and Work: A Historical and Critical Study*, (London: Penguin 1973), p. 6.

not. We shall see in section 4 below how such a process of self-definition by abnegation characterizes a sub-culture defining itself in contrary terms to its host culture.

It was to emphasize this socially constructed objectivity or facticity of the collective consciousness, as well as its non-metaphysical character, that Durkheim coined the term "collective representations" in his later writings.[5] Collective representations were states of the collective consciousness different in nature from the states of the individual consciousness.[6] "Representation" refers to the mode of cognizing a social object and the objects themselves which does not constitute the ambiguity that Lukes believed, since the whole point of a sociology of knowledge is that thought and object are not separable in the way presupposed by a naive realism.[7] By the general term "representation" social products whose meaning is defined by an implicit social and ideational consensus are grouped together, whether they be aesthetic objects, artifacts, symbols, linguistic concepts, stories, or myths, in interrelated systems of meanings. Thus when one group differs from another it is in terms of their collective representations, and we say that the two groups have different cultures.

On such a view a cultural system is a kind of linguistic system. Meaningless units of sound or written words acquire conventionally meanings so as to become the patterns of speech or writing known to linguists as "phonemes" and "morphemes." In the same way, so too do meaningless objects of the natural world, or stories or pictures, initially unrelated or told for purposeless entertainment, when they become incorporated into the social world as expressions or representations, in a concrete form, of the social consciousness. As such we may compare how Durkheim understood culture in terms of collective representations with what the latter Wittgenstein had to say about "forms of life." "Collective representations," we shall argue, are concrete symbolic, and therefore cultural, expressions of "forms of life."

---

[5] E. Durkheim, *Les Formes Élémentaires de la Vie Religieuse: Le Système Totémique en Australie,* (Paris: Alcan 1912).

[6] Lukes op. cit. p. 6.

3. *Wittgenstein and culture as agreement in form of life*

Wittgenstein's famous argument was that any agreement or disagreement presupposed a prior agreement, what he called "agreement in a form of life." We can imagine an argument about the use of sound and colour words which we had with a radical reviser of our sound and colour concepts. He tells us that "blue" is a sound and "ringing" is a colour. If we are naive realists, we might claim that we can refute him by referring to what we see under normal eyesight and normal conditions, on the reasonable assumption that human sensory organs are almost identically constructed for the majority of our species. But, of course, such a view obscures the complex relation between language and perception that cannot be reduced to a view of so-called ostensive concepts simply labeling sense-data.

The anthropologists have, for example, pointed to the way in which different cultures cut up the world in terms of different colour schemes, to the way in which, for example, eskimos have fifteen different words for snow. How would we settle the argument between someone who claimed that: "Eskimos see the same substance that we see but describe it in fifteen different ways," and someone who asserted to the contrary that: "We see fifteen different things but describe them all by the same term"?

Without subscribing to the extreme Sapir-Whorf hypothesis that we cut up reality in the way in which we do because of the absolute obligatory pattern that language imposes upon thinking, we can nevertheless regard the relationship between language and thought as complex and problematical.[8] The later Wittgenstein's solution was to say that we can disagree that "blue" is a sound or "ringing" a colour. But whether we agree or disagree, what makes that agreement or disagreement possible is our prior agreement or consensus, whether explicit or implicit, in the syntax and semantics of the language in which that agreement or disagreement is expressed. If there was not the semantic and

---

[7] Ibid. p. 7.

[8] B.L. Whorf, *Language, Thought, and Reality, Selected writings of B.L. Whorf*, Ed. J.B. Carroll, Forward S. Chase, (Cambridge Massachusetts: Harvard University Press 1956), and E. Sapir, *Language: an Introduction to the Study of Speech*, (London: Hart-Davis McGibbon 1978).

syntactical agreement as a back cloth, it would not be possible even to disagree. If we disregarded all such fundamental agreement, no communication would be possible, but instead an anarchic chaos of meaningless sounds in which there could not even be disagreement.

Such a semantic or syntactic backcloth was therefore part of what Wittgenstein meant by "form of life" in which we agree. The moral rebel arises within a form of life, and can never be so radical as to reject the form of life *in toto* otherwise he could not even express and communicate to others his program for moral change. The Marxist has learned moral principles like "justice," "fairness," "equality" etc. from the very community of judgment whose substantive contradictions he seeks to expose. Likewise the leaders of the European Reformation arose in a tradition of Augustinianism which they shared with their contemporary church, but in terms of which they sought to refute scholasticism, whilst labouring under the false-consciousness that they had swept all tradition aside and had made contact with the un-corrupted New Testament revelation.[9]

The association of "form of life" with "collective representation" is, I believe, a fruitful one in explicating what constitutes a culture. The incorporation of art and artifacts into the fundamental conceptual schemes of a society, in the context of which they acquire their symbolic meaning, makes the study of culture not unlike the study of language, for reasons that we have seen. Morphemes and phonemes are the product of the imposition of social rules upon otherwise meaningless entities. "Form of life" is often associated therefore with Wittgenstein's other well-worked notion of "language-games," the implicit ground rules of which are in a way set by the players simply by the way that they play. But indeed it is a far broader notion than the purely linguistic. It refers to the fundamental pattern and organization of social consciousness of which, partly language, partly tools, artifacts, art, and symbols, and partly agreed morals, are systematically interrelated into a cultural whole.

---

[9] For an account of reformation theology as radical Augustinianism, see J. Pelikan, *Reformation of Church and Dogma (1300-1700)*, (Chicago: Univeristy of Chicago Press 1984), p. 196-209, 224-228 ff.

4. *Form of life, collective representations, and sub-cultures*

The association of "form of life" in this sense with "collective representations" now enables us to give a more precise account of the use of "sub-culture" in contrast with culture. A subculture will arise where there is a partial but not absolute change in the consensus on rules for the meaning of the concept involved. Keeping to our extraordinary example of the sound blue and the colour ringing, if such changes were practiced by a group in a way that was systematically related to other such partial rule-changes so that the collective representations of the sub-group were still related to those of the host group, a sub-culture will have come into existence. Such a use of Wittgenstein has been used by Hudson to defend theistic discourse against the charge of being meaningless. A religious subculture can still engage in meaningful dialogue with its secular host culture because, although the host culture rejects its theistic assumptions, there are sufficient agreed rules of meaning regarding certain concepts even though many of the rules may appear altered.

One of Hudson's arguments was centred on the question how can God be said intelligibly to act or to meet with men without a physical body. Yet the theist is involved in a contradiction because he affirms the former, but denies the latter. The concept of "intention" and "will" are not however, despite behaviourists claims, reducible to statements about bodily movements.[10] It therefore becomes possible to speak of God "acting" or "meeting." Spatio-temporal events of certain kinds, like the parting of the waters of the Red Sea, can be intelligibly substituted for bodily movements in the case of God "acting" or "meeting."[11]

Players of the religious language-game may therefore be said to be using terms differently from others in Western, secular societies in that the rules of reference for willing agencies are changed in the case of God. But in this respect they are not unlike the radical revisers of colour and sound words in the famous example about disagreement in opinion. Theists are dependent

---

[10] See also A. Brent, *Philosophy and Educational Foundations*, (London: Allen and Unwin 1983), p. 24-44 ff.

on a shared form of life or interpersonal backcloth of semantic and syntactic rules in order to express intelligibly their claims about the acts of God. As Hudson says:

> In the logical map work of which I have been speaking, however, it is essential to notice where the frontier of the language-game we call religious belief unite it with other linguistic territories as well as where they mark it off from these. Religious discourse is not cut off from every other sort of discourse. Some, at least, of the language is used in non- religious contexts.[12]

In relation to an understanding of culture, therefore, and what constitutes a sub-culture, we propose interpreting Durkheim's concept of collective representations in terms of Wittgenstein's concept of a form of life. In Hudson's example of the relationship between theism and secular society we can as a result see how a distinct culture differs from a subculture. It is the parasitic relation between fundamental concepts used in a distinctive way by the subculture and those of the host-culture that may be said to constitute it as a subculture, and not as a separate culture in its own right. In terms of interdenominational relations we may say that the distinction between schism and heresy on such a sociological view becomes the difference between using religious concepts in a way that remains within the conditions of meaning presupposed by a shared, form of life (schism) albeit in new and unusual ways, and a radical reversal of such fundamental meanings (heresy).

We may therefore say, roughly, that denominations that accept, say, the common creeds of Christendom are therefore so many subcultures within a general, catholic culture, whereas those who do not constitute a separate culture. I say "roughly" because, as I have made clear, definition of "culture" remains problematic in sociological and anthropological terms. Furthermore, as will become clear, I believe that there is a strong case for regarding the distinction between different cultures and subcultures as not absolute but one purely of degree, and indeed dependent on the particular focus within which one finds the best

---

[11] W.D. Hudson, *A Philosophical Approach to Religion,* (London: MacMillan 1974), p. 12-13, 161-176.
[12] Ibid. p. 11.

examination of a particular problem. Hudson will presumably have described, in one such focus, all theistic belief systems as a common culture, parasitic for its concepts on the general usage of the wider group, and without distinctions between them in terms of further subcultural grouping. In another focus, adherents of a particular religious faith divided denominationally can be regarded as members of different subcultures of a common culture or form of life which diverges radically from secular culture.

The only grounds upon which "culture" and "subculture" on such a view could differ absolutely, and not simply by degree, would be on a thesis of epistemological relativism. Indeed the culture/subculture distinction appears to be the creation of a relativistic epistemology according to which cultures cannot really understand each other or translate each other's key concepts, whereas sub-cultures can. According to such a thesis, sub-cultures can communicate with their host cultures and engage in significant dialogue because, despite changes in so many conceptual agreements in opinion, both are still underlaid by agreement in form of life.

But such disagreements in opinion could theoretically come so to diverge from the host culture that there was no longer any possibility of dialogue and shared understanding about anything. The unexamined assumption of such a view is that there is no human form of life presupposed by particular social and cultural forms of life that enables cross-cultural dialogue meaningfully to proceed. If such epistemological relativism should be discounted, then it would follow that what in one focus are all human cultures in another focus are sub-cultures of a common, human culture or form of life. The conceptual force of the description "human culture" in such a context would be to show how human groups generally differ from non-human ones.

Indeed, unless such an epistemological relativism can be discounted, our theological concept of incarnation in a culture, with its implication for Order and the episcopate, will be quite vacuous. If one culture can in principle become so conceptually and symbolically isolated from another that any real communication must cease, then Christ as the Word made flesh, and whose reality is incarnated in specifically cultural forms, will be unrecognizable to those who do not share those cultural forms. Mutual recognition in dialogue of life, worship, and ministerial Orders will therefore become a pipe dream. Furthermore the fundamental assumptions of ecumenical dialogue, that there is a lost common ground between the churches divided at the Reformation and at the Eastern Schism will be radically denied, and we shall be ecumenically following a false trail. All that will be left will be a "live and let live" mentality between our existing ecclesiastical ghettos. Finally, such an account will not be without problems for Christianity as it claims to be a revealed religion with a historical dimension to what it reveals. Dialogue is not simply a trans-spatial phenomenon but, in terms of tradition and liturgy, a trans-temporal one as well.

We must therefore look for the foundations in epistemological and cultural theory that will give both ecumenism and enculturalization justification in non-relativistic terms.

5. Culture, the social construction of reality, and epistemological relativism

Before therefore we turn from our general definition of culture to specific theological understandings of "incarnation," "sacrament," and "Order" in such a perspective, we need to articulate two problems that will be faced by Christianity as a revealed religion when examined in such a perspective. The first is that a Christian culture does not simply grow and develop autochthonously, so to speak, and cannot be so regarded. The second is that a cultural relativism that also implies an epistemological relativism is in total contradiction to any notion of Christian orthodoxy.

In the first place, therefore, Christianity is not simply a revealed religion, but a revealed religion with a basis in history. Historical tradition will always therefore be an inescapable feature of the transmission of Word and Sacrament in missionary endeavour, with the result that the culture that bears the historical tradition will be incorporated into the culture that receives it. A truly Christian culture cannot grow autochthonously. Our present study makes no efforts to deny this fact, which is inescapable on any claim to Christian orthodoxy. What we are concerned with is the character and process of that cultural transmission. Any account of the enculturalization of Order such as that with which we are concerned will have, at an anthropological level, an inescapably "tranfusionalist" as opposed to a purely "functionalist" aspect.[13]

In the second place, functionalism implies a cultural relativism which in turn implies an epistemological relativism. The functionalist school of anthropologists, with whom the names of Durkheim's disciples Malinowski and Radcliffe-Brown are associated, asserts basically that the significance of a set of cultural practices are not to be found in their historical origins but in their present social utility in effecting the good functioning of the social system of which they form part. Religious beliefs and practices, on such a view, cannot be regarded as survivals in a technological culture made obsolete by evolutionary progress. They are as they are because of the social function that they now perform behind all their appearances of being of quite different significance. As such the "diffusionist" approach is also rejected, which seeks to explain cultural features in terms of their external origin in critical geographical centres from which they are imported, and by which they are influenced. It matters not to the functionalist theorist whether the influence is regarded as diachronic (historical) or synchronic (from external social interaction). The form of the culture is determined solely by its utility in present society.

Functionalism raises many theoretical problems within anthropology in their own right. The problem with a purely functionalist approach in terms of the theology of Order in a cultural perspective is that it leads, as we have said, to an epistemological relativism that runs quite contrary to the nature of Christianity as based upon a revelation grounded in history. If, following Durkheim, we defined culture in terms of collective representations, and Wittgenstein in terms of form of life, are we not committed to an epistemological relativism such as functionalism otherwise commits us to? In consequence, the Christianity of one culture could be quite different from the Christianity of another, just as the Christianity of one age could be regarded as

---

[13] For a more detailed account of these differing anthropological schools, see I.M. Lewis, *Social Anthropology in Perspective*, (London: Penguin 1976), p. 60-65.

different from another. The prospect of an ecumenical unity developing between them could never as such be supported on the grounds of their sharing a common revelation, historically grounded, about the nature of God, the world, the human condition, and mankind's redemption. It would be a case of creating a new, twentieth century, world-wide Christian culture rather than rediscovering and developing what already exists.

There are, however, two reasons for rejecting the claim that cultural theory necessarily leads us to epistemological relativism. The first is that such a claim is arguably founded upon a misreading of Wittgenstein's thesis since it assimilates that thesis too closely with Quine's notion of the indeterminacy of translation. The second is that the structural-functionalism of Lévi-Strauss points to a concept of culture that sees the various cultures of mankind, like their languages, arising in a rule-governed way from a common human consciousness, as sketched by the deep-structure grammarians. Lévi-Strauss, in other words, claims to be able to reveal the process by which, in dialogue, different sacred stories can be retold in a new synthesis which reconciles the antinomies of each story when told apart. Let us review briefly these two points.

Wittgenstein once said that we should be less interested in someone who denied the existence of the earth 150 years ago than someone who denied the existence of Napoleon. This was because in the former instance our whole system of evidence was being called into question.[14] In consequence, it is possible to interpret Wittgenstein's "language-game" in terms of the fundamental rules for making objective judgments that are socially relative. Any claim to knowledge presupposes an interpersonal backcloth of rules against which claims can be tested. It is therefore possible that, in the course of playing our social and cultural games, such games can come to so differ so radically that they are mutually incomprehensible. They will then have no agreed backcloth in common, and the two cultures will either be, or have come to be, so divergent in this respect that no communication between them is possible. But what is interesting is that if we substitute for Wittgenstein's fictitious example a real-life ex-

---

[14] L. Wittgenstein, *On Certainty*, (Oxford: Blackwell 1969), p. 190 cf. Brent (1983) op. cit. p. 294-304 ff.

ample to make his point, his relativist conclusion is denied and his point unmade. A religious fundamentalist will tell us that the world was created in 4004 B.C. as was taught in the 17th Century by Archbishop Ussher, and generally then believed. We may reject his thesis and yet we claim to be understanding what he is claiming and why, mistaken though we may hold his confusion of a scientific with a religious statement to be. Moreover our claimant for a world history of only 150 years would be able to in dialogue make contact with the fundamentalist group and accept some of their patterns of argumentation in order to make and communicate his point to them as well as to us.

But to put our objection more formally, a relativistic view of Wittgenstein, albeit from a different epistemological stance, will be regarded as supporting a thesis not dissimilar to Quine's indeterminacy of translation. Quine believed it was possible for two human languages to be virtually untranslatable within each other's terms, though with the deceptive appearance of having been translated. An anthropologist might, while trying to study the language of another culture, say "gavagai" whenever he saw what was for his culture a rabbit. But "gavagai" could mean not a whole or enduring rabbit but stages or brief temporal segments of rabbits. Despite an apparent translation, if all such concepts generally throughout the language differed, there would be no semantic contact between the linguistic culture of the anthropologist and that which he was trying to observe. The two languages, like two Wittgensteinian forms of life, could so utterly diverge so that there could be no real communication between them at all.[15] But Yudkin, in a most perceptive paper, has challenged such an understanding of the later-Wittgenstein. She points out that one particular insight of Wittgenstein was his notion of concepts definable in terms of "family-resemblance." To be comprehensible, or, if you like, usable in a language-game, certain critical concepts have to possess a certain kind of vagueness. By "vagueness" he meant "not exhaustively definable" so as to produce precise conceptual equivalences, but identifiable rather in terms of resemblance rather like that which exists between members of families.

---

[15] W. Van O. Quine, *Word and Object*, (Cambridge Mass.: MIT Press 1959), p. 51-52 and Brent (1983) op. cit. p. 59-68.

Members of the Churchill family are not identified as such because an exhaustive definition of the features of each member allows identification in terms of equivalence. There is the Churchill nose, scowl, eyebrows, forehead, etc. As a result, if we try to identify members of the family in terms of all these features exhaustively spelled out we shall fail to classify since someone will lack the Churchill nose, someone else the eyes, and yet a third the scowl and so on, whilst possessing all other features. Yet somewhere along the line there will occur two members of the family who have no common features. One has the Churchill scowl and forehead, but not the eyebrows or stoop, but the other will possess the eyebrows and stoop but not the scowl or forehead.[16] What as it were allows admission into the Churchill family is that the features of a given member form with the features of others a kind of pattern or chain which permits the new non-exhaustively definable class. Tables, after all, come in all sorts of shapes and sizes and there is no one or set of common features that establish them as members of the same class. And so do rabbits or "gavagai."

Yudkin charges Quine with attributing to the member of the tribe whose expression is allegedly so intranslatable "a passion for exactness that only someone familiar with metaphysical hairsplitting in our own language could manifest."[17] She then quotes from Leach the example of asking whether the sketch of a car upon a blackboard is a Ford or a Cadillac. Such a question is like asking a Kachin who is in the process of killing a pig, and claiming that he is giving it to the ants, whether ants have legs. Our question is idiotic because it ignores the vagueness or special kind of imprecision exhibited by such as our concept of a car, or the Kachin's concept of an ant, that constitute their communicative strength. This special kind of imprecision that allows new discoveries to be incorporated into existing schemes (or open-classes) exemplifies a general feature of human languages

---

[16] I am indebted for these examples and my general discussion to R. Bambrough, Universals and Family Resemblances, in *Proceedings of the Aristotelian Society*, LX (1960-1), p. 209-211. See also H. Staniland, *Universals*, (New York: Doubleday Anchor 1972), p. 74-77 ff.

[17] M. Yudkin, "On Quine's contretemps of translation," in *Mind* 88 (1979), p. 93-96.

that, arguably, enables mutual understanding of conceptual schemes initially alien when members of different cultures meet. Its existence dissolves Quine's problem, founded upon some mistaken notion that definition be exhaustive, that leads him to the equally mistaken notion that it is in principle possible that one language could be so radically translated in terms of another that it meant something utterly different from what its native user intended.

Another way of expressing this point about language has been deployed by the deep-structure grammarians. Katz, for example, argues for semantic universals as the basis of any human language system in his thesis of the "effability" of any human language in terms of another. At first sight it appears improbable that, say, the language of a south sea island culture that deals with natural events in terms of such categories as the human-like spirits that control them can be translated into the language world of twentieth century, Western man. But let us imagine such a native language user learning English and taking a course in physics, and then returning to his native culture in order to communicate the fruits of his learning. As Katz says:

> What he must therefore do is either use English words for concepts not in his language or else make up words that more readily fit into the phonology of his language. In either case he will have to introduce a large stock of new words, but will have to rely on the already existing semantic structure of the native language to define them on the already existing phonological and syntactic structure of native language to make it possible to form sentences with them that express the laws of modern physics.. We do not suppose that by so enlarging the vocabulary of his native language he has in fact changed the language essentially, just as we do not assume that English has changed essentially as a result of the increase in the number of vocabulary items brought about by the rise of science in the last hundred years.[18]

We have sought to assimilate, therefore, Wittgenstein's notion of a language-game to both a linguistic thesis about meaning and a cultural thesis that understands the symbols, artifacts, tools, rituals etc that define a culture by analogy with a linguistic system. In so doing, however, our mention of Quine, "family re-

---

[18] J.J. Katz, *Semantic Theory*, (New York: Harper 1972), p. 20-21.

semblance" and Katz on semantic universals have served to emphasize that we are not thereby committed to a thesis of cultural relativism such that cultures could become or already be so linguistically, semantically, and culturally insulated from one another that no real cross cultural communication or adaptation could proceed without destroying the original semantic and cultural systems of at least one of the social groups in the interchange. Historical traditions can affect and determine the range of options available to the present, as can present traditions of other cultures. Both diachronic and synchronic influences will, therefore, belie a purely functionalist view of culture. In consequence, ecumenical dialogue will have a point and purpose, since no human linguistic system could be so logically insulated from another as to make communication impossible. But so far our account only lays bare the possibility of mutual understanding of different cultural and subcultural perspectives. Why should dialogue in which theological differences can be understood also in fact hold out the possibility of such disagreements being transcended by new agreements?

At this point of overlap in our discussion between linguistic, semantic and cultural theory we are inevitably lead to the structural functionalism of Lévi-Strauss. We shall see how, in his own way, this great, though highly controversial, anthropologist is opposed to an unrestricted relativism in his analysis of human cultures. Though human cultures assume a diversity of appearances which develop and unfurl with great fecundity, Lévi-Strauss will nevertheless claim that they are limited in form by the fundamental nature of the human mind which is able to be given algebraic expression in terms of binary logic. A human society cannot simply develop just any cultural form. Furthermore, identifying theologies with Straussian sacred stories by establishing formal similarities between them, we shall show how the logic of sacred stories (theologies), in mutual reflection that is the process of their retelling by communities in dialogue, transcend differences by synthesizing antinomies into new syntheses.

6. *Lévi-Strauss: the limits of cultural relativism*

Lévi-Strauss and his disciples regard a cultural system by analogy with a linguistic system as conceived by deep-structural grammarians such as Chomsky and Katz, to whom we made reference above. A linguistic system is, after all, a symbolic system with the basic subject-predicate sentence about the rules for distinguishing different classes of things (*langue*), and the making of statements about particular things (*parole*). In *langue* we have the total semantic system in the context of which the various categories of language map out the various entities recognized by the culture. No one distinction can be established by one person alone in isolation since the "I" of any language user only has meaning if the contrast with "we" is understood.

To classify means not only to discern similarities but to distinguish them, and in terms of a conceptual scheme which is meaningful in terms of shared agreement on contrasts and similarities expressed in terms of agreed symbols. That classificatory scheme, being independent of any particular individual, has to be available to any individual but not necessarily used in its entirety by him. It is the sum total of what Durkheim called the collective representations of the social group. It is that availability of the scheme, without in fact ever being used by an individual in its entirety, that is termed by the structural-functionalists as an individual's "langue."

Thus in terms of Chomskyan linguistics we may say that a person's *langue* describes his particular competence in a particular language as opposed to his actual performance in that language. A person, after all, only ever performs, due to the shortness of life and its limited opportunities, part of what the rules of his language make him competent to perform. His actual performances Lévi-Strauss calls his "parole" where symbols are joined together according to syntactical rules to form particular sentences. The variety of possible human languages are limited, according to the deep-structural grammarians, by human linguistic competence, even though all the linguistic possibilities have not yet been realized. So too for the Straussians, though all possible expressions of human cultures have not yet been realized, the possible new expressions are nevertheless formally limited in terms of the algebraically conceived, possible permutations of

langue. In the context of the present discussion, though not just
anything can count as a version of the sacred story that justifies
ecclesial Order as a collective representation, nevertheless there
are still as yet unrealized forms of such a sacred story to which
ecumenical dialogue can progress. From our analysis of some
ARCIC and Lima examples (section 8), we shall show is in fact
in process of realization.

It is the achievement of symbolic thought which marks the
evolutionary transition from nature to society. The ability to
make natural distinctions is common in the world of animal nature. Man is like the animals in that he recognizes the difference
between members of his own species and those of others, differences between men and women, between what is edible and
inedible, dominance and submission, sexual availability or non-
availability, etc. But the development of symbolic thought enables raw animal categorizations to be transformed into social
ones, as the totemism to be witnessed in any human society
bears witness, particularly in our animal metaphors used as
moral classifications.

If this was the whole of the Straussian argument, it would not
be incompatible with epistemological relativism regarding cultural differences. But in a way analogous to the search of the
deep-structure linguists for a universal grammar common to all
human language, Lévi-Strauss seeks an algebra that will account
for the way in which the human mind as such, independent of a
particular culture, will process cultural artifacts and symbols.
The algebra proceeds according to the logic of binary relations.
But it also involves mental processes that synthesize antitheses
that arise as a culture develops and which can be particularly observed in those collective representations of a social order found
in a society's mythology.

Lévi-Strauss points out that an almost universal character of
myths— interpreted as the sacred story associated with ritual and
without prejudice to the presence or absence of historical cores—
is their focus upon the violation of prohibited or incestuous sexual relations. In classical mythology, for example, Zeus, the father of the gods and men, marries his mother Hera, and
Oedipus, unknown to himself, marries his own mother.
Chronos eats his own children and so on.

In his famous analysis of the Oedipus myth, Lévi-Strauss seeks to draw out in detail the paradoxes that it is the purpose of the logical structure of the myth to overcome.[19] The antinomies he sees in terms of the over- and under-evaluation of kinship and in terms of the affirmation and denial of the autochthonous origin of man. When Kadmos seeks his sister Europa ravished by Zeus, or Oedipus marries his mother, Jokasta, or Antigone buries her brother Polyneikes despite prohibition, the concern with family relationships clearly overrides all other considerations. When the Spartoi, who are born from the dragon's teeth sown in the earth, kill one another in what is in fact fratricide, or Oedipus kills his father Laios, or Eteokles his brother Polyneikes, there is an under-evaluation of kinship. As the myth is created, revised, and new features added in the course of oral and written transmission, the same logical process remains in evidence shaping the transformation of such antitheses as the sacred story is developed.

There is another set of antinomies to be observed in the Oedipus myth, and that set is characterized by the theme of the denial and affirmation of the autochthonous origin of man. Lévi-Strauss' interpretation at this point revolves around the meaning assigned to certain names. Labdacos, who is the father of Laios, connotes someone who is lame. Laios' name connoted "left-sided" and his son's name, Oedipus, connotes someone with a swollen foot. These features can be illuminated by comparative mythology. It can be asserted from comparative studies that generally, (though not "universally" as in the following), such are the physical deformities of the first men springing to life autochthonously from the earth. As Lévi-Strauss says:

> In mythology it is a universal characteristic of men born from the Earth that at the moment they emerge from the depth they either cannot walk or they walk clumsily. This is the case of the chthonian beings in the mythology of the Pueblo: Muyingwu, who leads the emergence, and the chthonian Shumaikoli are lame ("bleeding-foot," "sore-foot"). The same happens to the Koskimo of the Kwakiutl after they have been swallowed by the chthonian monster, Tsiakish:

---

[19] C. Lévi-Strauss, *Structural Anthropology*, (London: Allen Lane 1968), chpts 10-12.

When they returned to the surface of the earth "they limped forward or tripped sideways."[20]

The antithetic features of the story to those of the autochthonous origin of mankind are Cadmos killing the dragon, or Oedipus killing the Sphinx. As the sowing of the dragon's teeth implies the autochthonous origin of mankind, the slaying of the dragon implies the denial of that origin. Furthermore the Sphinx rises from the ashes and its destruction implies the negation of autochthony.

Thus in the Oedipus myth we detect two kinds of antitheses, one which overrates and underrates kinship, and the other which affirms and denies the autochthonous origin of man. But the two kinds of antithesis are related to one another. The mutual destruction of each other by the Spartoi, who were born from the dragon's teeth, unite into a pattern the the under evaluation of kinship and the denial of autochthony. The converse of over evaluation (under evaluation) of destroyed autochthony (autochthony) in their relation to each other thus combine into a pattern the two sets of binary relations.

Lévi-Strauss thus believes that in such formal features as these, quantifiable in terms of a logic of binary-relations, we can locate the invariant, formal dimensions of that expression of culture that is a myth or sacred story. Such a sacred story cannot have just simply any form, however apparently limitless in their fecundity the particular and substantive features of the mythological productions of human cultures may appear. His structuralism is a version of functionalism in that the universal dimensions of mind that account for such formal invariance are deployed in order to solve fundamental problems of social theory prescinding from diachronic and synchronic influences.

One such particular problem in the transition from nature to society is to be seen in sexual prohibitions arising from laws or customs against incest. The state of nature for the Straussians ends when human beings exchange certain women with others and thus set up an extended familial structure. Without such an exchange, the war of nature would not give way to reciprocal

---

[20] Ibid. p. 215-216, see also E. Leach, *Claude Lévi Strauss*, (New York: Viking Press 1970), chpts 3-4.

exchanges that produce civil peace. Thus the social bond requires the denial of sexual relations with what beyond nature become defined as immediate kin. Myth, for reasons that may be attributed to Freud, thus becomes the means of working through and reconciling the tensions produced by the natural libid.inous drive by means of a set rationalizing solutions. That is why mythology is concerned with incestuous relations and their resolution.

Furthermore, mythology has its own problem-solving logic that addresses the facts of social experience disconsonant with nature. Unless the process of marrying and giving birth is not eternal, as Aristotle appears to have believed it to be, then the first man and woman must have been created or come into existence spontaneously (or autochthonously). But if this is the case, then the fact of the proliferation of the human species to this day points to the intermarrying of brothers and sisters, and even of sons and mothers, or fathers and daughters in the case of the primeval pair. The fundamental, moral conflicts that arise from this very point are synthesized and harmonized by the kind of binary logic to which we have already made reference.

It must be admitted that the Straussian account is a controversial one. Leach, for example, criticizes it at a number of points.[21] The assumption that incest taboos are universal is questionable as are a number of other of Lévi-Strauss' sweeping generalizations. However, the tentative and provisional character of any sociological or anthropological thesis should not pre-empt the use of such a thesis in an exploratory work of the kind that we intend pursuing regarding cultural episcopacy. Indeed Leach himself was not so inhibited, despite his skepticism about the universal claims for structuralist explanation, from applying structural analysis to biblical myth and the formation of Christian doctrine. Let us now look at some examples of structuralist approaches to theology which a structuralist would regard very much as a mythopoeic exercise in telling a sacred story. We shall be adopting a qualified use of this anthropological method in understanding the development of a theology of episcopacy.

---

[21] Leach (1970) op. cit. p. 69, 90-91 ff.

7. *Structuralism, myth, and the sacred stories of Christian revelation*

The weakness of both Lévi-Strauss' and Leach's approach is that although both claim not to make any judgment about history in analyzing the biblical sacred stories, they fail in practice to keep both concepts distinct.[22] Because history is described theologically, the theological description cannot be held necessarily to deny the historical core. The structuralist "logic" will assist our understanding of the language of the description, but will not necessarily say anything about the true nature of what is described.

The biblical revelation is given in the historical and cultural context in which the texts were written, and in the transformation of those isolated texts as they are received in the period 200 B.C. to A.D. 337 and interpreted as telling a single sacred story. The cultural expression of them as sacred stories will as such bear a structuralist form, if structuralism is valid. Moreover, if the stronger, Straussian form of structuralism is valid, any human culture, by virtue of a common human mental endowment, will think formally about its metaphysical and social constructs in such a structuralist way.

Leach takes the Egyptian Horus myth as the exemplar for the structural features that he observes in the biblical sacred stories. Whether he does this because he believes there was a historical influence either in the early Old Testament case of Moses or in the syncretism of the immediately pre-Christian, pagan Roman Empire, or whether because he is losing his scepticism about Straussian universal properties of mind, he does not make clear. In the myth, Osiris marries his sister Isis, and is murdered by his brother Seth. Isis then gives birth to Horus, son of the dead Osiris. The old Pharaoh is Osiris, and his son and successor is Horus. But their wives, both mother and daughter-in-law are both equally representations of Isis.

---

[22] Cf. for example what is claimed about the Jesus of History in E. Leach, and J.A. Aycock, *Structuralist Interpetation of Biblical Myth*, (London: Cambridge University Press), p. 107 where Leach says: "I do not believe that Jesus was a historical personage at all."

A number of structuralist antitheses in consequence result. Thus Isis becomes both queen-mother and queen-wife. Furthermore, Horus and Osiris are interchangeable in so far as the son who represents Horus is destined himself to become the father and hence Osiris. Since myth is timeless, temporal succession can be reversed and what is old can become young and *vice-versa*. Leach applies this to Trinitarian theology, with some gnostic nuances where Mary is Mother of God the Son and, in some sense, bride of Christ. Though orthodoxy would deny that she is so in any direct sense, orthodoxy will itself apply the logic described by structuralists as "mythopoeic" in effecting a kind of connection. "Mother Church" is the bride of Christ. Moreover any nun in representing in her life the Virgin Mary also claims to be the bride of Christ, and so continues the paradox of the virgin who is also wife and mother. The various images and their inter-relationships, through association, therefore, overcome the antithesis that involves the contradiction that she who is the Mother of God cannot be his bride and remain a true virgin.

Leach perceptively distinguishes in the biblical revelation fundamental antitheses in such images as master/servant in contradistinction to kingship, and in turn to husband/wife. Moses' kingship represents a transformation of the Osiris-Horus myth. The scene of the bulrushes and the ark involve Moses' mother and sister, and Pharaoh's daughter and implies, as the Dura-Europos murals make clear, symbols of death and resurrection. The ark is depicted like a Roman sarcophagus. Jochabed (Moses' mother) and Miriam (his sister) are painted as disguised midwives in identical clothes, with a naked and goddess-like figure moving out of the water with the infant Moses in her arms. Thus Pharaoh's daughter, Moses' mother and sister each operate in the role of Isis who is daughter, mother, and sister combined in the mythopoeic logic. The equivalence is indicated by the similarity of Miriam and Jochabed, and the divine characteristics of the goddess who arises with Moses in her arms (Pharaoh's daughter). The sarcophagus-tomb like bulrushes determine the sacred tale as symbolizing death and resurrection, with Pharaoh playing the role of Seth.

The myth is further transformed in the sacred story of the birth of Jesus. As Leach says:

> ..if we follow the lead of Christian artists down the centuries and transform the "wise men" of Matthew Chapter 2, together with the Shepherds of Luke Chapter 2, into "three Kings" then the "babe lying in a manger" discovered by the Kings equates with the baby lying in "an ark of bulrushes" discovered by a Princess. Notice that both the kings and the Princess arrive on the scene as emissaries of Seth (Herod in the one case; Pharaoh in the other). So Jesus, like Moses, is a Horus figure and we are led to start thinking about possible connections between Mary (Miriam), the virgin mother, virgin sister of Moses, and the figure of Isis who managed to be mother, sister, daughter, wife, daughter all at once.[23]

The basis for Leach's structuralism is not, as I have said, clear. It may be that he believes a direct and substantive, historical influence of the Horus myth either on the composition of the Old Testament stories or in the context of the pagan world of the first Christian centuries on the Christian texts. However, a structuralist need not so argue.

The comparison made between one sacred story and another does not establish historical borrowing for the Straussians. The purpose of the comparison is to show how human beings, in any culture, formulate their sacred stories by a kind of mythopoeic logic which synthesizes antitheses, which harmonizes and makes equivalent opposites such as virgins and married women, life and death, royal power and human defencelessness, mothers and daughters etc. On such a view, even if the first Christians or their Jewish predecessors had never heard of the Horus myth, their sacred stories would have been formally comparable in this way. The telling of a sacred story, or if you like, the construction of a theology, is the product of a human endowment arguably culturally universal whose precise logico-mythopoeic dimensions structuralism is trying to unravel.

Because this monograph is concerned with the sacred story associated with the development of church Order in terms of the development of a culture— myth is the spoken part of ritual and both may be said to develop *pari passu*— we will continue our exposition of Leach's structuralist interpretation, in terms of the

---

[23] Leach (1983) op. cit. p. 43-44.

Ignatian ritual that creates Order. So far we have been concerned with sacred stories predominantly on the theme of kingship but there are themes of master/servant as well. Moreover Leach is sensitive regarding the relationship between christology and theology of Order, however questionable in detail some of his reading of church history may be in this regard.[24] As Leach says:

> In contrast to the Master/Servant image, which fits with a pentecostal ideology and an egalitarian, congregationalist type of church-organization, the Kingship pattern is systematically hierarchical. In Christianity this latter aspect of Deity is given special emphasis in Roman Catholicism and in episcopal forms of Protestantism.[25]

In both the sacred stories of Moses and of Jesus the antitheses of servant/prophet and king are synthesized in a way that can be represented by structuralist accounts of mythopoeic logic. The king lives in a palace surrounded by symbols of power and luxury like Moses, adopted son of Pharaoh's daughter. Yet in the wilderness he adopts the prophetic role of a prophet's natural habitation as the son-in-law of the Priest in Midian. God appears to him directly as God does with prophets, but not with kings. Kings represent or embody God's person, power and immortality in their persons, rather than standing before God and listening to his voice as apart from him.

Prophets however are equal to one another and Miriam and Aaron also prophesy. The prophetic and the monarchic is, however, reconciled when it is said that Moses speaks to God face to face but Aaron and Miriam only in dreams and visions. Moreover Miriam is stricken with leprosy for prophesying against Moses' irregular, ectogamic marriage with an Ethiopian. (*Num.* 12) Thus the hierocratic principle is asserted against charismatic equality. But rather the myth or sacred story accomplishes this by means of its internal, mythopoeic logic. In myth semi-divine rulers are marked out by their infringement of kinship taboos. Oedipus married Jokasta his mother. So too Moses' mother, Jochabed was his father's (Amram's) sister so

---

[24] His treatment of Arianism as a populist movement, without regard to the role that this played in the legitimation of imperial power with the church in subordination is a case in point, see ibid. p. 74-78.

[25] Ibid. p. 38.

that he was conceived in an incestuous marriage. Moses' own marriage first to Zipporah, daughter of Jethro, priest of Midian, and then to the unnamed Ethiopian, broke the rule of endogamy. Thus Miriam's equality with Moses is denied by the mythopoeic logic which generally marks out the status of sacred heroes by making them signs of broken kinship taboos. Kingship and prophecy are synthesized by the introduction of the logic of broken incest taboos in the case of rulers.

So also in the New Testament there is clearly an antithesis between Jesus born to be king in the Nativity Stories, and the baptism with the Spirit and his fasting in the Wilderness in which the image of the servant/prophet preponderates. His miracles, like the feeding of the five and four thousand, takes place in dessert places, and both incidents are followed by Jesus going to a mountain to pray, and going to the mountain for the Transfiguration. The images of kingship only replace those of the prophet when the scene shifts to Jerusalem where his disciples become his servants, and he orders people out of the Temple as his own palace. The movement of the sacred story therefore synthesizes the antitheses of kingship and charisma, and of masterhood and servanthood. It does so in this instance by images, common in sacred stories, regarding the mountain or desert location of the prophet in his poverty, and the urban location of the king in his wealth and power, and in the interrelationship between these localities in the story of the servant/king. Moses too removed from a palace to the wilderness and thence to a mountain.

Now at this juncture we must point out that a structuralist approach has implications for accounts of the development of church Order in terms of contemporary redaction-criticism that has not so far been noticed. No-one as far as I am aware has sought to take the antinomies of prophet/servant and king in the gospel accounts and, in association with different geographical terrains, sought to attribute these to separate Christian communities, some of whom regard Jesus as a king, and others as a servant/prophet, with both traditions combined by the editors/redactors of the four gospels. Yet as we shall see in Chapter 4, similar features applied to groups of disciples have been used in propounding the theory that charismatic, prophetic, and apostolic strands in the gospel and other, early Christian texts emanate from different and rival groups with distinct ministerial patterns. Structuralism shows us that this is not necessarily so, but that the Christian sacred story, like any other sacred story, will necessarily exhibit such antinomies *ab initio*. In our next chapter we shall return to the mythopoeic logic of a theology or sacred story of church Order in Ignatius of Antioch, the martyr-prophet bishop, who does not command and yet demands obedience towards those who, together with their presbyters and deacons, share his episcopal office. We shall in our next chapter show how Ignatius' theology of Order reflects both the creation of a society through the creation of collective representations, and the construction of a sacred story in which the antinomies of hierarchy and the charisma of the Spirit-filled community are synthesized by a structuralist logic. For the moment, let us summarize where our account has so far led us, drawing out its implications for both modern ecumenism and recognition of divine revelation.

8. *In Conclusion: the sociological context for ARCIC and the Lima Liturgy*

We concluded our first chapter with a theological argument, namely (i) that as grace completes nature but does not destroy it, and (ii) as human nature together with human understanding are inextricably bound up with the cultural forms in which that nature and that understanding is expressed, then (iii) individual human cultures are to be valued in their own right as that which the redemptive action of God in Christ's completes but does not destroy. As both liturgy and Order have the sacramental purpose of symbolizing what they effect and effecting what they symbolize, liturgical forms and ordained persons will share the cultural character of the particular redeemed community which they represent. We proposed seeing this theological argument not simply as an instrument for understanding the communication of the gospel in terms of missions, but also for illuminating the character of ecumenical divergence, as well as giving point to ecumenical dialogue.

The validity of such a theological argument rested on principally two anthropological assumptions which we have examined in this chapter, and for which we sought to argue. The first of these was that what Wittgenstein called "agreement in form of life" could never so radically diverge from one society to another so as to make communication and dialogue absolutely impossible. Our grounds were that there is at the level of highest generality a peculiar kind of vagueness about certain fundamental concepts that are their communicative strength, enabling through their open-textured character new concepts to be linked within existing conceptual schemes whether those concepts were intra or cross cultural.

Thus it is possible to regard the church as the extension of the incarnation as existing in a number of distinct cultural forms in terms of a common Christianity of shared meanings. It was furthermore a consequence of that conclusion that the difference between sub-cultures within a society and different cultures between societies became one of degree. At the highest level of generality, a common, human form of life, witnessed in what Katz calls the "effability" of human languages, implies a subcultural relationship between what cease to be distinct human cultures. Subcultural denominational differences in consequence differ only in degree from cross cultural differences regarding the church as the extension of the incarnation in a culture.

The second assumption is that any dialogue establishing epistemological agreement will also be marked by sociological accompaniments in terms of the formation of new united or re-united groups. Epistemological agreements will be accompanied by the creation or re-assertion of what Durkheim called "collective representations," and here, in ecclesial terms, Order will inevitably be involved. Such collective representations are, however, created by means of sacred stories in which antinomies are reconciled and which proceed by their own, structuralist logic. Bread, water, wine, and oil are never only such, but their nature is defined in terms of the shared categories of the group, and of the sacred story woven around them, as for that matter are such figures as bishops, presbyters, deacons, apostles, prophets, pastors and teachers.

As a further exemplification of our theme it will be well, therefore, in conclusion to take some examples from two ecumenical documents, namely the Lima Statement on ministry and the Final Report of the Anglican-Roman Catholic International Commission.[26] One example, found in the Lima Statement, is the quest in that statement for general and open-textured concepts to express the fundamental agreements of the representatives of various ecclesial traditions in a dialogue over disagreements in opinion. Those believing in church government on the basis of a threefold Order the focus of whose unity is the bishop, and those believing in presbyteral or some form of charismatic church government, look in their dialogue to the general, open-textured concept of ἐπισκοπή, rather than the "closed" concept of priest, bishop, deacon, minister, pastor etc.

As the *Lima Statement* says:

> The Church as the body of Christ and the eschatological people of God is constituted by the Holy Spirit through a diversity of gifts or ministries. Amongst these gifts a ministry of *episkopé* is necessary to express and safeguard the unity of the body. Every church needs this ministry of unity in some form in order to be the Church of God, the one body of Christ, a sign of the unity of all in the Kingdom.[27]

Thus representatives of episcopalianism, presbyterianism, and congregationalism, when facing one another in dialogue appeal to a shared agreement in "form of life" in terms of a general principle of "oversight" (*episkopé*). The "ministry of *episkopé* is necessary" to the ordering of the community, but whether that ministry resides in a single bishop remains an unresolved issue of the dialogue. Indeed we are informed that there are general presbyteral, diaconal, as well as episcopal functions, expressed and performed "in different ways." Moreover, "in some cases, churches which have not formally kept the threefold form have, in fact, maintained certain of its original patterns."[28] Patterns of family resemblances rather than exhaustively defined, closed classes are therefore being pursued in dialogue, in a way that our earlier, general sociological and epistemological discussion sug-

---

[26] Anglican-Roman Catholic International Commission, *The Final Report*, (London: S.P.C.K. and C.T.S. 1981); *Baptism, Eucharist and Ministry. Faith and Order Paper No, 111* (Geneva: World Council of Churches 1982).

[27] *Baptism, Eucharist and Ministry*, op. cit. p. 25 para 23.

[28] Ibid. p. 25 paras 22 and 24. See also ARCIC, op. cit. p. 42 and p. 63-64.

gested would take place. Thus dialogue is able to proceed, because one community of judgment cannot insulate its concepts and categories against the encroachments of another, as would occur if we could produce exhaustive definition of closed-class concepts.

Whether the existence of general episcopal, diaconal, and presbyteral functions within the community not located in concrete persons can fulfil other demands acknowledged in the Lima Statement is, however, another matter. Frequently we are informed what the cultural argument which we are developing would also demand, namely that Order arises out of and reflects the character and life of the Christian community:

> Finally, the intimate relationship between the ordained ministry, and the communal dimension where the exercise of the ordained ministry, is rooted in the life of the community, and requires the community's effective participation in the discovery of God's will and the guidance of the Spirit.[29]

The ordained ministry can only fulfil its calling "in and for the community" with whose recognition they cannot dispense.[30] "Any member of the Body of Christ," in preaching, teaching, or in other ways, "may contribute to the sacramental life of that body. The ordained ministry fulfil these functions in a representative way, providing the focus for the unity of the life and witness of the community."[31] We shall ask in our consideration of the development of the ministry and its theology in Ignatius of Antioch, whether the "representative" function of ministers of the general presbyteral, diaconal, and episcopal functions of the body of Christ do not require such ministers to be understood in terms of what Durkheim described as the community's "collective representations,"to which we referred earlier in this chapter, and which distinguish a debating society or a philosophic school from an ordered community with a distinctively cultural form.

We saw earlier that cultural artifacts, symbols, or representations had no meaningful existence as part of some putative state

---

[29] Ibid. p. 26 para 26.
[30] Ibid. p. 22 para 12.
[31] Ibid. p. 22 *Commentary* (13).

of nature apart from the network of fundamental concepts and ritual acts against the backcloth of which they were considered to be what they were by their communities. But the diversity of such concepts and acts required ordering into a meaningful, cultural whole by means of the dialectical logic by which the community's sacred story is created synthetically, as analyzed by the structuralists. We see in such contemporary ecumenical statements that we are examining examples of antinomies arising that require for their resolution the construction of a sacred story (or, as I would prefer, a theology) in a way that we shall see to be strikingly similar to the rise of the threefold Order in the early second century.

The *Lima Statement* requires the reconciliation of the antinomy between the community's participation in the priesthood of Christ and the priest as representative of Christ's priesthood to the community.[32] The antinomy appears to be partly resolved in terms of the representative character of ordained ministry of the functions of the community as a whole, to which we have already made reference. But the reconciliation of episcopal, presbyteral and congregational elements in the ordained ministry remains uncompleted.[33] Indeed if we now turn to the Anglican Roman Catholic discussion there is insistence that the priesthood of Christ, and the priesthood of the community, are "two distinct realities." Priestly ministry is "not an extension of the common Christian priesthood but belongs to another realm of the Spirit."[34] The unsynthesized antinomy thus remains.

In the ARCIC account of authority, a further fundamental antinomy appears. There is an emphasis at the beginning their report which is what we described in our first chapter as jurisdictional in contrast to representational:

An essential element in the ordained ministry is its responsibility for "oversight"(episcope). This responsibility involves fidelity to the apostolic faith, its embodiment in the life of the church today, and its transmission to the church of tomorrow.. Church and people

---

32 Ibid. p. 13 para 17 and *Commentary* (17).
33 Ibid. p. 26 *Commentary* (26).
34 ARCIC op. cit. p. 36 and p. 41-43.

have continually to be brought under the guidance of the apostolic
faith.[35]

Continuity in the apostolic faith is not enough in itself but must
also involve "the commission given to the apostles."[36] Thus there
appears an authority conceived as external to the community and
imposing the apostolic tradition from without.

But as the report continues, another perspective begins to
emerge. The ordained ministry is about building and strengthening *koinonia* within the local church and also with strengthening
and developing *koinonia* between the churches which is the
function of the *collegium* of bishops united under the universal
primacy of the Roman Pontiff.[37] *Koinonia* in consequence is the
product of the internal faith of the community, not imposed
externally, which the ordained minister "discerns" and expresses
representatively and not jurisdictionally:

> All who live faithfully within the *koinonia* may become sensitive to
> the leading of the Spirit and be brought towards a deeper under-
> standing of the Gospel and its implications in diverse ordained min-
> isters commissioned *to discern these insights and give authoritative*
> *expression to them, are part of the community,* sharing its quest for
> understanding in obedience to Christ, and receptive to the needs and
> concerns of all.[38]

In consequence one criterion for the authority of a credal statement is its reception by the faithful who "discern a harmony between what is proposed to them and the *sensus fidelium* of the
whole church."[39] There thus emerges an antinomy between
jurisdiction and tradition transmitted from without and the faith
of the community within, since the later is by no means passive,
but rather itself actively affirms and questions what is brought to
it.

We shall be seeking a theological account rooted in the classical
and patristic statement of the threefold Order which will synthesize these and other, fundamental antinomies in our theology of

---

[35] *ARCIC* op. cit . p. 33-34.

[36] Ibid. p. 43.

[37] Ibid. p. 55-67.

[38] Ibid. p. 54 my italics.

[39] Ibid. p. 72.

Christian ministry, on the basis of a sacred story about ecclesial Order as the cultural incarnation of the events of human redemption.

CHAPTER THREE

ORDER IN IGNATIUS OF ANTIOCH

The ordained ministry as sacramental representation

We have not chosen to begin the historical part of our discussion of cultural *episcope* with Ignatius simply because he represents the earliest, late first to early second century account of an episcopal form of church government. Had we done so, our choice might be considered at best arbitrary and at worst an example of that kind of special pleading which selects the most favourable example in support of a case. Undoubtedly ministry in the early church assumed far more diverse forms than that of the threefold Order which emerges unambiguously for the first time only with Ignatius.[1]

The significance of Ignatius for our argument is that his account of church Order fits well the requirements of the sociological and cultural ecclesiology which we adumbrated in general terms in the last chapter. We shall show that the threefold Order for Ignatius, in contrast to earlier glimpses of church life before him, exhibits a social organization with a cultural form. We argued in our last chapter that to speak of community in social terms is to study similarities between social organizations, but to study them in cultural terms is to draw out what makes one society different from another. Furthermore, those differences cannot be regarded in a naively realistic way as artifacts, customs, or possessions that a society contingently owns and can in a piecemeal way cast aside. Rather artifacts, symbols, and rituals

---

[1] H. Koestler, ΓΝΩΜΑΙ ΔΙΑΦΟΡΟΙ the origin and nature of diversification in the history of the early church, in *HThR* 58 (1965), p. 290-306 and W. Bauer Rechtgläubigkeit und Ketzerei im ältesten Christentum, in *BZHT* 10 (Tübingen: Mohr 1964). Cf. H.E.W. Turner, *The Pattern of Christian Truth*, (Oxford: Bampton Lectures, 1954); F.W. Norris, Ignatius, Polycarp and 1 Clement: Walter Bauer reconsidered, in *VCh* 30 (1976), p. 23-44.

derive their meaning from what Wittgenstein described as "form of life" and are what Durkheim called "collective representations" of the "collective consciousness." It was thus artifacts, symbols and rituals, as interweaved with an interpersonal conceptual backcloth that constituted the society's "culture."

We shall argue in this chapter that Ignatius of Antioch, in arguing the unique form of Christian society in terms of the threefold Order, exemplifies the emergence of a Christian community in an unambiguous social and cultural form. Bishops, priests, and deacons are "collective representations" of what the community affirms about its redeemed character. As "collective representations" they fulfil what the medieval definition of a sacrament requires, namely that a sacrament "symbolizes what it effects and effects what it symbolizes." What however the description of a sacrament in terms of a "collective representation" achieves in terms of increased theological understanding is to unite what it is to be sacramental to what it is to be a community. A "collective representation" both represents a culture and extends its social cohesion by reinforcing its cultural identity, thus symbolizing what it effects and effecting what it symbolizes.

Both Schillebeeckx and Rahner have pointed out the defectiveness of medieval and post-medieval views of sacramental validity which left out of account the ecclesial dimension to the sacramental act. In the case of the Eucharist, to use the central example of a sacrament, by omitting the ecclesial dimension, the medieval view made the consecration of bread and wine, which becomes the body and blood of Christ, a kind of personal action of the priest standing over against the community, and providing the fruits of his act to the community, to be either consumed or simply adored in the highly individualistic office of benediction. The intention of the priest to do "what the church does" became, therefore, a highly individualistic act. The emphasis of Schillebeeckx is to regard the priest's act as a representative act of the Church, and thus to make the community's conceptual backcloth of faith as important as the priest's individual act in constituting the substance of what is sacramentally represented.

Indeed, from what we have argued in the last chapter regarding collective representation, sacraments cannot be otherwise. Bread and wine are not things in isolation, to be made a more composite thing by being combined with a form of words, albeit attended by miraculous grace. "Bread" and "wine" like "hat" or "helmet" or "heart" or "womb" come already endowed with meaning by the interpersonal conceptual backcloth with which they are woven into the community's collective consciousness or form of life. Such things are already cultural symbols, and as symbolic as the verbal formulae with which they are combined. As Schillebeeckx says:

> In the sacraments grace comes to us in an ecclesial visibility. A sacrament is valid only when it is ecclesial. So if the intention of the minister is necessary for validity, it means that this intention must in some way concern at least the visible character of the sacrament. The minister performs the ritual act in the name of the church and thus in the name of Christ. the sacraments are not things but rather spiritual and religious symbolic acts of the Church- that is to say they are "incarnation."[2]

Thus in the Eucharist the statement made by symbols, ritual words and acts, and elements is the collective representation of the fact that "we are the Body of Christ," which creates and extends the reality that it expresses. A collective representation, like a Schillebeeckxian sacrament, does not represent something external to the community but "incarnates" the life of Christ found in and not apart from the community.

The ordained ministry was almost always in patristic thought interlinked with the ministry of the whole Church, and what it means to be an ordained minister has been part of what it means to offer as a community the eucharistic offering. Ignatius' of Antioch gives us, we shall argue, the first systematic statement of what makes a group of Christian individuals into a corporate society. The Christian society is created by its forming collective representations in terms of bishops, presbyters and deacons, who enact liturgically what it is that makes a Christian society different, that is to say what makes that society a distinct culture. Such collective representations have as their backcloth the form of life expressed in terms of a sacred story about the Father who sent the Son, who was really incarnate, and who truly suffered

---

[2] E. Schillebeeckx, *Christ the Sacrament*, (London: Sheed and Ward, 1963), p. 128, 162. See also K. Rahner, *Theological Investigations*, Vol. IV, (New York: Herder 1971), p. 242-243, 269-286 ff.

and rose again. Collective representations therefore express concretely the collective consciousness or central value system of the community. As, however, what binds office to community, and community to its self-understanding, is a sacred story, the logic of that sacred story, as we shall see, will proceed in terms of structuralist antinomies of the kind that we described in the last chapter.

Let us now make our case in a detailed analysis of the theology of Ignatius of Antioch.

1. *Ignatius and the apostolic ministry*

For Ignatius the church is the means by which the events of human salvation can be found and experienced concretely in a shared, form of life. Those events, basically, are the birth of Christ, his truly human life, his real sufferings and resurrection. (*Smyr.* 1; 2; *Tral.* 9; 10) The result of experiencing such events is union with God. Moreover that experience is made possible by the continuance in the present of the apostolic ministry. For Ignatius, despite his apparent mysticism, the δόγματα and δι- ατάγματα of the Lord and his apostles remain important (*Mag.* 13,1; *Tral.* 7,1). But also important is that the Father not only sent the Son, but that from both came the apostles too. Ignatius wishes to be found "in the company (ἐν κλήρῳ) of the Ephesian Christians, who were ever in agreement with the apostles in the power of Jesus Christ (οἳ καὶ τοῖς ἀποστόλοις πάντοτε συν- ήνεσαν ἐν δυνάμει Ἰησοῦ Χριστοῦ)." (*Eph.* 11) It is through membership of such a company that union with God is achieved. The Ephesians are exhorted to be united amongst themselves and with the threefold Order because: "it is useful (χρήσιμον) to be in blameless unity (ἀμώμῳ ἑνότητι) in order that you may also always share in God (ἵνα καὶ θεοῦ πάντοτε μετέχητε)." (*Eph.* 4, 1-2)[3]

But for Ignatius the apostolic ministry is experienced not through a collection by the community of remembered historical

---

[3] See also *Tral.* 1,2, where μιμητὰς ὄντας θεοῦ reflects hellenistic religious notions of identification by imitation. Cf. *Mag.* 14. In *Pol.* 8,3 there is the prayer διαμείνητε ἐν ἑνότητι θεοῦ καὶ ἐπισκοπῇ. Cf. W.R. Schoedel, *Ignatius of Antioch*, (Philadelphia: Fortress Press), p. 18-20.

events in past time, but through the present reality of the church gathered for the Eucharist. The gathered ἐκκλησία "incarnates" the heavenly realities in which the Father continues to send the Son, and from both the Spirit-filled apostles continue to proceed. The mark of the true church is the exhibition of this heavenly reality in the liturgy, in the context of which the bishop, surrounded by the presbyters and attended by the deacons, find their significance. The bishop represents the fatherhood of God, the deacons the ministry of Jesus Christ, and the presbyters the Spirit-filled council of the apostles. The Philadelphians are to "flee to the gospel as to the flesh of Jesus and to the apostles as the presbyterate of the church (τοῖς ἀποστολοῖς ὡς πρεσβυτερίῳ ἐκκλησίας)." (*Philad.* 5,2) By achieving union with the threefold Order, they achieve union with God the Father who sent the Son and from whom proceeded the Spirit-filled apostles.

Thus for Ignatius "to be grounded in the teachings of the Lord and of the apostles" (βεβαιωθῆναι ἐν τοῖς δόγμασιν τοῦ κυρίου καὶ τῶν ἀποστόλων) is not merely to possess remembered oral history but to act "in the Son and the Father and the Spirit" (ἐν υἱῷ καὶ πατρὶ καὶ ἐν πνεύματι). That union is expressed, in a timeless, eschatological, liturgical moment (ἐν ἀρχῇ καὶ ἐν τέλει) when they are gathered "with your bishop worthy of praise, the finely woven spiritual crown of your presbyterate, and your deacons according to God (μετὰ τοῦ ἀξιοπρεπεστάτου ἐπισκόπου ὑμῶν καὶ ἀξιοπλόκου στεφάνου τοῦ πρεσβυτερίου ὑμῶν καὶ τῶν κατὰ θεὸν διακόνων)." (*Mag.* 13,1) Here the liturgical assembly or ἐκκλησία appears as the place where, not once, but in an ever timeless "now," the Father sends the Son, and the Son sends the spirit-filled apostles. These are the events represented liturgically in the bishop sending the deacons to serve the people in the liturgy. The spirit-filled apostles are there in the presbyterate forming a unity around bishop and deacons in their seated liturgical circle, and accepting their father-bishop's commands through his standing and circulating diaconal emissaries.[4]

---

[4] *Mag.* 13,2, where being in unity involves subjection to the bishop and each other, corresponding to Christ's subjection to the Father, and the subjection of the apostles to both.

2. *The threefold Order as* τύποι *of the heavenly Church*

Thus Ignatius can claim that the members of the threefold Order are τύποι. The the root meaning of the word τύπος is "impression" or "mark" from which it comes to be applied in Ignatius in the sense of "representation," "image" or "model."[5] The bishop in this sense is a "type" of the Father, the deacons a "type" of the Son, and the presbyterate a "type" of the spirit-filled apostles. Bishop, presbyters, and deacons become the "marks" or τύποι of the "true" church because they reflect eternal, transcendent and super-historical realities which they incarnate in the life of the church on earth.

Validity of Orders is not for Ignatius a question of an act of ordination which he never mentions,[6] let alone an act of ordination in terms of a chain stretching through secular history back to the apostles. As we have seen, bishops "represent" or "incarnate" the fatherhood of God whereas it is the presbyters who collectively represent the "council (σύνεδριον, σύνδεσμος) of the apostles." (*Tral.* 3,1; *Mag.* 6,1) All that is necessary is the type corresponding to the antitype, the *Urbild* corresponding to the *Abbild,* which is able to incarnate the heavenly church Order. Even if the recent trend away from regarding Ignatian theology as proto-gnostic is correct, there is still a common caste of mind shared by Ignatius with the Seer of the *Apocalypse* in this respect. Such a shared perspective is not, after all, surprising since both write to churches in Asia Minor, many of which are in the same cities, at a distance of some ten years from each other.[7]

---

[5] G.W. Lampe (Ed.), *A Patristic Greek Lexicon*, (Oxford: Clarendon Press 1961), p. 1418-1420, notes other meanings such as "form," "principle," "outline," or Old Testament "type."

[6] Ignatius does use the later word for "ordain," but in its earlier sense of "elect," when the Philadelphians are requested χειροτονῆσαι διακονον εἰς τὸ πρεσβεῦσαι ἐκεῖ θεοῦ πρεσβείαν (*Philad.* 10,1). Elsewhere this same appointee is simply called θεοπρεσβύτης ("ambassador of God"), (*Smyr.* 11,2) or θεοδρόμος "God's courier"). (*Pol.* 7,2) The person in question is to take Ignatius' news back to Antioch so that his election (χειροτονῆσαι) has no necessary connection with his diaconal office.

[7] Instead of regarding Ignatius and the Seer as inhabiting radically different communities of judgment, the former clerical, and the later prophetic/charismatic (with whom *Matthew* and the *Didache* are grouped), as Koestler

The Seer describes a heavenly church Order to which the earthly church is a counterpart. The twenty-four presbyters gather around God's throne and the heavenly altar, just like Ignatius' presbyterate forming its liturgical circle around their bishop. (*Apoc.* 4,4; 6,9; 7,11-14; 8,3-6 etc.) Ignatius describes the χόρος or "choir" singing around the heavenly θυσιαστήριον (*Eph.* 11,1; 13; 19,3), and unity with the hierarchy is described in terms of the cords of a lyre reminiscent of the heavenly lyres of the *Apocalypse.* (*Eph.* 5,2; *Mag.* 7,2; *Philad.* 4 cf. *Apoc.* 5,8; 14,2; 15,2) The Ephesians are stones in the temple of God's building (*Eph.* 9,1) in similar terms to those in which the Seer describes the Church as the New Jerusalem. (*Apoc.* 21,19) The symbol of the cross as a tree bearing the fruit of immortality, and the healing image for the properties of true doctrine, and the poisonous character of false, characterizes both works. (*Eph.* 10,3; 20,2; *Tral.* 6,11; *Philad.* 3,3; *Smyr.* 1,2 cf. *Apoc.* 2,7; 22,2) As with Ignatius, so with the Seer, therefore, the transcendental, eternal world is concealed behind contemporary events and revealed symbolically in the contemporary liturgy. The liturgical assembly or ἐκκλησία is the incarnation or "type" (τύπος) of the heavenly church Order which is its antitype.[8]

At first sight, therefore, it is arguable that the church in Ignatius reflects, in its Order, the heavenly hierarchy and its validity is in that reflection. Bishops, presbyters, and deacons stand for the Father, the apostolic council, and Christ as suprahistorical realities. Thus no act of ordination is important nor any series of such acts leading back to the apostles. All that is necessary is the type corresponding to the antitype, the *Abbild* corresponding to the *Urbild*, which is able to realize in the present the heavenly church Order. The obedience of the Son to the Father, and the sending of the spirit-filled apostles from both, is realized

---

(1965) op. cit. p. 287-290 does, we are seeing in our analysis rather a shared fundamental perspective with colourful variations. Cf. Turner, op.cit. passim.

[8] For an analysis of the foundations of Order in liturgy in both Ignatius and the Apocalypse, see W. Padberg, Vom gottesdienstlichen Leben in den Briefen des Ignatius von Antiochien, in *ThG* 53 (1963), p. 338-339 and Geordnete Liebe, Amt, und Pneuma, und kirchliche Einheit bei Ignatius von Antiochien, in *Unio Christianorum: Festschrift für Erzbischof Lorenz Jäger*, (Paderborn: Bonifacius 1962), p. 206-207.

in the acts and words of bishops, deacons, and presbyters in the present ἐκκλησία or eucharistic assembly.

As a result of such considerations, it has become fashionable in contemporary discussion of Ignatius to claim that his vision of the church is completely supra-historical.[9] Ignatius is charged with a Platonist account of church Order in which "he is certainly not thinking of the Gospel accounts. but of some supra- historical reality. in which the Apostles have a continuing place in the universal church."[10] Thus the heavenly church Order has no "historical anchorage" (historische Begründung).[11] It is, however, quite false to divorce Ignatius' theology from any historical grounding in this way, as we shall now argue.[12]

3. The extension of the historical incarnation

It is important not to oversimplify the transcendental and a-historical character of the Father, Son and apostles as though they were incarnated as it were out of the open air in their τύποι that are the bishop, deacons, and presbyters. Though Padberg is right to stress this fundamentally liturgical context to Ignatius' understanding of Order in terms of liturgical functions as expressing the *Urbild-Abbild* relation, it is quite wrong to make this relationship totally unconditioned historically.[13] What takes

---

[9] H. Paulsen, *Studien zur Theologie des Ignatius von Antiochien*, (Göttingen: Vandenhoek and Ruprecht 1977), V. Corwin, *St. Ignatius and Christianity in Antioch*, (New Haven: Yale 1960), etc.

[10] Corwin (1960) op. cit. p. 196-199.

[11] Paulsen (1977) op. cit. p. 145-157, who claims: "Es ist dem Ignatius durchaus nicht um eine historische Begründung des Verfassungsbegriffes zu tun, so wenig diesem traditionsgeschichtliche Implikate fehlen. Charakteristisch dafür ist, dass Ignatius nicht auf den Gedanken der Sukzession verweist. Die ignatianische Betönung der Hierarchie und vor allem monarchischen Episkopates— wobei der Bischof in der Stelle Gottes tritt— lässt sich zunächst einmal nicht einfach historisch herleiten, sondern nur als Konsequenz ignatianischer Theologie (und ihrer Verschränkung vom Himmlischen und Irdischen) begreiffen; in diesem Zusammenhang muss sie deshalb zunächst erläutert werden," p. 151-153.

[12] For a more detailed discussion of these points, see A. Brent, History and Eschatological Mysticism in Ignatius of Antioch, in *ETL* 65 4 (1989) p. 309-329.

[13] Padberg (1972), op. cit. p. 51-2, Padberg, (1962) op.cit. p. 201-217, and Padberg (1963), op. cit. p. 337-347.

place in the timelessness of liturgy for Ignatius once had a beginning in time.

Being in unity with the presbyteral apostles, and through them with the Father and the Son, is a process that has a historical dimension. Unity for Ignatius is described in terms of "commingling". The Ephesians are commended for being "as mingled together (ἀνακεκραμένους) as the church is with Jesus Christ and as Jesus Christ is to the Father in order that all things may be in harmonious unity (ἐν ἑνότητι σύμφωνα)." (Eph. 5,1) But this "commingling" had a beginning in time (ἐν ἀρχη). As the famous passage in Smyrnaeans makes clear, the timeless Order is not caught out of the empty air, but the "commingling" begins at Christ's resurrection. Those around Peter touch the risen Lord and believed, "mingling with his flesh and blood (κραθέντες τῇ σαρκὶ αὐτοῦ καὶ τῷ αἵματι)," and this mingling was with one who was "as fleshly, even though he was spiritually united (πνευματικῶς ἡνωμένος) with the Father." (Smyr. 3,1-3)

Thus it is in unity with a historical community, transmitting and representing the fact of the saving events through its present Orders, constituting and conducting the liturgical community, that salvation is received. Though Ignatius may quote from the Teaching of Peter to make this point, it is nevertheless reinforced by his allusions, however circumspect, to the Johannine tradition. The "spiritual crown" of the presbyter-apostles, corresponding to those who wish for an apostolic union that will enable them to act in the Spirit as in the Father and the Son, reminds us of John's account of the Upper Room and the inbreathing on the Twelve.[14] So too does Ignatius' comment that "the Lord received ointment on his head that he might breath incorruption on the church" (ἵνα πνέῃ τῇ ἐκκλησίᾳ ἀφθαρσίαν). (Eph. 17,1) For Ignatius therefore the gathered, liturgical assembly, through what its Orders as τύποι represent, continues

---

[14] Jn. 20,21-2. That the "disciples" here were in fact the Twelve, see 20,24. H. Köster, Geschichte und Kultus im Johannesevangelium und bei Ignatius, in ZThK 54 (1957), p. 56-59 argues for a distinction between a putatively Johannine sense of history, and that of Ignatius' a-historical sacramentalism, only by failing to grasp that the latter has the kind of historical concern for which I am arguing in this chapter.

in the present the historical reality of the saving acts of God in Christ. This is the significance for Ignatius of "coming together."[15]

We may describe the church according to Ignatius, therefore, as the "extension of the incarnation." For not only does the threefold Order, by constituting the τύποι, incarnate the transcendental church Order, but continues what began in the facts of salvation history. What Padberg described as "the presence of Jesus Christ in his church" (die Anwesenheit Jesu Christi in seiner Kirche) as a "concretely experienced reality" (konkret erfahrene Realität) is nevertheless a reality which is not purely Platonic but grounded in history.[16]

But at this point we might well ask Ignatius why what we have described as the church as the extension of the incarnation needs to be expressed in terms of a threefold Order of office holders? We have already made reference to Ignatius and the Johannine tradition, and, according to many modern commentators, *John* focuses on the community, undifferentiated hierarchically, as the organ of the Spirit and the continuance of the life of the incarnate λόγος in the world. Let us therefore examine how and to what degree such an objection to Ignatius' account is valid.

4. *Ignatius and the Johannine Tradition a: the* ἐμφύσησις

Ignatius speaks of the Lord "breathing incorruption on the church," as we mentioned above. Parallel with Ignatius' account of the beginning of the church with the "commingling of flesh and spirit" between the risen Christ and "those around Peter," is the scene in the Upper Room in *Jn.* 20,19-23. The risen Christ says "Even as the Father has sent me (ἀπέσταλκέν με), so I am sending you (πέμπω ὑμᾶς). Saying this, he breathed into them (ἐνεφύσησεν) and said to them: Receive the Holy Spirit." The

---

[15] Padberg (1963) op. cit. p. 339 says: "Der christliche Gottesdienst wird als "Zusammenkommen" oder ganz allgemein als "Tun" bezeichnet (*Eph.* 13; *Mag.* 4; 7,1; *Tral.* 7,2; *Philad.* 7,2; *Smyr.* 8,1)," and "Die Anwesenheit Jesu Christi in seiner Kirche ist nicht abstrakte Lehre, sondern konkret erfahrene Realität." (1972) op. cit. p. 51.

[16] R. Padberg, Das Amtsverständnis der Ignatiusbriefe, in *ThG* 62 (1972), p. 51.

commission to forgive sins then follows. At first sight the comparison between Ignatius' κραθέντες τῇ σαρκὶ αὐτοῦ and John's ἐνεφύσησεν appears strained since the latter is concerned with immortality and not the forgiveness of sins. However in Ignatius' claim that Jesus received oil on his head "in order to breathe incorruption on the church" (ἵνα πνέῃ τῇ ἐκκλησίᾳ ἀφθαρσίαν), he reveals that "breathing" was related in his mind with the immortality gained through the "commingling" at the resurrection.[17]

The inbreathing of the Spirit constitutes, according to *John*, the church as the extension of the incarnation. The λόγος, as the mind of God where are found those eternal realities which Plato described as the transcendental world of Forms, was incarnated in the life of Jesus of Nazareth. In that life the incarnate λόγος reveals himself as the "real light," the "true bread," and the "real vine," who comes from the God who is also "real." (*Jn.* 1,9; 6,32; 7,28; 15,1; 17,3) ἀληθινός is the characteristic Platonist description of the transcendental world, as is καλός ("good, beautiful") in the "good wine" (καλὸν οἶνον), or the "good shepherd" (ὁ ποιμὴν ὁ καλός). (*Jn.* 2,10; 10,11) The "works" that Jesus "reveals" are also "good" (πολλὰ ἔργα ἔδειξα ὑμῖν καλά) (*Jn.* 10,32). The "works" in question are the miracles which are σημεῖα or "signs" that reveal the λόγος as the bearer of the transcendent realities, the light, life, glory, judgment, exaltation and reign.

The Holy Spirit in *John* acts as Jesus' *alter ego* , and as such cannot yet be before Jesus is glorified. (*Jn.* 7,39) The function of the Paraclete who comes, is to continue what was done and revealed in the incarnate life of Jesus. (*Jn.* 15,26; 16,13) Thus it is important that the Spirit as the *alter Christus* should be given on the very evening of the resurrection itself, and "breathed into"

---

[17] The relationship between Ignatius and the fourth gospel is nevertheless problematic as such implicit allusions make clear, see C. Hammond Bammel, Ignatian Problems, in *JThS* N.S. (1982), p. 85-97. Cf. also C. Maurer, *Ignatius von Antiochien und das Johannesevangelium*, (Zürich: Zwingli 1949); H. Köster (1957) op. cit. p. 56-59; R.M. Grant, Hermeneutics and Tradition in Ignatius of Antioch, in *ArFil* 1-2 (1963), p. 194; L. Wehr, Artznei der Unsterblichkeit : die Eucharistie bei Ignatius von Antiochien und im Johannesevangelium, in *NA* n.f. 18, (Münster: Aschendorf 1987).

the community in which the heavenly realities will continue to be revealed in word and act, in the σημεῖα which will continue. (*Jn.* 14,12; 16,13-15; 17,20) [18]

For *John*, therefore, the "inbreathing" is important because it marks the church as the extension of the incarnation. The λόγος as the bearer of the transcendental realities becomes flesh in history, and the *logos-pneuma* continues that transcendental life, the living water, the true bread, the real vine, the light, life, glory, judgment, exaltation etc., seen in the signs which Jesus did, in the life of the church. In the fourth gospel, neither baptism nor the Eucharist is specifically inaugurated by any one special act of Jesus, which has misled some scholars into thinking that the author's religion was purely spiritual with no sacraments. Rather the fourth evangelist has no such special acts of Jesus because he wishes to locate the validity of the sacraments in the total sacramental fact of the incarnation. The christ-event in its totality creates its ecclesial representations or ikons.

In this respect the fourth evangelist again parallels Ignatius in the way in which the church's liturgy, through the threefold Order, as we have seen, incarnates the eternal, transcendent saving events that have entered history and continue historically in the present church. The church has the sacrament of baptism because Jesus "was conceived of Mary according to the divine plan (κατ᾽ οἰκονομίαν) of the seed of David and the Holy Spirit; who was born and baptized in order that by his passion (τῷ πάθει) he might cleanse the water." (*Eph.* 18,2) The baptism "to fulfil all righteousness" took place in history at the hands of John (*Smyr.*1), as did Christ's death, ἐν σαρκὶ, "in the time of Pontius Pilate and Herod the Tetrarch." (*Smyr.* 1,1; *Mag.* 11) He received oil upon his head, and thus the rite of unction is historically grounded. (*Eph.* 17,1) The Eucharist is the true bread of God because it is the true body and blood of him who suffered under Pontius Pilate. (*Smyr.* 6,2; *Eph.* 20; *Philad.* 4)[19] It is thus the historical facticity of the life of Jesus of Nazareth

---

[18] C. H. Dodd, *The Fourth Gospel*, (Cambridge: University Press 1958), p. 226-227, and C.K. Barrett, *The Gospel According to St. John*, (London: S.P.C.K. 1958), p. 61-62, 71, 118-119, 475.

[19] G.R. Snyder, The Historical Jesus in the Letters of Ignatius of Antioch, in *BR* 8 (1963), p. 3-12.

that grounds the sacramental nature of the church according to
both Ignatius and the fourth evangelist.

But at this juncture the critical question now arises is the character of the change between John and Ignatius regarding church
Order.

5. *Ignatius and the Johannine Tradition b: church Order*

Granted that, according to the fourth evangelist, the Holy Spirit
is inbreathed into the disciples and not into the open atmosphere,
why cannot the Spirit as the *alter Christus* simply be passed on
to individual, charismatic leaders who from time to time will
pass on the Spirit to other Christians? Why, on the other hand,
should not the Spirit be given to the community as a whole
without any formal representatives of the community holding
any office akin to Holy Orders. Why, in other words, do the
σημεῖα which incarnate in particular objects like bread, wine,
and water, or in events like miraculous healing the eternal acts of
redemption have to be located in individual persons in a threefold
Order acting as liturgical τύποι of those events?

Recent work on the fourth gospel has tended to support the
point of view that there is no ministerial Order apart from the
community implied in that work, and as such can be contrasted
with Ignatius' alleged *Frühkatholizismus*.[20] Those in the Upper
Room into whom the "inbreathing" takes place are called
"disciples" (μαθηταί and not "apostles" (ἀπόστολοι), since the
word ἀπόστολος is used strictly in the Jewish sense of *Shaliah*
as a synagogal ambassador. (*Jn.* 13,16) The fourth evangelist
does however refer to "the Twelve" as the inner circle of disci-

---

[20] J.W. von Walter, Ignatius von Antiochien und die Entstehung des
Frühkatholizismus, in W. Koepp (Ed.), *Reinhold Seeberg Festschrift, Vol.
12, Zur Praxis des Christentum,* (Leipzig: Deichert 1929); H. von
Campenhausen, *Ecclesiastical Authority and Spiritual Power in the Church
of the First Three Centuries,* (London: Adam and Charles Black 1969), p.
138-141 ff.; E. Schillebeeckx, *Ministry: A Case for Change,* (London:
S.C.M. 1981), p. 25-27; C. Clifton-Black II, The Johannine Epistles and
the Question of Early Catholicism, in *NT* XXVIII 2 (1986), p. 131-58; G.
Strecker, Die Anfänge der Johanneischen Schule, in *NTS* vol. 32 (1986), p.
31-47; J. Rhode, Häresie und Schisma im ersten Clementbrief und in den
Ignatius-Briefen, in *NT* 10 (1968) p. 214-217.

ples who remain faithful when the rest fall away, including the
natural brothers of Jesus. (*Jn.* 7,3 & 5; 6,67-71) But no account
of their commissioning is given as in the synoptic gospels, as
opposed to the "call" of individuals such as Simon and Andrew,
Philip and Nathaniel (*Jn.* 1,35-51), with the result that it is argued that the fourth evangelist set no store by a distinctive ministerial office upon which the church is founded and ordered.

But although the term μαθηταί is used of both the disciples in
general and of the Twelve as the faithful remnant, this cannot
mean that no distinction is drawn between them. As we have
seen, the Twelve are the faithful remnant of the μαθηταί in general and owe their position to that fact. Furthermore, in the,
scene in the Upper Room at the inbreathing, the Twelve are
clearly intended by the term μαθηταί. In the Thomas passage
which immediately follows we are informed that "Thomas, one
of the Twelve, was not with them when Jesus came, (*Jn.*
20,24), and that the "other disciples" (ἄλλοι μαθηταί) have to
tell him that they have seen the Lord. ἄλλος refers to "another of
the same kind," so that clearly it is the Twelve (without Thomas)
who receive the inbreathing, and not the general company of
disciples. The Spirit which they receive, moreover, is the fulfilment of the promise made to the Twelve at the Last Supper. (*Jn.*
16,13).

John has the Twelve functioning as representatives of the
community in that it is by virtue of their faith that the community
stands when the rest of its members fall away. It is in such a representative role that they receive the inbreathing. The Spirit is not
breathed into the Twelve disciples as isolated individuals but into
a corporate community. The very expression ἐνεφύσησεν is related to the description in *Gen.* 2,7, according to Philo of
Alexandria, where God breathes into Adam's nostrils the breath
of life.[21] It is, I believe, not without significance that the description of the group in the Upper Room should be "the
Twelve," even though the absence of Judas ("the son of perdition" *Jn.* 17,12), and Thomas, means that in fact their number
was only ten individuals.[22] Thus the ommission of any inaugu-

---

[21] *Jn.* 20,22 cf. Dodd (1958) op. cit. p. 226-227.

[22] E. Schweizer, Der johannneische Kirchenbegriff, in *TU* 73 (1959), p.
363-381 clearly misreads the situation with his bewildered comment: "Nur

ration of an ordained ministry is consistent with the ommission of the unauguration of the Eucharist or Baptism. The sacraments of Baptism, Eucharist, or Order rise out of the total historical fact of the incarnation.

I believe, therefore, that contemporary critics, of whom Schweizer is typical, have consistently underestimated the corporate and representative role of the Twelve in the fourth gospel, however sensitive Schweizer was to the presentation of individual disciples in that gospel, and the way in which the ecclesial metaphors are chosen to emphasize the individuality of participants in the community (Vine, Flock, Wheat, and Corn, etc).[23] Although at one point he was prepared to follow Barrett in regarding the disciples as "representatives of the whole community (überal Repräsentanten der Gesamtgemeinde)," he consistently divorced such representation from the notion of "office" (Amt) or "priesthood" (Priestertum).[24] As a result, and in his further desire to downgrade the Twelve, he interprets the figure of "the beloved disciple" as an ideal individual figure whose closeness to Jesus downgrades the role of the Twelve.[25]

Schweizer's case for the abnegation of church Order in the fourth gospel founders, in a way that is typical of proponents of such a case, on two objections The first is that it rests on the fundamental assumptiom that the evangelist is interested psychologically in the individual characters described in his gospel, from which is derived his allegedly general, anti-ecclesiastical perspective.[26] But his historical *mileu* is one in which the characterization of individuals as in the modern novel is as yet undis-

---

im Nachtrag (21,5 ff.) ist ein besonderer Auftrag erwähnt...der nicht hier gehörig ist 20,22 ff., wo nicht einmal klar ist, ob die zehn (!) Jünger oder eine grössere Gruppe gemeint sind," p. 373. I have argued that the immediately following passage (20,24) makes it "einmal klar" that ten individuals with the corporate title "the Twelve" is purposely intended.

[23] Ibid. 70-375.

[24] Ibid. p. 373 and 365.

[25] "Die Zwölf sind zwar nicht verschwunden—— wie könnten sie das?— Wohl aber treten sie gegenüber dem Lieblingsjünger stark zurück. Er aber charakterisiert eben diese innige Verbundenheit des Glaubenden mit dem Herrn— er "liegt an Jesu Brust" (13,23)." Ibid. p. 373.

[26] "Erst im vierten Evangelium werden einige, namentlich genannt Jünger auch psychologisch geschildert," Ibid. p. 371.

covered. The character of Nathaniel is that of a typical representative, that of "an Israelite in whom there is no guile," (*Jn* 1,47) and who therefore stands as a dodecal (I will not use the non-Johannine term "apostolic"), representative of the redeemed human response to Jesus. In Samaria's daughter, we have a like representative, redeemed human response, (*Jn.* 4,7-30) and so too with Nicodemus. (*Jn.* 3)

In regarding the sub-theme of the Beloved Disciple in terms of similar individualism, Schweizer fails to see the implied ecclesiastical polemic which would damage his case for the fourth gospel as an anti-ecclesiastical document. The Beloved Disciple is, like the other individuals, a representative figure, and, as the fragment of Polycrates of Ephesus was later to show, a figure standing for a tradition of Ephesian primacy around the apostle John used in the former's letter to pope Victor against the tradition of Roman primacy around the apostles Peter and Paul.[27]

The Beloved Disciple is not set against the Twelve in general, but against Peter. Peter knows of the identity of the betrayer only because the Beloved Disciple informs him from Jesus. (*Jn.* 13,23-26) Peter could not have got into the courtyard of the High Priest had it not been for the relation of the Beloved Disciple to the latter. (*Jn.* 18,15) It is this disciple to whom Jesus entrusts his own mother and not to Peter. (*Jn.* 19,26-7) It is he who gets to the Tomb before Peter on the morning of the resurrection, and who first witnessed its emptiness without entering the Tomb, but who stands without and believes. (*Jn.* 20,2-8) And finally in the Johannine community's appendix it is the Beloved Disciple who identifies the risen Christ to Peter by the lakeside. The figure of the Beloved Disciple, historically the apostle John, functions therefore as the representative of the Ephesian tradition of the primacy of John, for which Polycrates provides background historical evidence.

I stated that there was a second objection to Schweizer's thesis, in addition to his fundamentally incorrect assumption about the fourth evangelist's individualism. The second fundamental assumption is that because the Twelve are representatives of the whole community, no differentiation of the community in terms

---

[27] Eusebius, *H. E.* Book 5,24.

of office can been implied. Thus "office" (Amt) is set against "representation." But we shall see now how Ignatius regards office in terms of a sacral representation of the saving events experienced concretely in the community in process of salvation. We shall argue that his representative view of Order places him far closer to the Johannine view of the Twelve as constituting the community by acting, in a metaphysical sense, as its representatives. By contrast, in the later Church Orders, exemplified by the *Didascalia Apostolorum*, we shall see that the originally Ignatian and Johannine, representative view of Order has been pressed into a monarchical mold. (Chapter 4) The scene in the Upper Room inaugurates the sacrament of Order as obliquely and mystically as the Feeding of the Five Thousand inaugurated the Eucharist, or the Feet Washing inaugurated Baptism.

6. *The typology of representation in Ignatius*

In sections 3.2 and 3.3 above, we saw that according to Ignatius the bishop with the presbyters and deacons were τύποι or "representations" of the saving events not as it were caught out of the empty air but as incarnated in the present community, "commingled with" (ἀνακεκραμένους), that is to say in historical continuity with, those who touched the risen and glorified Jesus. Thus they do not represent what Padberg described as the "concretely experienced reality" of the saving events *to* the laity from some transcendental world of which the latter had no previous knowledge, but rather "represent" or "typify" the experience *of* the community in process of redemption.

It may be asked to whom what we must describe as the threefold typology (rather than "hierarchy") of the community presents or displays the saving events, if not to the community which is finding union with God in redemption? The answer to this lies in the early eschatology still reflected in Ignatius, the significance of which is, nevertheless, unperceived by the authors of the recent attacks on the genuineness of the Middle Recension.[28] It is through the threefold typology, representing

---

[28] M.P. Brown, *The Authentic Writings of Ignatius of Antioch: A Study in Linguistic Criteria*, (Durham N.C.: Duke University 1963); H.J. Sieben, Die Ignatien als Briefe: Einige Formkritische Bermerkungen, in *VCh*

the saving acts in the clergy's liturgical roles, that the demonic powers are shaken. The saving events of Christ's conception and death, as well as Mary's virginity, were, by God's plan or design, (κατ' οἰκονομίαν) "hidden from the ruler of this age,... three mysteries to be cried aloud, which were wrought in the silence of God." (*Eph*. 18,1; 19,1) This was why, when the star shone, the "old kingdom was destroyed. from then on everything was shaken (συνεκινεῖτο) because the abolition of death was in progress." (*Eph*. 19,3) The demonic powers now see the saving events as the church displays these through the threefold typology of its Order. This is why the community should more often gather liturgically for the Eucharist (πυκνότερον συν-έρχεσθαι εἰς εὐχαριστίαν), for when they so gather (ὅταν γὰρ ἐπὶ τὸ αὐτὸ γίνεσθε) "the powers of Satan are destroyed, and his destructiveness dissolved in the harmony (ὁμονοίᾳ) of your faith." (*Eph*. 13,1; *Smyr*. 6,1)

There is however one objection that can be raised against such a representative as opposed to jurisdictional role for the Ignatian bishop, which centers upon the meaning of προκαθέζεσθαι. Undoubtedly this verb is used in the sense of "preside over" in the church Fathers of the two centuries after Ignatius in a sense almost equivalent to προεστὼς as the eucharistic president of Justin *1 Apol*. 65,3. But the former term (as is the latter in the first example) is also are used in the sense of a prostitute "sitting out" in public and "exhibiting" herself (Athanasius, *Gent*. 26; Origen *Celsus*. 4,63), or of a city being pre-eminent in its region (Basil of Seleucia *Vitae Thecl*. 1). The term is then used in a

---

(1978), p. 1-18.; R. Joly, *Le Dossier d'Ignace d'Antioche*, (Université Libre de Bruxelles: Faculté de Philosophie et Lettres: LXIX 1978); C. Kannengiesser, Bulletin de Théologie Patristique: Ignace d'Antioche et Irénée de Lyon, in *RSR* 67 (1979), p. 599-623; G. Pelland, Le dossier des Lettres d'Ignace d'Antioche. A propos d'un livre récent, in *SciEspirit* 32,3 (1980), p. 261-297: W. Schoedel, Are the Letters of Ignatius of Antioch Authentic? in *RelStRev* 6 (1980), p. 261-297; R. Winling, A propos de la Datation des Lettres d'Ignace d'Antioche, in *RSR* 54 (1980), p. 259-265; J. Rius-Camps, *The Four Letters of Ignatius the Martyr*, (Rome: Pontificium Institutum Orientalium Studiorum 1980); J. Fischer, Bibliographic Note, in *ThRev* 2,77 (1981), p. 119-222. Joly's particular line of attack is continued in C. Munier, A propos d'Ignace d'Antioche, in *RevSR* 54 (1980), p. 55 (1981) p. 126-131. Cf. Hammond Bammel op. cit.

sense which falls short of "rule" in terms of the president of a council (John Damascene, *Vita Barlam et Joas*. 26-7), or of a judge "standing out" or being pre-eminent in his court appearance, or at one point in the *Clementines* of being "outstanding in truth" (τὸν ἀληθείας προκαθεζόμενον), where the reference can be neither to "presiding over" nor to "ruling" truth. (*Ep. ad Iacob*. II) In what sense is this term used in Ignatius?

The answer must be in the sense of "stand out" or "be pre-eminent." Our first reason is because nowhere in Ignatius is the bishop or anyone else regarded as προκαθεζόμενος alone and without qualification. Indeed, as we shall see, only the Christian community as a whole and without reference to the triple τύποι is so described without qualification in *Romans*. The qualification always is some variation of προκαθεζόμενος εἰς τύπον. To so translate this phrase as "rule over as a type" would be grotesque. "Preside over as a type" might, on the other hand, have appeared plausible had we not seen that, even if τύποι can be said to "preside over" a community, these particular ones possess no transcendental reality snatched out of the open air apart from the community by virtue of which they can claim such power. Rather they are "pre-eminent as a type" because they "stand out" from the community as signs or ikons of the common community experience of the saving events.

There is, however, a second reason which strikes at the almost general tendency to describe Ignatius' concept of episcopacy as "monarchical." Ignatius does not use the term προκαθημένος of the authority of the bishop alone, but of all three Orders in the threefold typology. To the Magnesians he speaks of προκαθημέ-νου τοῦ ἐπικόπου εἰς τύπον θεοῦ καὶ τῶν πρεσβυτέρων εἰς τύπον συνεδρίου τῶν ἀποστόλων, and appears at first sight to leave the deacons out of this pre-eminence or presidency by merely describing them as τῶν διακόνων τῶν ἐμοὶ γλυκυ-τάτων πεπιστευμένων διακονίαν Ἰησοῦ Χριστοῦ.[29] But that this is a stylistic variation in his usual description of the co-

---

[29] *Mag*. 6,1. Cf. however J.B. Lightfoot, *Apostolic Fathers* Pt. II Vol. II Sect. 1 p. 119 note 6. See also E. Sausser, Tritt der Bischof an die Stelle Christus? Zur Frage der Stellung des Bischofs in der Theologie des hl. Ignatios von Antiocheia, in *Festschrift für Franz Loidl*, Ed. Viktor Flieder, (Vienna: Hollinck 1970), p. 325-329.

equal, triple typology is shown by the fact that further on in this passage the Magnesians are exhorted to "be united with the bishop and those who are pre-eminent as type and teaching of of incorruption (ἐνώθητε τῷ ἐπισκόπῳ καὶ τοῖς προκαθημένοις εἰς τύπον καὶ διδαχὴν ἀφθαρσίας)." (*Mag.* 6,2)

In *Trallians*, moreover, although the bishop is described formally as ὄντα εἰς τύπον πατρός, equality of status is preserved by mentioning the deacons before the bishop, and connecting them with his typology by means of ὡς καὶ as part of the indispensable threefold Order to the bearing of the name of "church" or to the summoning of the eucharistic assembly: ὁμοίως πάντες ἐντρεπέσθωσαν τοὺς διακόνους ὡς καὶ τὸν ἐπίσκοπον ὄντα εἰς τύπον πατρός, τοὺς δὲ πρεσβυτέρους ὡς συνέδριον θεοῦ καὶ σύνδεσμον ἀποστόλων. χωρὶς τούτων ἐκκλησία οὐ καλ-εῖται.[30] If, finally, we look at the one place where προκαθη-μένος is unqualified by εἰς τύπον, we find further corroboration of our thesis. Without such a qualification, the term is applied by Ignatius to the community represented and not those who typify or represent. This is why I believe that Ignatius can refer to the Roman community in its entirety, without reference to presbyters and deacons which it certainly had at this time, as *1 Clement* makes clear, if not in fact a presiding *presbyter-episcopus,* as προκαθημένη τῆς ἀγάπης and προκαθήται ἐν τόπῳ χωρίου Ῥωμαίων. (*Rom.* insc) There is here no reference to the nascent jurisdiction of the Papacy, as has often been claimed, but rather that the whole community "sits forward," "stands out," or "is pre-eminent (προκαθημένη)."

Thus the community can display its character as a communion fellowship (ἀγάπη), in itself or through type-representation of its Orders. Thus it is arguable that Harnack's original understanding of the latter term in *Rom.* insc. in terms of pre-eminence rather than presidency should be adopted on grounds of its general consistency with the use of the term throughout the

---

[30] *Tral.* 3,1. It is tempting to translate χωρὶς τούτων ἐκκλησία οὐ καλεῖται as "without these the eucharistic assembly cannot be summonsed," although καλεῖται is used in Ignatius in the sense of "called" or "named," *Mag.* 4.

Ignatian corpus.[31] As a result, when the church of Antioch is deprived of its bishop, another church, in this case Rome, can display to it the quality of its fellowship directly and not through its clerical ikons. The communion-fellowship of the church as a whole, along with Jesus Christ, can be the church of Antioch's bishop (Ἰησοῦ Χριστός ἐπισκοπήσει καὶ ἡ ὑμῶν ἀγάπη). (*Rom.* 9,1).

Although προκαθημένος could, therefore, be translated in these preceding passages as "preside," the propriety of so doing we have seen to be questionable. This word may be comprehensibly applied to a single episcopal person in such a sense, but it has a plural subject in Ignatius, in terms of the people of the three Orders to which its action applies. "Sitting forward," which is the alternative to its derived sense of "pre-eminent," ought therefore arguably to be used in translation in these passages. Certainly when the phrase προκαθημένοι or such like is modified by the addition of εἰς τύπον the sense "pre-eminent as a type of" would appear more natural than "presiding as a type of." The charge of "monarchical" *episcope*, moreover, is belied once one continues the quotations on which it is based to find all

---

[31] A. Harnack, Das Zeugnis des Ignatius über das Ansehen der römischen Gemeinde, in *SPAW* (1896) VII, p. 123; O. Perler, Ignatius von Antiochien und die römischen Christengemeinde, in *FZPhTh* 22 (1944), p. 413-451, cf. J. McCue, The Roman Primacy in the Second Century and the Problem of the Development of Dogma, in *TS* 25 (1964), p. 171-175; V.B. Kötting, Zur Frage der "successio apostolica", in *Catholica* 27 (1973), p. 234-247; P. Meinhold, *Studien zur Ignatius von Antiochien*, (Veröffentlichungen des Instituts für europäische Geschichte, Mainz: Wiesbaden Steiner 1979). R. Staats, Die Martyrbegründung des Romprimats bei Ignatius von Antiochien, in *ZThK* 73 (1976), p. 463 rejects the interpretation that I have given here because: "kann Ignatius an anderer Stelle das Wort "Vorsitz" durchaus im amtlich-hierarchischen Sinn gebrauchen (Mag. 6,10), so dass die Möglichkeit ausscheidet, das Verbum προκαθῆσθαι im Sinne von "hervorragen" oder "sich auszeichnen" zu deuten." What I have argued is that in all other places the word is not "amtlich- hierarchischen" but representative and liturgical, and so fully consistent with this sense in the *Romans'* passage. Staats argues against Harnack (op.cit. p. 123) that the genitive τῆς ἀγάπης following προκαθημένη must make it mean "rule over" and not "be preeminent in." But in Basil of Seleucia *Vit. Theclae* 1 the capital city is described as "pre-eminent in every city of Isauris" (πόλις προκαθεζομένη πάσης τῆς Ἰσαυρίδος πολέως), using a genitive to express the object of the pre-eminence.

three τύποι included in the action of the verb which clearly bears the sense of "pre-eminent" rather than "rule." Finally, though one church could not be said to "rule" another except through official delegates, a church such as Rome can be said to be "pre-eminent" in a locality or outstanding for the communion-fellowship or ἀγάπη that it displays.

Thus Ignatius' insights help us to illuminate one strand in our argument, namely that *episcope* can be representative as opposed to being jurisdictional. But our other strand is cultural, namely that the representative bishop takes on the representation of the common, community experience of union with God through Christ in the particular cultural form of that community. We shall now see the extent to which this strand of our argument is also present in Ignatius' view of church Order.

7. Ignatius' clerical visitors as corporate personalities of their communities

We saw that, for the fourth evangelist, individual characters are typical representatives of the responses of particular communities as in the case of the Samaritan woman, Nathaniel, or even of the Beloved Disciple as representative of an ecclesial tradition. Though Ignatius would have difficulties with our notion of cultural pluralism, nevertheless it would be true to say that his clerical representatives are not simply the ikons of the divine and transcendental side of the events of salvation history incarnated, in a dualistic mode, in the communities to whom he writes. Indeed, Köster established that such a dualistic mode was quite foreign to Ignatius whose antinomies of σάρξ and πνεῦμα are brought into a soteriological monism.[32] When his clerical visitors represent their communities, they represent not simply the saving events shared by the community, but also the gifts and qualities of the individual communities themselves, as we shall now see.

---

[32] H. Köster, Geschichte und Kultus im Johannesevangelium und bei Ignatius, in *ZThK* 54 (1957), p. 57-58: "Wenn auch diese Terminologie in ihrem Ursprung dualistisch ist, so zeigen doch die angeführten Stellen (die sich beliebig vermehren lassen), dass Ignatius keineswegs dualistisch, vielmehr im Sinne eines soteriologischen "Monismus" denkt." It will be clear from my argument (sect. 3 above) that I strongly disagree with the distinction made here between history (in John) and cultus (in Ignatius).

Apart from the resident Polycarp, called by Ignatius "the bishop" of Smyrna, and his clergy visiting him as a transit prisoner, or the bishops of the nearest churches, and the presbyters and deacons of the more distant (*Philad*. 10,2), Ignatius had no direct contact at the time of writing with the churches of Asia Minor. He makes this quite clear in each letter, apart from *Romans* from which church he had no visitors, in the way in which he always begins his reflections with named clergy— with the exception of *Philadelphians* regarding names. Their qualities in his description are idealized qualities from which he hypothesizes the character and way of life of the communities that they represent.

He gives no information about those communities apart from his mystical musings on the essence of the personality of the clerics with whom he has his prison conversation. Thus Ignatius' knowledge of Ephesians comes from seeing their "whole multitude" in Onesimus "your bishop," where πολυπλ– ήθειαν contains the word πλῆθος which is Ignatius' usual theological term for the gathered ἐκκλησία. (*Mag*. 6,1; *Smyr*. 7,2) He prays that they will enjoy "communion fellowship" (ἀγάπη) with Onesimus, and so reflect his likeness (ἀγαπᾶν καὶ πάντας ὑμᾶς αὐτῷ ἐν ὁμοιότητι εἶναι). (*Eph*. 1,3)[33] Crocus, mentioned after the deacon Burrhus, is also the one through whom he receives an example of their communion fellowship (ἐξεμπλάριον τῆς ἀφ ' ὑμῶν ἀγάπης)— a communion fellowship which he also sees in Onesimus, Euplous, and Phronto. (*Eph*. 2,1)

The Magnesians he sees through "Damas your god-worthy bishop and the worthy presbyters Bassus and Apollonius, and my fellow slave, the deacon Zotion." (*Mag*. 2) "In these aforementioned persons" he claims to see and have communion fellowship with their whole gathered church (τὸ πᾶν πλῆθος ὑμῶν ἐθεώρησα ἐν πίστει καὶ ἠγάπησα). (*Mag*. 6,1) "Polybius your bishop" reveals to Ignatius the "unwavering and blameless mind" of the Trallians, and gives him such joy that he sees their

---

[33] ἀγαπή is translated "communion fellowship" following F.X. Funk, *Der Primat der römischen Kirche nach Ignatius und Irenäus: Kirchengeschichtliche Abhandlungen und Untersuchungen*, 1 Bd. (Paderborn 1897), p. 8-11, and Padberg (1962) op. cit. p. 216-217.

whole gathered church in him (ὥστε με τὸ πᾶν πλῆθος ὑμῶν ἐν αὐτῷ θεωρῆσαι). (*Tral.* 1,1) In Polybius he receives the example of their communion fellowship as he had done previously with Onesimus of Ephesus. (*Tral.* 2,2) The Smyrnaeans are commended as "joined together (κατηρτισμένους) in unshakable faith (ἐν ἀκινήτῳ πίστει),.and established (ἡδρασμένους) in communion fellowship in the blood of Christ," (*Smyr.* 1,1) just as Polycarp their bishop is "established as on an unshakable rock (ὡς ἐπὶ πέτραν ἀκίνητον)." (*Pol.* 1,1) In place of any description of them as individuals, he gives us his mystical vision of the corporate personality of the churches in their bishops, presbyters, and deacons at his prison meeting with them.

That Ignatius is not simply engaging in hyperbolic metaphor can be clearly seen from what he says regarding Onesimus of Ephesus. He claims that, in the course of meeting their bishop, their conversation was a supernatural exchange in which the divine characteristics of the community, of which Onesimus was a sacral representative, was disclosed to his mystical vision. As he says:

> For if in such a short time I had such converse of mind (τοιαύτην συνήθειαν) with your bishop, as was not human but spiritual, how much more do I consider you blessed as you are blended together as the church to Jesus Christ, and as Jesus Christ is to the Father.
> (*Eph.* 5,1)

The three Orders, in union with each other, in their personalities, (ἐν τοῖς προγεγραμμένοις προσώποις), represent sacramentally the corporate personality of their churches. In Ignatius' non-human, spiritual communication (συνήθεια) with Onesimus, he was able to bless the community itself "mingled" (ἀνακεκραμένους) with each other and with him as the Church to Christ and Christ to the Father. (*Eph.* 5,1) This is why the prayer of the bishop on behalf of the whole church has far more power than the prayers of one or two. (*Eph.* 5,2 and *Mag.* 6,1)

Thus Ignatius' description of church Order arises from a kind of mystical interchange as he grasps the hidden qualities of the visiting clerics, and develops fully fledged descriptions of the spiritual qualities of the communities of which he holds them to be the sacral representatives. Outside of *Romans* where no individuals are named, wherever actual and for the most part named members of the three Orders are mentioned, they are therefore type-representatives of their communities, though the words preferred in connection with such individuals are ἐξεμπλάριον and ὁμοιότης and not τύπος. They wear the corporate personalities of their communities and for this reason too are τύποι of the communities' spiritual possessions. The threefold Order are therefore the τύποι of redemptive acts of Father sending the Son, and the spirit-filled apostles proceeding from both, and embodied in their communities. As such the hierarchy do not so much display the acts of redemption to the laity, whose redeemed state they represent, but rather to the cosmic powers shaken by the gathering together of the liturgical assembly.

Having now completed our theological account of Ignatius' understanding of Order, let us now see how such an account fits with our definition of culture in terms of the structural- functionalist, sociological model that we have been pursuing in this monograph.

8. Ignatius' church Order in a sociological perspective

The sociological model which we sought to construct in Chapter 2 regarded a sociological description and a cultural description as both having reference to the same reality. The former described similarities between societies in terms of class, status, power, government, authority, etc whereas the latter described differences. Different cultures— between the which and sub-cultures there was only a difference of degree on a non-relativist theory of translation— were distinguishable in terms of the way in which they made concrete their central value systems, collective consciousness, or forms of life. The social expressions of these Durkheim called "collective representations," which consisted of artifacts, material symbols, symbolic acts, and distinctive concepts bound together and interpreted in terms of a shared, community form of discourse. Such "collective representations," giving an outward and visible form to the value system only partly understood by any particular participating member, constituted a collection of disparate individuals into a common society with concrete and observable signs of identification, operating with an interpersonal backcloth of fundamental rules and values.

Ignatius of Antioch was, of course, unaware of such details of modern, sociological analysis. But in the theological account that he gives to justify the kind of church Order which he prescribes we can witness an early, second century ecclesiastical development that conforms to the requirements of such a sociological model. In turn, such a model will help account for the spectacular success of the threefold Order in becoming practically universal by the end of that century. Ignatius' question was how did a collection of isolated individuals become a society, and his answer was a theological one about three Orders which were ikons of the one Father who sent his Son and the Spirit filled apostles. The Son came from the one Father and returned to the Father who was one. (*Mag.* 7,2) The Son did nothing either through himself or through the apostles, without the Father with whom he was in union (ἡνωμένος ὢν). The community, therefore, must do nothing without the τύποι of the Father-bishop, or the presbyter-apostles, and their solidarity as a community becomes what is signified and signifies what it becomes when liturgically the presbyters sit around the central bishop and deacons come and go with the gifts that he offers from and to the people.

Thus we see the development of a distinct society in Ignatius in which the collective representations, creative of the community, have been established. The sacred story of the saving acts is part of those representations of the collective consciousness, but a story alone cannot create a community. It must receive a concrete and tangible form in terms of material symbols, symbolic acts, artifacts etc. along with the conceptual web presupposed by the sacred story. But the availability of material symbols for the developing collective consciousness of a distinctively Christian culture was severely limited, given the existence of an infinite variety of these already in existence in existing Mediterranean cultures, and endowed with their own Jewish or pagan meanings.

Thus there could be, at this early period, no sacred vestments, sacerdotal families, or sacred buildings and altars. The chasuble, stole, and alb grew from the secular dress of the Roman magistrate. We shall see in the next chapter that James, the Lord's

trate. We shall see in the next chapter that James, the Lord's brother, has a very tenuous claim as the holder of an hereditary ecclesiastical office. Furthermore, though Ignatius may use the term "altar" metaphorically with reference to the Old Testament cultus, the locus of the eucharistic offering in the early church was always called a "table."[34]

Where, therefore, could the tangible fabric, as it were, of the collective representations of a distinctively Christian culture be found in Ignatius' time? Not in sacred objects such as altars, nor in sacred vestments could the church find any unambiguous cultural distinctiveness given the pagan and Jewish associations of these. Instead these were found in sacred persons– representative persons or τύποι— who derived their authority at this time not from simply holding a quasi-magical office *per se* but because of the three distinct roles in unison that they performed in the symbolic acts of the liturgical drama, creative of one community out of many individuals. The cultural focus, in terms of our definition, had in other words to be away from material symbols associated with symbolic acts and, instead, on symbolic acts associated with distinct cultural persons. Indeed it is arguably here that we find the real origin of the distinctively Christian conception of the role of the ordained minister, namely that of an indelible office, held for life, of a "separated" person but with no hereditary requirements, in comparison with lay worshippers.

The presbyterate in the synagogue had no sacerdotal role in the liturgy in so far as any literate, male adult could participate under the chairmanship of the ἀρχισυνάγωγος.[35] In the temple the office of priest was derived from a single hereditary family. In terms of Roman paganism, the *paterfamilias* presided over ceremonies concerned with the *lares et penates*, and offices like *fla-*

---

[34] The "one altar" is the "one bishop" in *Philad.* 4,1 cf. *Eph.* 5,2; *Mag.* 7,2. For *Tral.* 7,2, see Schoedel op. cit. p. 5, who points out that early christian writers deny that the τράπεζα was an altar (Minucius Felix, *Octavius* 32,2; Origen, *Contra Celsum* 8,17). See also Padberg (1963) op.cit. p. 238.

[35] E. Schürer, *The History of the Jewish People in the Age of Jesus*, (Ed.) G. Vermes, F. Millar, and M. Black, (Edinburgh: T. and T. Clark 1979), vol. 2, p. 434-439.

ject to *protem* appointment and resignation, though some indeed
were for life and restricted to patrician families. Nowhere here
do we find the Christian notion of persons who arise out of, and
are identified by, their congregations as "sacred"— or if that is
not anachronistic, "set apart,"— invariably for life. Models were
available but not adopted, since the second century, historical
process at work in the Christian community was not one of cultural assimilation but of a distinctive culture intentionally created.

In the earliest Christian ἐκκλησία, therefore, such offices
could not be identified in terms of an hereditary caste, nor were
there material scrolls like those of the Torah of which the presbyters of the synagogue might be the custodians and pass on.
The development of such a theory of tradition, and the notion of
the canon of scripture to which it gave rise, was a late second-
century development. There were no shrines with associated
rites with material sacred stones, plants, or vestments, the legal,
pro tem possession of which could identify the office holder.
Thus the cultural, collective representations of the earliest church
evolved, not in terms of sacred objects, but in terms of sacred
persons who possessed nothing material but a liturgical role in
the weekly enactment of the community experience of finding,
through the ministry of the presbyter-apostles and the diaconal-
Christ, union with the Father-bishop. The cultural artifacts and
material symbolic representations, making concrete the collective
consciousness, were very small, consisting of ceremonies focusing on water, bread and wine in the context of a private house.

Thus the collective representations of the nascent Christian
society became highly personalized in terms of representative
persons, rather than objects which stood for, and with, the sacred story expressing the central norms, values, and beliefs of
the group. It is this culturally and sociologically conceived situation that we find reflected in the letters of Ignatius of Antioch and
their theology. The centrality of the liturgy to those concrete expressions of unambiguous social identity that Durkheim called
"collective representations" meant that the sacred story control-
ling liturgy also controlled the emergence of one ἐπίσκοπος out
of the situation in the more ambiguous, Jewish-Christian synagogue with its multiple πρεσβύτεροι who might also be called
ἐπίσκοποι. The bishop as the type of the one Father in the liturgy

must himself be one if his liturgical role is also to function as an unambiguous collective representation. Person and role must equally be inseparable if this unambiguity is to be maintained. The bishop stands as God's type in Ignatius because, according to the Johannine tradition, "it is my Father who gives you the bread from heaven to eat."[36]

The sociological model outlined in Chapter 2 did, moreover, understand the sacred story developed by the culture in structuralist terms. The sacred story was part of the web of meaning in terms of which distinct cultural organization and identity was both developed and maintained. Let us now see how Ignatius' particular form of the Christian sacred story functions in achieving this end.

9. *Ignatius' sacred story*

In Chapter 2 we presented in general terms Lévi-Strauss' argument that cultures create their sacred stories or "myths" in terms of a particular kind of logic, not relative to any one culture, which synthesized antinomies that arose in the development of the sacred story. We emphasized there our view that the historical basis or otherwise of such sacred stories was in no way prejudged by such an account, which dealt simply with the logic of linguistic description. It is not mere piety, therefore, that lead us to prefer the term "sacred story" to that of "myth" in view of the historical claims of orthodox Christianity.

It will be recalled that the original Straussian examples were from classical mythology. The Oedipus myth dealt with antinomies in the over and under evaluation of family relations. On the one hand Antigone buries her brother Polyneikes despite prohibition. On the other hand, Oedipus marries his mother and kills his father. Another antinomy was the affirmation and denial of the autochthonous origin of man. Cadmos killed the dragon from whose teeth mankind arises as sprung from the earth, and Oedipus kills the Sphinx that rises from the ashes. Both antinomies are both related and overcome as the telling of the sacred

---

[36] *Jn.* 6,50 cf. *Eph.* 20,1 and Hippolytus, *Ap.Trad.* 3,5 ff. See G. Dix, *The Shape of the Liturgy,* (London: Adam and Charles Black 1945), p. 136-137.

story proceeds combining both into a pattern of binary relations. The Spartoi born from the dragon's teeth autochthonously destroy one another in fratricide and thus undervalue their fraternal relation. Converse relations are thus combined into binary patterns. As the myth is created, revised, and new features added in the course of transmission, whether oral or written, the same logical process remains in evidence shaping the transformation of such antitheses.

Let us now look at the sacred story as Ignatius took it over and developed it, to the extent of course that that sacred story can be recovered in the pre-Ignatian, ecclesiastical situation. The Antiochene gospel of *Matthew* reflects prophetic strands within the early church in tension with teaching ones as does the *Didache*, though in neither work is there mention of the office of presbyter within the community of Jesus.[37] The first evangelist, however, portrays a tendency to attack the excesses of both groups, and we hear of attacks both upon false-prophets and against teachers seeking too great honour, as we do also in the *Didache*.[38] As a result, and following the procedures of redaction criticism, there is a tendency in the literature to regard the Ignatian situation as the early catholic forging of disparate groups into a single church.[39]

There is, however, an objection to atomizing the extant literature, in this way, insightful within certain limits that redaction criticism might otherwise be. Such an approach has the tendency to equate people who teach and who prophesy, whether humbly and truly, or arrogantly and falsely, with holders of distinct offices characterizing distinct schismatic groups. The *Didache,* at least, can only with difficulty be fitted into such a mold since there an "apostle" can prophecy (11,6), and a "prophet" can be

---

[37] *Mat.* 10,16-23, 40-2; 23,34 cf. *Did.* 10,7; 13,1-7; 15,1-2.

[38] *Mat.* 7,15-23; 24,11, 23-5 cf. 23,8-12; *Did.* 11,1-12 cf. 13,2.

[39] See e.g. C. Trevett, Prophecy and Anti-Episcopal Activity: A Third Error Combatted by Ignatius? in *JEH* 34 (1983), p. 1-5; J.L. Ash, The Decline of Prophecy in the Early Church, in *TS* 37 (1978), p. 227-252; J.D. Kingsbury, The Figure of St. Peter in Matthew's Gospel as a theological problem, in *JBL* 48 (1979), p. 78-80 ff.

described as "teaching" (11,10).[40] Furthermore, such an approach detaches the phenomena thus atomized from their place in the total pattern of development to which their place in the sacred story that is the canon of the New Testament testifies. There are prophets and teachers from Antioch who play an early role in the church of Antioch as witnessed by the Acts of the Apostles, who recognized the ministry of Barnabas and Paul as "apostles" or "traveling missionaries" by imposition of hands. (*Acts* 13,1-3) The antinomies between appointment, Order, and charisma thus run through the sacred story of the New Testament.

Let us therefore see how that story may be read in a structuralist perspective. We may say that antinomies or converse relations combined into a pattern of binary relations in this instance form the pairs: order/ charisma, and in history/ beyond history. As such they form a structuralist parallel with such binary relations in the Oedipus myth as the over evaluation (order) and under evaluation (charisma) of kinship, and the denial (history) and affirmation (beyond history) of the autochthonous origin of man. We may say that the two binary relations are related to each other in that the charismatic element, claiming to be essentially a religion of the Spirit, will tend to emphasize as it were the autochthonous origin of the Church, sprung from the mysterious realm of the Spirit without natural origin. Order, on the other hand, will emphasize the validity of the the community in terms of the tangible sources of its legitimacy, and this in turn will imply a sense of history and succession.

But in the logic of the Oedipus myth this connection between two sets of binary relations was not established in terms of conceptual analysis of words like "charisma," "order," "kinship" or "autochthonous." Indeed such concepts are themselves the theoretical constructs of the interpreter and do not form part of the data themselves. The mythopoeic logic of the sacred story associated unrelated ,ets of binary relations by developing further that story. The Spartoi, born autochthonously from the dragon's teeth, mutually destroy each other and thus unite the denial of kinship in fratricide with the assertion of autochthonous origin.

---

[40] For my criticism of Trevett in this respect see A. Brent, Pseudonymity and Charisma in the Ministry of the Early Church, in *Aug* 27,3 (1987), p. 347-376.

How, in the Christian sacred story, are the relations order/ charisma related to in history/ beyond history?

As we have already said, the problems of charisma and Order did not originate in the pre-Ignatian, Matthaean or Didascalian church of Antioch. Indeed, the earliest New Testament records, namely the epistles of Paul, reveal such tensions as endemic in the community from the first. Paul claims to be an "apostle," and therefore a member of a group originally far larger than the Twelve, despite the later insistence by the author of *Luke-Acts* that the two groups were originally identical. "The Twelve," "James the Lord's brother," "five hundred brethren," "all the apostles," and Paul himself are all mentioned as the various groups that shared in the uniqueness of the immediate, post-Easter experience.[41] But quite clearly Paul's controversies reveal the tension between Order and charisma.

Paul lays claim to charismatic experiences such as *glossolalia*, (*1 Cor.* 14,18) and also claims to have received supernaturally a revelation (ἀποκάλυψις). (*2 Cor.* 12,1-10) Indeed at one point he asserts his independence from "those who were apostles before me" on the basis of that ἀποκάλυψις. (*Gal.* 1,11-12, 16-17) One of the marks of such an apostle is that he "has seen the Lord" (*1 Cor.* 9,1-2), and for him resurrection seems to have a physical basis (*1 Cor.* 15,12-19), although he is indeed studiously vague about the story of the empty tomb. Jesus died, "was entombed," "was raised," and "appeared."[42] After all, to have lain stress on having witnessed the events surrounding the

---

[41] *1 Cor.* 15,3-9 cf. H. von Campenhausen, Der Urchristliche Apostelbegriff, in *StTh* vol. 1 Fasc. I-II (1947), p. 112-114; W. Schmitals, Das Kirchliche Apostelamt: Eine historische Untersuchung, in *FRLANT* n.f. 61, (Göttingen: Vandenhoek & Ruprecht 1961); G.G. Blum, *Tradition und Sukzession: Studien zum Normbegriff des Apostolischen von Paulus bis Irenäus,* (Berlin: Lutherisches Verlaghaus 1962); K.H. Rengstorf, ΑΠΟΣΤΟΛΟΣ, in *TWNT*, p. 100-101; J. Roloff, Apostel/Apostolat/ Apostolizität, in *Theologische Realenzyklopädie*, Band III (Berlin: Walter de Gruyter 1978), p. 432-439; E. Larsen, Die Paulinischen Schriften als Quellen zur Geschichte des Urchristentums, in *StTh* 17 (1983), p. 33-53.

[42] *1 Cor.* 11,23-6, see W.L. Craig, The History of the Empty Tomb of Jesus, in *NTS* 31 (1985), p. 40-41 ff. and E. Bammel, Herkunft und Funktion der Traditionselemente in 1 Kor. 15,1-11, in *ThZ* 11 (1955), p. 401-419.

empty tomb would have emphasized the authority of the witness of the Twelve against the ἀποκάλυψις of the wider group of "all the apostles," the last of whom Paul claimed to be.

But it was not with the Twelve and their authority, or at least with two of their number, Peter and John, (with whom was joined the member of that other group, James the Lord's brother) that Paul experienced his sole conflict. For when he describes elsewhere the mark of an apostle, in whose number the Twelve were included, he does not emphasize having "seen the Lord," but rather signs, wonders, revelations, and miracle working. Against such a predominantly charismatic, apostolic ministry Paul has to insist about those whom he terms "superlative apostles" (τῶν ὑπερλίαν ἀποστόλων) that he too has visions (ὀπτασίας), and revelations (ἀποκαλύψεις). (2 Cor. 11,5; 12,1, 11) He has performed in their presence the "miracles of the apostle (τὰ σημεῖα τοῦ ἀποστόλου), with signs and wonders and powers (σημείοις τε καὶ τέρασιν καὶ δυνάμεσιν)." (2 Cor. 12,12) In this respect his apostolate is self-authenticating and can grow as it were autochthonously without connection with certain, historically specific spatio-temporal experiences at the Empty Tomb to which the Twelve at Jerusalem could lay claim.

As the sacred story of the Christian ministry proceeds, however, these antinomies between order and charisma, history and the purely transcendent are synthesized as the story is retold. In Luke-Acts, for example, we have one retelling of the sacred story which accords with structuralist, synthesizing logic. The Twelve are the final authorities in the church because they are the recipients of the Easter experience and the church is thus founded on historic Order. However, they are recorded also as called and commissioned during Christ's ministry, where he gives them "power" (δύναμιν) and "authority" (ἐξουσίαν) "over all the daemons (ἐπὶ πάντα τὰ δαιμόνια)."

Luke has thus described the commissioning and ministry of the Twelve, taken from the common tradition, in highly charismatic terms, where it is found only in Mark and expressed in a far lower key. Furthermore, it is a charismatic ministry which they share with a wider group which he calls the Seventy Two and to which he will not give the original name of "apostle" since he reserves this title for the Twelve alone. To these also Jesus gives ἐξουσία over the daemons, and when they return Jesus sees "Satan falling as lightening from heaven." (*Lk.* 9,1; 10,17-20; *Mat.* 10,5-42; *Mk.* 9,7) Thus in Luke's version of the sacred story of the Christian ministry, the binary relation of charisma/order assumes a higher order patterning.

It should be noted that within this patterning, one antinomy does not wholly negate the other. It is not the case that the ministry of the Twelve, standing for historically based Order, negates and obliterates the charismatic strand by appropriating it, and thus makes its charismatic legitimacy dependent upon the particular historical origin of Order. The commissioning and ministry of the Seventy Two remains part of the sacred story, and is the converse of the ministry of the Twelve. In other words the antinomies experience synthesis in the new version of the sacred story without there being any final contradiction. The Seventy Two never become witnesses of the Empty Tomb as do the Twelve. The continuance of their ministry remains self-authenticating and autochthonous, flowing from the transcendent beyond history, and in that sense denying legitimating historical relations.

We saw too that in the sacred story of the Christian ministry emanating from the Johannine circle, in the form that Ignatius immediately took it over, there is a similar synthesizing of antinomies. Only Jesus can perform σημεῖα before his glorification, before which the Spirit is not yet (given). (*Jn.* 7,38-9) The Twelve, whom *John,* as we have seen, calls "disciples," though the inner, more obedient group of disciples, cannot accordingly be commissioned for a charismatic ministry during Jesus' ministry, though they are promised that they will do greater works, because he goes to the Father. (*Jn.* 6,66-7; 14,12) But on the evening of the resurrection the Spirit is given in the ἐμφύσησις, and they can bind and loose from sin. (*Jn.* 20,22-3)

But in the Johannine sacred story of the Christian ministry, the charismatic and autochthonous does not stand alone and transcendent, without historical relations. The other side of the charisma/order binary relation is there also. In so far as the "ten" or "eleven" disciples whose presence is implied by the succeeding Thomas narrative, (*Jn.* 20,24) and the clear identification of

Judas as the "son of perdition" (*Jn.* 13,29; 17,12), are described as Twelve, it is as representatives of a corporate body, the church as the new Israel, that the ten or eleven disciples receive the Holy Spirit. Thus the antinomies of the charismatic powers of the community and its historical order are synthesized by means of the notion of representation. The Twelve represent the new people of God and offer the obedience that the many disciples who had fallen away could not offer on behalf of all the faithful whose gifts and calling they represent. Thus the notion of Order as representation holds in tension the strands of Order and charisma, and these in turn are further developed as the sacred story continues to unfold through its underlying structuralist logic.

Finally we saw that Ignatius retold the sacred story of the Christian ministry in terms of the pre-eminence of the threefold typology which represented the common community experience of finding union with God the Father, through the Son who came from him, and the spirit-filled apostles who in their turn were sent. Just as the Twelve in *John* stood for the Spirit-filled community, so too does the threefold typology in Ignatius. The sacred story explains according to its mythopoeic logic how the charismatic community can gather in Order, and shake the daemonic powers, only by being grounded in history and denying autochthony. Just as Jesus Christ departs from and return to the one Father, so the deacons depart from and return to the bishop seated in the presbyteral circle in the liturgy. The "spiritual crown" of the spirit-filled presbyter/apostles form a unity through their harmony with their central bishop. Thus the antinomies of order/ charisma are synthesized into the converses of binary relations.

Similarly, the antinomies of history and beyond history are both synthesized and related to the binary relations of charisma/ order. The final victory of charismatic transcendentalism would be a docetic victory that negated the historical incarnation of Christ come in flesh. Thus the retelling of the sacred story in terms of the representative threefold typology will not allow that negation. The concrete representation of the saving events in the liturgy resolve the tension in the sacred story between he who can be both Son of Man and son of God:

Assemble yourselves together man by man as a common body (οἱ κατ᾽ ἄνδρα κοινῇ) in one faith and in one Jesus Christ who physically (κατὰ σάρκα) as son of David was both Son of Man and Son of God, so that in consequence you obey the bishop and presbytery without distraction of mind, breaking one bread, which is the salve of immortality, the antidote for living in Christ eternally and not dying.

(*Eph.* 20)

Through the representation of the threefold typology, therefore, the antinomy of in history/ beyond history is synthesized by association with the sacred story of the Christian ministry. According to the flesh Jesus Christ was David's descendant so that he was Son of Man as well as being Son of God. The church, assembled through its ikons as a corporate entity and not as a collection of individuals, as a common body (κοινῇ), will exhibit these two relations of divine sonship and human existence in synthesis. There emerges therefore a clear pattern amongst the Ignatian antinomies of passible/ impassible, physical/spiritual, begotten/ unbegotten, of Mary/of God (*Eph.* 7,2), which combined the antinomies of charisma and Order in terms of the role played in the sacred story by the representative typology that is the ordained ministry.

Let us now summarize where this chapter has brought us in terms of our discussion of cultural episcopacy and ecumenism.

10. *In conclusion*

In Chapter 1 we explored the notion that episcopacy could be representative, in a cultural sense, as opposed to being defined wholly in terms of territorial jurisdiction. We saw that, although the Anglican view of episcopacy was decidedly jurisdictional, and reflected its late medieval, immediately pre-Reformation origins, the Roman Catholic view was far more ambiguous. Although the practice of consecrating titular bishops *in partibus* presupposed that there could not be a bishop without a prescribed territory, however fictional, Rome nevertheless does recognize, in the patriarchies of the Eastern Rites, bishops who represent traditions and cultures and who occupy both in eastern Europe and north America the same geographical area as western bishops with their different congregations and cultures. We saw however that the justification given in the documents of Vatican II regarding such Eastern Rite bishops was ambiguous. Not only did those documents lack a clear concept of culture, but they were ambiguous regarding whether the eastern patriarchs are bishops simply because they represent a Christian tradition of spirituality and devotions, or because they represent this in addition to having historically founding apostles in the history of the episcopal succession of their Sees. We shall return to this problem, involving a questionable historical claim about apostolic foundations, in our next chapter.

In Chapter 2 we sought to look at tentatively the outlines of both a theology and sociology of cultural representation which would ground our argument for cultural episcopacy. In Aquinas' principle that grace perfects nature but does not destroy it we found the basis for our argument that if "culture" is inseparable from nature, then grace completes culture too. We then associated the indigenization of liturgy with the indigenization of ministry, and claimed for both the theological insight of the church as the extension of the incarnation in a culture. We expressed our conviction here, as in Chapter 1, that our argument had implications not simply for the missionary and post-missionary situations of the third world but also for the prospect of ecumenical reconciliation where there would inevitably have to be intercommunion and mutual recognition between geographically overlapping, ecclesiastical jurisdictions.

At this point the need for a sociological definition of culture became pressing. We regarded culture in terms of that which individuated a given social group and defined it in terms of a phenomenological version of Durkheimian functionalism. A culture was a set of material and conceptual symbols interwoven with the discourse which formed a backcloth to it as its "collective consciousness," or, in Wittgensteinian terms, "form of life," expressing the fundamental norms and values that distinguish the group from others. Following Durkheim, however, we insisted that the collective consciousness or form of life had to have a concrete and tangible expression for it to function in ordering the life and social identity of a community. A culture makes itself visible through its "collective representations" which involve rituals and liturgies, behind which, and developing and continuing which, is a sacred story itself in process of continuous development.

We proposed regarding the logic of the sacred story, formally general if not universal between cultures, in terms of Straussian structuralism. We further pointed to the phenomenon of "family-resemblance," observed by the later-Wittgenstein, and saw there the key to the translatability of human languages, which requires the possibility of being able to associate new meanings into known conceptual schemes and to incorporate the former into the latter. The more open-class and non exhaustively definable such general concepts were, the more the possibility emerged of genuine dialogue and cross-cultural consensus. Thus we saw both in the antinomies of ecumenical discussion, and in the search for consensus in abstracting and generalizing the concepts of ministry, an example of the working of our sociological thesis.

In our present chapter, we began by noting the view of both Schillebeeckx and Rahner regarding the inadequacy of the medieval view of a sacrament in that it divorced the act of the priest from the act of the whole church. We then showed in term of our sociological account how by understanding a sacrament in terms of collective representation we were able to understand how a sacrament effects what it signifies and signifies what it effects, in a way that makes it part of expression of the life and values of the whole community and not simply of a clerical caste. We saw, moreover, in our subsequent discussion of the classical statement of episcopal church government, that of the epistles of Ignatius of Antioch, that though Ignatius represents a theological typology in which the threefold Order represents the experience of a community achieving union with God in Christ, what that theology effects fulfils the conditions of our sociological thesis regarding collective representations.

The threefold Order thus became, through its enactment of the liturgical drama, the collective representations that give to the community its cultural identity by expressing its central, valued experiences, norms, and beliefs. Moreover we have analyzed Ignatius' sacred story in structuralist terms and found it to unfold according to the same mythopoeic logic that shaped and controlled early versions of that story. Both the Lukan and the

Johannine versions represented the synthesis of antinomies in the early history of the development of Order in a way that paralleled Strauss' analysis of the Oedipus myth in classical antiquity. And thus the themes of our second chapter were brought into parallelism with the themes of our third.

It would of course be wrong to try to draw prescriptive conclusions from a descriptively theological, allied with a descriptively sociological account that we have so far produced. Such an account can show us the logic, both theological and cultural, that lead to the emergence of the threefold Order of the catholic church in the early second century. It can also show us by the same theological and sociological logic how and why ecumenical dialogue will proceed as it does by seeking a new form of the sacred story of the Christian ministry. The development of that story, in the twentieth century as in the first, will proceed by a kind of mythopoeic, binary logic which establishes new patterns of integration for its antinomies, and which seeks to express its concerns in open and general categories conducive to new consensuses. But it does not tell us how far such a new pattern of integration achieved by the new sacred story of the ministry of the twentieth century church will, or ought, to resemble that of the first.

What our account does however show— and to this extent it is by no means unhelpful— is that there is nothing strange about what developed with Ignatius' in the first century and what is developing now ecumenically in the twentieth. It simply makes no sense to regard the development of the second century as the kind of aberration or distortion called *Frühkatholizismus*, any more than it makes sense to regard contemporary ecumenism in such a light. As we have shown, the historical and cultural conditions for the development of the collective representations of a distinctively Christian culture made inevitable the expression of those representations by individual persons, as other kinds of symbolic representations were not sufficiently distinctive of Christian culture in the second century. As Clifton Black II and others have pointed out, we do require a new set of analytic criteria for understanding the development of early Christianity than those yielded by the *Frühkatholizismus* model.[43]

In the following chapters, we shall pursue the theme of sacred ministry in terms of representation and not jurisdiction in the historical situation prior to Ignatius, and endeavour to account for the rise of jurisdictional episcopacy subsequent to Ignatius' time.

---

[43] C. Clifton Black II, The Johannine Epistles and the Question of Early Catholicism, in *NT* 28 2 (1986), p. 131-158, who finds himself confronted at the conclusion of his discussion by two mutually contradictory sets of conclusions, and says: "... it is unsettling that two such highly divergent reconstructions such as those just presented could arguably have emerged from the application of the same analytic criteria. If these dozen canons have been fairly manipulated, then the criteria themselves must be flawed. Thus if anything be clear at this end of the study, it is that *the very model of "early Catholicism", as it is customarily defined, ultimately obscures rather than clarifies.*" p. 157, his italics.

CHAPTER FOUR

PSEUDONYMITY AND APOSTOLIC TRADITION

Concepts of Order and representation
in early Christian pseudepigrapha

In Chapter 1 we saw that, in its decree on Churches of the
Eastern Rite in communion with Rome, the second Vatican
Council approved the notion of existing and new patriarchs or
archbishops consecrated with responsibility for a rite rather than
having jurisdiction over a territory. (*Orientalium Ecclesiarum* 9;
10) Such patriarchs or archbishops had the right "to establish
new eparchies," (ibid. 9) and, "wherever an Ordinary of any rite
is appointed outside the territorial bounds of its patriarchate, he
remains attached to the patriarchy of that rite." (ibid. 7) But we
saw that there was an ambiguity about why what in our terms are
cultural episcopates should be so recognized. Was it because in
representing a rite they represented "discipline, doctrine, history,
and characteristics of Easterners" (ibid. 6) alone, or because
there was in addition a historic link with the ancient church and
alleged apostolic foundation? Of Eastern Orthodoxy separated
from Rome, *Unitatis Redintegratio* had said of the Patriarchies:
"many glory in taking their origins from the apostles themselves." (ibid. 14) As a comment on this text, Abbott and
Gallagher wrote:

> We read in the Acts of the Apostles and St. Paul's epistles that
> James the Less was at Jerusalem (Gal. 1:18-19); Peter at Antioch,
> (Gal. 2:11-14), Paul at Cyprus and Athens (Acts 13:4-12; 17:16-
> 34). Alexandria was traditionally the See of Mark.[1]

No mention is made in this note about the association between
the Apostle John and Ephesus, no doubt owing to the historical
problems raised by the relevant texts.

---

[1] W.M. Abbott and J. Gallagher, *The Documents of Vatican II*, (London:
Geoffrey Chapman 1966), p. 375.

There is, nevertheless, a problem posed for an account of episcopacy that sees cultural representation, in a sacramental sense, as the sole criterion of validity. The mutual recognition of bishops who so represent their cultures in process of redemption must be on the basis of conformity to historic tradition in some sense. Thus we must now deal with the vexed question of ministry and the apostolic succession. In so doing, we are faced with still disputed questions regarding whether, and in what sense, certain historical experiences of the ministry and events of the first Easter legitimated ministerial office, as distinct from the general faith of the whole community. Given that the view of the apostolic faith as a kind of field-marshal's baton that could be handed from apostle to bishop, and then from bishop to his successor (albeit protected by the charism of interpretation) was the invention of Irenaeus, in what form if any was there prior to him such a historical dependence for ecclesiastical authority?

It is my view that the whole issue has been obscured by a tendency in the literature to set charisma and historical succession at variance with each other as alternative forms of legitimation only to be later combined by Irenaeus.[2] I have already, in Chapter 3, criticized reading the Christian sacred story in this way from a structuralist perspective. In this chapter I will begin by taking as my first example the writer of the *Apocalypse* in order to show that, despite many surface dissimilarities, he shares with Ignatius both the view of ministry as representative of the corporate character of the community, as requiring historical continuity with the teaching of Jesus, and as essentially requiring charismatic, mystagogical gifts.

I shall then show that both the device of literary pseudonymity, and the figure of Peter in *Matthew,* also presuppose *both* a kind of mystagogical charisma *and* a contact with oral historical tradition. I shall in conclusion argue that the very nature of an oral historical tradition presupposes both transmitters held in authority in whom, nevertheless, the community sees

---

[2] For a recent example see E. Schillebeeckx, *Ministry: A Case for Change,* (London: SCM 1981); R.E. Brown and J.P. Meier, *Antioch and Rome,* (New York: Paulist Press 1983), chpts III and IV.

the representatives of its own faith and life.[3] What the pseudonymous letter writer will represent is a communally recognized reflection and articulation of the faith that the community received from its founding apostle, and which continues orally in its corporate life.

In conclusion, we shall look at James as a possible counter example to such a thesis, on the grounds that he holds office in terms of a caliphate representing Christ's natural relations. We shall see as we proceed that, to the contrary, his original authority, like Paul's, rested upon an oral *paradosis* that by its very nature rested upon particular historical experiences of particular people, yet also by that very oral nature was inseparable from the corporate life of an ongoing community.

1. *The Apocalypse and ecclesial representation*

In the *Apocalypse* the Spirit-filled John writes in his own name what the "Spirit says to the churches." (*Apoc.* 1,10-11) He is therefore an ecclesiastical letter writer who, though a witness to "the word of God" and "the witness of Jesus," and to this extent to the deposit or παραθήκη, may nevertheless be said to claim a charismatic right as he writes to the "angels" of the churches. (*Apoc.* 2, 1,8,12,18; 3,1,7,14) Indeed, at first sight this writer might well be regarded as the charismatic *Doppelganger* to an Ignatian bishop, since the Seer writes from Asia Minor some ten years before Ignatius, and indeed to the same churches in the case of Smyrna, Philadelphia, and Ephesus. But we should not allow the surface differences between the apocalyptic pageant on the one hand, and Ignatius' episcopal exhortations on the other, to blind us to an essential similarity of thought and interest.

A facile reading of the *Apocalypse* may initially suggest a world of difference between the churches of Asia Minor to which John was writing and the churches to which Ignatius was

---

[3] For an earlier version of this argument, see A. Brent, Pseudonymity and Charisma in the Ministry of the Early Church, in *Aug* 27 3 (1987), p. 347-376

to write a decade later.[4] At first sight we seem to be dealing with an apocalyptic writing– a prophecy of immediately impending events– of which there is almost a complete absence in the Ignatian correspondence.[5] Furthermore, far from resting on or reflecting any church Order, the document seems to presuppose a charismatic church Order in which a prophet such as John, imprisoned on the Isle of Patmos, addresses whole Christian communities without distinction in the seven letters. But there are grounds for rejecting such *prima facie* impressions as misleading.

To begin with, there is the much discussed question of the nature of the "angels" of the churches to whom the seven letters are addressed. Following Hemer,[6] we may record that these have been identified with (i) heavenly guardians of the churches, (ii) human representatives of them, (iii) personifications of the churches, and (iv) human messengers. But we dissent from Hemer's view that they cannot represent the bishops of the churches in anything approaching the Ignatian sense that were to appear there some ten years later.

If John had regarded them as purely heavenly guardians of the churches as (i) suggests, he would not have been able to attribute to them the sins and failures of their people. Furthermore, he could not have addressed and transmitted letters with quill and ink to purely heavenly figures.[7] The common apocalyptic con-

---

[4] See e.g. E. Schüssler Fiorenza, *The Book of Revelation: Justice and Judgment*, (Philadelphia: Fortress Press 1985), p. 142-146 for the latest reading of this relationship in terms of an *a priori* charismatic-episcopal disjunction. See also P. Prigent, L'Hérésie Asiatique et l'Église confessante de l'Apocalypse à Ignace, in *VCh* 31 (1977), p. 1-22.

[5] But see e.g. *Eph.* 13; 19.

[6] C.J. Hemer, *The Letters to the Seven Churches in their Local Setting*, in *JSNT.S* 11 (1986), p. 32-34.

[7] This interpretation was defended by J. Colson, *L'Évêque dans les Communautés Primitives*, (Paris: Les Éditions du Cerf 1951), and more recently by A. Lemaire, *Les Ministères aux Origines de l'Église: Naissance de la triple hiérarchie: évêques, presbytres, diacres*, (Paris: Les Éditions du Cerf 1971), p. 118-122, and M. Thurian, L'Organisation du Ministère dans l'Église Primitive selon Saint Ignace d'Antioche, in *VC* 21 (1967), p. 28. This human identity of the angel-bishops is assailed by those who argue that the middle recension of the Ignatian corpus is a forgery later than the early second century, see Joly op. cit. p. 75-77. Dassmann, op. cit. p. 75-76,

cept of an individual angel as a corporate symbol of a nation or people (*Dan.* 10,10-21; 12,1) has thus been combined with a human representative, as is suggested by the equation of the seven angels with the seven stars (*Apoc.* 1,16 cf. 1,20), where the former are clearly the earthly counterparts of their latter, heavenly images.

It should be emphasized, moreover, that such an interpretation does not require the support of the variant reading: τὴν γυναῖκα σοῦ Ἰαζάβελ in *Apoc.* 2,20 so that it becomes a reference to the angel- bishop's wife. Textually the variant is uncertain and, in terms of my understanding of apocalyptic imagery, "Jezebel" is the Old Testament reference which locates she who acts in her spirit in the writer's time in the events of salvation history. Such a reading would therefore falsify my interpretation rather than confirm it by making "Jezebel" an actual person rather than the apocalyptic image. Hemer was far too quick in concluding, therefore, that the role of the angel as standing for an individual, corporate representative was somehow falsified by the falseness of such a variant reading.[8]

We have also, furthermore, shown in Chapter 3 how Ignatius' idealized description of bishops such as Polybius of Tralles, Damasus of Magnesia, and Onesimus of Ephesus, or for that matter deacons such as Bourrus, Zotion and Krokus refer to them not as individuals but as wearing the corporate personalities (ἐν ὁμοιότητι, ἐξεμπλάριον) of their communities. It was they who were thus wearing the very corporate personality, personified as an angelic form, that the Seer describes in the *Apocalypse.* As Colson pointed out, an Ignatian bishop was very much a combination of a human representative who personified his church and acted as a messenger of God, and thus fulfils the roles of the angels of the churches in (ii), (iii) and (iv)

---

whilst accepting the genuineness of the middle recension, assails the existence of the angel-bishops before Ignatius, and endevours to explain Ignatius' "invention" of monepiscopacy with reference to his alleged subordinationist christology, despite the modalism of *Eph.* 1,1.

[8] Hemer (1986) op. cit. p. 3. See also A. Satake, Die Gemeindeordnung in der Johannesapokalypse, *WMANT* 21 (1966), p. 150-155 ff.; R. Zollitsch, *Amt und Funktion des Priesters: Eine Untersuchung zum Ursprung und zur Gestalt des Presbyterats in den ersten zwei Jahrhunderten*, (Freiburg: Herder 1974), p. 125-136.

above, combined.[9] Despite the angelic symbolism, unless the corporate personality had an individual location, it is difficult to see how it could be written to, and addressed personally in, the way that the Seer does in the letters to the seven churches.

In this respect, many of Satake's objections to the identity of the angels with church officials can be refuted with reference to this interconnectedness of the visionary images of Ignatius and the *Apocalypse*, and with particular reference to Ignatius' mystical vision of the corporate qualities of a given Christian community, which he saw intuitively in the personalities of its clerical representatives, as we argued in Chapter 3. To claim, as Satake[10] does, that the movement between the second person singular, and the second person plural, means that no individual can be addressed but rather a community as a whole, misses the point about contemporary exchange of ecclesiastical letters as witnessed by both *1 Clement* and Ignatius' *Polycarp*.

Firstly, as *1 Clement* (inscr.) makes clear, in time of both Ignatius and the *Apocalypse* letters were written in the name of one church to another, namely from the church of Rome to that of Corinth, even though the author was known who both wrote in the name of the church externally, and presumably received inward correspondence in turn addressed by his counterpart in the name of another church. We shall be later giving our reasons for questioning Clement's status as a "mere" secretary in this regard.

---

[9] Colson op. cit. p. 97: "Et il écrit aux Tralliens à propos de Polybe, leur évêque: "C'est votre Église tout entière que je contemple en sa personne." Tel est, selon saint Ignace et dans la ligne de l'Apocalypse, le rôle de l'évêque, sa place dans l'Église."

[10] Op. cit. p. 149-155. Satake's other objection was that outside the letters to the seven churches, the *Apocalypse* uses "angel" "also Bezeichnung himmlischer Wesen." He concludes that, since "in keiner Stelle bezieht es sich auf ein Gemeindeamt," this is evidence that we should "in unserem Fall keine Ausnahme annehmen." But my position has been that "angel" as the corporate personality of the community is used in approximately the same sense elsewhere, only the heavenly reality does have as elsewhere an earthly counterpart, namely someone like Polybius, bishop of Ephesus who, behind phenomenal appearances, wore the transcendental character of his community.

Secondly, six of Ignatius' letters are addressed to the churches as communities even though presumably their bishop was the initial recipient. When, however, an individual bishop is addressed as in *Polycarp,* the second person singular easily gives way to the second person plural as now the exhortations are for the bishop individually, now for the community in general. (cf. *Pol.* 1-5; 7,2 with 6-7,1,3; 8,3) The switch between the singular and plural form here is directly comparable with what takes place in the letters to the seven churches in the *Apocalypse,* especially when the mention of the collective prayer of the community is qualified by the second person plural. (7,1) Thus we are reminded about the "prayer of the bishop and of the whole church" that had far more strength than "the prayer of one or two" (*Eph.* 5,2), and which prefigured as one of the key texts in our discussion of Ignatius' view of representative episcopacy.

But in Ignatius' case, by contrast with that of Clement, the letter writer saw the corporate personality of the redeemed community in a conversation with its bishop that required a spiritual discernment which could apprehend the realm of the Spirit behind the accidents of the present. His "conversation" (συνήθειαν) with Onesimus was not human (οὐκ ἀνθρωπίνην) but spiritual (πνευματικήν). (*Eph.* 5,1) In this respect, the kind of qualities required of John the Seer, to see in the angels of the churches their communities, is not unlike the kind of eschatologically mystical ability that characterizes the office of an Ignatian bishop.

In Chapter 3 we saw that the Ignatian bishop, in possession of the δόγματα and διατάγματα (*Mag.* 13,1; *Tral.* 7,1) of the Lord and the Apostles, must nevertheless be critically part of the acts of realizing the saving events in the present liturgy. As a τύπος himself, he must be able to see beyond the phenomenal present to the unseen, transcendental drama taking place beyond time and history where the Father continues to send the Son, and from both come the Spirit-filled apostles. It is interesting therefore to note that Ignatius' eschatological understanding of the church points to something of significance about the qualities of an Ignatian bishop. As the focus of the church's unity he must witness to the history of the incarnation and must therefore identify and safeguard historical events, particular that salvific event of Christ come in flesh. But he is not merely the transmitter of the "brute facts" of secular history— if ever there are such things— but their mystagogical interpreter.

The Ignatian bishop must be capable of the mystical vision which is able to see the incarnated events of salvation history behind the accidental appearances and accretions of the structure of the present liturgical assembly (ἐκκλησία). Ignatius does not simply claim that he personally functions in this interpretive and prophetic role (*Philad.* 7), but that in so functioning he is characteristic of the bishop's role in general. He reminds Polycarp that as a bishop Polycarp shares the ἐπισκοπή of God the Father and Jesus Christ. But it is Christ as mystagogue who is here intended, who as high priest knows the mysteries of God as in *John* only the Son knows the Father. (*Jn.* 17,24-6)

Polycarp is to pray that the "invisible things" will be revealed to him, and as with Ignatius these invisible things include "heavenly things and the arrays of angels and the musterings of principalities." (*Pol.* 2,2) Like Christ the high priest, therefore, for Ignatius the bishop is "entrusted with the holy of holies, that is entrusted with the hidden things of God." (*Tral.* 5,2) Moreover, part of those "hidden things" involve taking the historical facts of history and interpreting them within the schema of salvation history. The passion and resurrection of Christ are taken and interpreted as the "good prophets pointed out in their preaching."[11] Ignatius therefore regards his mystagogical gifts as characteristic of the office of any bishop, and not simply as a product of his own personal charism.

We have seen in this section, therefore, that there is a connection between the charismatic and visionary qualities of both Ignatian bishops, and the Seer of the *Apocalypse*, and how these qualities extend to the ability to communicate with churches as letter writers on the grounds of being able to grasp, through spiritual intercommunication, the corporate qualities of the communities concerned, as worn by their angel-bishops. The similarities between Ignatius' and the *Apocalypse* extend further, therefore, than the corporate and representative functions of an-

---

[11] *Philad.* 9,1. I am indebted thus far to H. von Campenhausen, *Ecclesiastical Authority and Spiritual Power in the church of the First Three Centuries*, (London: SPCK 1969), p. 104-105.

gel/bishops. Both share general images and, at a psychological level, a common visionary process. Let us develop further this point in more general detail.

2. *Visionary process in Ignatius and the Apocalypse*

There is great consistency between the imagery of the *Apocalypse* and that of Ignatius of Antioch. Furthermore this imagery in both writers in developed through the medium of visionary experiences that move from the mundane to the transcendental in similar ways. The idealized descriptions of the various congregations moves them in Ignatius' vision out of their present earthly context into the heavenly sphere. Ignatius imagines those whom he addresses to be a χόρος or choir singing around the heavenly θυσιάστηριον (*Eph.* 5,2; *Mag.* 7,2; *Philad.* 4), and the unity with the threefold hierarchy is described in terms of the harmony of the cords of a lyre. (*Eph.* 4,1; *Philad.* 1,4) The image of the lyre in the vision of the heavenly church prefigures in the *Apocalypse* as the twenty four presbyters gather around God's throne and the heavenly altar. (*Apoc.* 4,4; 6,9; 7,11-14; 8,3-6 etc) The Ephesians are stones in the shrine of God's building (*Eph.* 9,1), just as the Church as the New Jerusalem is so described in the *Apocalypse*. (*Apoc.* 21,19) The symbol of the cross as a tree bearing fruit of immortality, and the healing properties of right doctrines in comparison with the poisonous character of heresy prefigures in both works. (*Eph.* 10,3; 20,2; *Tral.* 6; 11; *Philad.* 3,3; *Smyr.* 1,2; cf. *Apoc.* 2,7; 22,2)

Unlike other apocalyptic writings, such as *II Esdras, Enoch*, or the *Testaments of the Twelve Patriarchs*, the *Apocalypse* does not make reference to a future separated by a space of time however short or long, from the writer's own. The eschatological events are already beginning to take place in terms of the action of Christ "who was and is and is to come." (*Apoc.* 1,8) Christ is already, as "firstborn from the dead, also the ruler of the kings of the earth" (*Apoc.* 1,6) and, in the church, is already establishing his kingdom. In Ignatius, as we have seen, there is a formally similar eschatology, with the Father sending the Son and the Son sending the Spirit filled apostles still timelessly continuing behind the contingent human action in each liturgical assembly.

Furthermore, although the Seer is to announce "what must necessarily follow these events" (*Apoc.* 4,1), angelic and other supernatural beings are already at work in the seven letters behind the visible events of world history. The letters are, after all, addressed to a church official whose human features fade into insignificance in the invisible eternal drama, of eternal and invisible realities, as part of the angelic array. Just as other transcendental and heavenly entities and persons have earthly counterparts, so too the angels of the churches nevertheless have actual ecclesiastical counterparts, with whom a veritable fusion of imagery has taken place. In like manner we saw that the human features of Ignatius' clerical representatives faded into their τύποι which represented the saving events incarnated in the corporate personalities of their communities.

Moreover, the present church, and the future events that are to befall it, are taken out of the ordinary events of secular history and are located in salvation history by the device, well known and well used by the Apostolic Fathers, of identifying them as antitypes of Old Testament types. The Seer, with his eyes on the invisible and eternal drama which proceeds, with barriers of time, space, and particular circumstances removed, talks of "the teaching of Balaam who taught Balak" at Pergamon, and of "that Jezebel, the woman who claims to be a prophetess" at Thyatira. (*Apoc.* 2,14 & 20) In fact so transfixed is his gaze on what the "synagogue of Satan" represents in terms of the eternal, eschatological conflict which (Old Testament) Scripture describes, that we can hardly and but speculatively identify their this-worldly counterparts in terms of the secular history of the Seer's contemporary situation.

In his tendency to see contemporary events as expressions of a continuing and eternal salvation history, with the precise nature of the secular events obscured from view, the Seer, to an important extent, parallels Ignatius' own method of eschatological mysticism that we have noted. The Seer's own view of salvation history is more baroquely embellished with apocalyptic symbolism, and may be wider in its Old Testament allusions than Ignatius'. Indeed in Ignatius, by comparison, the presence in the

Church of Father, Son, and Holy Spirit continuing eschatologically their work, and grounding the church in salvation history, in the threefold Order, with barriers of time, space, and intervening secular historical events removed, seem to be a quite restricted view of the ongoing process of mankind's redemption. But a similar theological perspective as one of eschatological mysticism is nevertheless thus revealed. But are there closer connections in terms of a less defined version of what in Ignatius is to appear ten years later as a fully defined, threefold Order?

Remember that, in the eschatological mysticism that characterizes the Seer's vision, the future-becoming-present events that he describes, heavenly and other worldly though they may be, always have a concrete, earthly counterparts. When the Seer then describes the scene that is and shall be in heaven of the throne of God and the Lamb around which the twenty four elders sing their praises, we must ask what were the earthly counterparts that were the initial stimulus to these parts of the vision? These elders are mentioned in some five further chapters of the *Apocalypse*. (7, 11, 14, and 19) In each case, with perhaps the one exception[12], they are associated with the Lamb. The "Lamb standing as slain " stands in the midst of the elders (5,6) who fall at his feet. (*Apoc.* 5,8; 5,14; 19,4) The Elders, with many angels and living creatures are in a circle (ἐν κύκλῳ) around the Lamb's throne, and they praise him as "the Lamb which was slain." (*Apoc.* 5,11-12; 7,11-12; 19,7) The throne on which the Lamb sits is not his alone but it is the "throne of God and of the Lamb." (*Apoc.* 5,13; 6,16-17; 7,9,10,15,17; 19,4; 22,1,3) The Lamb is sometimes described as seated on the throne but at other times as "in the midst of the throne." (e.g. 7,17)

The apocalyptic drama proceeds from the present to the future, and as it does the slain Lamb is replaced more and more by the victorious Lamb, and the hymns of the later chapters celebrate his triumph and rule rather than his sacrifice. But what is the focus in the Seer's normal experience which generates the abnormal vision? The focus is the eucharistic assembly offering in the liturgy the Eucharistic sacrifice. There is, I submit, a reasonably clear reference to the liturgy in the *Apocalypse*, amongst all the

---

[12] *Apoc.* 4 where they even there are described as "seated robed in white garments" associated with being "washed in the blood of the Lamb."

mysterious analogies with often unidentifiable objects and persons in this world.

The "elders" or "presbyters" are twenty four in number and are seated on thrones around the central throne of God (and the Lamb) just as in Hippolytus and the early liturgies in general the presbyters are seated likewise in a circle (ἐν κύκλῳ) around the presiding bishop, and just as Ignatius, describing a similar scene, speaks of "the spiritual circle so fitly adorned of your presbytery."[13] It is in such a context and with such a liturgical reference, moreover, that we should understand the rather odd image of "the throne of God and the Lamb," where sometimes the Lamb is the slain Lamb and sometimes appears "in the midst of the throne." It is very difficult trying to envisage a royal figure holding an animal in his lap or with an animal sitting by his side, let alone a slain animal. But the real reference is to the presiding bishop (or presbyter) offering the "pure sacrifice" of the gentiles, which is indeed the "slain Lamb."[14]

The fulfilment in the Eucharist of Malachi's prophecy of the pure sacrifice that the gentiles would offer was a common theme in the Fathers from the early second century onwards. Thus we find that the *Apocalypse* becomes, on our interpretation, a kind of eschatological-mystical meditation upon the corporate, eucharistic and liturgical acts of the church of the late first century. Barriers of time and space are removed so that the whole action takes place in one eternal eschatological "now" as the sacrifice of Christ is regarded as the climax to the eternal process of human salvation, "as a Lamb slain from the foundation of the world." (*Apoc.* 13,18; 17,8)

The Eucharistic offering in the Anaphora therefore becomes the offering of the whole created order destroyed and recreated.

---

[13] *Mag.* 13 cf. B. Botte, Hippolyte de Rome, La Tradition Apostolique, in *SC* 11 (1968), sect. 4 p. 46.

[14] *Did.* 14,3; Justin Martyr, *Trypho* 41, etc. The liturgical interpretation of the *Apocalypse*, common in Augustine and the Fathers, was defended by Dom Gregory Dix, in *The Shape of the Liturgy*, (London: Adam and Charles Black 1946), p. 28 and 134. Dix's cogent though neglected argument was: "the symbolism of the book.. has been suggested by the current practice of the church in the first century, and not *vice versa*, because the arrangement described was that which was traditional in churches which disputed the inspiration and canonicity of the book."

But in the midst of the scene stands a throne which is God's throne but where also the slain lamb is to be found. The twenty four presbyters sit around and sing their anthems whilst they pour out their incense. (5,8) But in their midst stands the representative, in Ignatius' words, of God the Father as not only the president of the presbytery but as the president of the Eucharist also.[15] Thus it is here that we glimpse Ignatius' *mileu* in a document which is by no means so alike as to imply direct borrowing, but in which the Ignatian themes of eschatological mysticism and its implications for a theology of salvation history mark a common tradition of theological reflection.[16]

We observe therefore a matrix which exists between ministry that represents the community, and ministry which represents the apostolic tradition, and that emerges from our discussion of Ignatius and the *Apocalypse*. For one community to recognize another's possession of the apostolic tradition, there can be no culture-free deposit of faith to which reference can be made as the criterion of validity. There are no certain, brute facts of history or tabulated "command-ments" (διατάγματα) or "ordinances" (δόγματα) that both communities can mutually recognize that they have both received from a third source, or

---

[15] Note that there is a close connection between the *Apocalypse* and Ignatius on the one hand, and the Johannine tradition on the other, which finds its development in the Hippolytan liturgy, where the typical words of administration at communion are: "The Bread of Heaven in Jesus Christ." (Botte (1968) op. cit. sect. 21 p. 92. Ignatius' bishop as president of the Eucharist, like the Seer's, sits in God's place because: "It is my Father who gives you the Bread from Heaven to eat." *Jn.* 6,32.

[16] *Apoc.* 4,9; 5,7,11, etc. Perhaps the deacon is the one member of the tripartite Order of which we fail to find even the shadowy of traces that is all that a work like the *Apocalypse* will ever permit. Are they the four living creatures who invariably accompany the presbyters around the episcopal throne, but who stand at the central throne of the presiding presbyter-bishop, whilst the non-presiding presbyters sit on their own seats? The deacons, ordained "for the service of the bishop," were invariably smaller in number than the council of presbyters. Are they the angels who suddenly multiply in their thousands around the (liturgical) circle (κύκλῳ) of the throne (*Apoc.* 5,1)? It is perhaps to be urged in support of such an interpretation that a later Eastern Father, Theodore of Mopsuestia, makes such a symbolic equation between the deacons in their liturgical function, and angels, in *Cat. Hom.* 21-23.

otherwise one can pass on to the other. For Ignatius the saving events are incarnated in living communities, and have to be recognized as being there by the exercise of spiritual charisma. Mutual recognition is when corporate personality meets, and has fellowship with, corporate personality in the representative clerical persons. Recognizing, in the words of Vatican II with which we began this chapter, "being bright with the tradition of the apostles," is not therefore at variance with recognizing the "church as the extension of the incarnation in a culture."

We saw that this was also the case with the Seer of the *Apocalypse* in that he addresses in his letters the corporate persons of communities in a church official corresponding to the angelic personality. Nor must it be thought that we are ignoring the fact that there is no indication that he himself was the officer of a community so that there can be no community behind him that he is representing. Christian prophets in the New Testament do not stand alone. The prophets and teachers of Antioch were church officers because of (or despite) their charismatic gifts. Furthermore, their possession of the charisma did not prevent them laying their hands collectively on those who thereby became their representative *Shelikim*, Barnabas and Paul. (*Acts* 13,1-3) And Antioch, after all, was to be latter the church of Ignatius, and to stand in a relation of mutual recognition with at least most of the seven churches in Asia Minor to whom the Seer wrote.

Having traced such patterns linking Ignatian bishops and the transmission of the παραθήκη, and the prophetic and mystical vision of the letter writer of the *Apocalypse*, let us now examine the concept and theology of ministry presupposed by the literary device of pseudonymity. After all, the very notion of a letter written in the name of a dead apostle may, at first sight, imply an appeal to past authority against present charisma. Schillebeeckx, clearly, was convinced that the pseudonymous letter which arose after the death of the apostles "conceals a whole theology of ministry." On this basic point I have no formal disagreement. Where I shall differ is over the substantive character of that ministry in terms of the polarism of charisma and Order in the early church. Schillebeeckx regards the pseudonymity of the *Pastorals* and *Ephesians* in the Pauline corpus, as witnessing to the institutionalizing of specific ministers who are bearers of the παραθήκη.[17]

What I shall argue is that it is quite false to see such a development as the "apostolic" in contrast to the "prophetic" legitimation of church Order. What we have seen in Ignatius, and in the *Apocalypse* read in the light of Ignatius, we shall now see see in the pseudonymous epistles, in particular the pastoral epistles and the Matthaean community, namely that there is no final distinction between the prophetic and apostolic strands in the tradition, nor between themes of representation and authority in the ministry. Our distinction is located in a separation between the recording of objective history and salvation history which we shall argue was never made before Irenaeus. But salvation history in the New Testament and Fathers involved both an objective historical core, and the interpretation of prophetical insight, such that there could be no witnesses to apostolic tradition who were not prophets, and no Christian prophets who had no particular historical relationship to the apostolic tradition. There could be furthermore neither a prophetic nor an apostolic ministry that did not have as its backcloth a community with which its message interrelated.

3. *Charisma, pseudonymity, and the* παραθήκη

It is a mistake, for reasons that we have partly already argued, to regard the role of a church official writing an ecclesial letter, whether Ignatius the bishop, or the Seer of the *Apocalypse,* as purely incidental to his ministry. We saw that particularly in Polycarp's case where to receive a letter was to be addressed partly as an individual and partly as a corporate person, just as in the cases of the angels of the churches in the *Apocalypse*. Our case can be strengthened by considering at the outset the instance of Clement of Rome, who writes anonymously, though everyone appears to know his identity, though we shall argue that the same will hold true also for pseudonymous, ecclesial letter writers.

Clement of Rome, who appears on the later succession lists as the bishop of Rome, if he was instead a presiding presbyter, was

---

[17] Schillebeeckx (1981) op. cit. p. 12, 16-20 ff.

such because he was regarded by the community as the authorized letter writer. His famous letter to the Corinthians does not
bear his name but the name of "the Church of God which dwells
at Rome (ἡ ἐκκλησία τοῦ Θεοῦ ἡ παροικοῦσα Ῥώμην)." (*Cor.*
inscr.) Because of this there is a tendency to regard Clement as
standing in relationship to his fellow presbyters as a "mere secretary" in contrast to the allegedly later triumph of Ignatian monepiscopacy in his successors on the succession lists.[18] However,
when we meet with Clement in *Hermas*, we find that his letter
writing activity is more than merely secretarial. It is Clement's
official function to communicate Hermas' vision to the cities
outside Rome since Clement "has been entrusted with this
responsibility (ἐκείνῳ   γὰρ   ἐπιτετράπται)." (*Vis.* 2,4) His
alleged status as a "mere" secretary, moreover, does not square
easily with the fact that not only is he well known as its author
by both Irenaeus (*Adv. Haer.* 3,3,3) and Dionysius of Corinth
(Eusebius *H.E.* 4,23), but is regarded by both as his church's
bishop.

Clearly Hermas has the prophetic gift, but the communication
or otherwise of what he prophesies is in the hands of Clement,
who is surely one of the presiding presbyters (οἱ   πρεσβύτεροι
προϊστάμενοι) to whom he writes and who is distinguished in
their company by his status as the authorized letter writer. We
shall now see how, in the age before Clement and Ignatius when
such letters as theirs were written pseudonymously in the names
of apostles, a similar status to theirs arguably equally applied to
the letter writer.

It was in the literary device of pseudonymity that, as we stated
at the beginning of this chapter, Schillebeeckx saw the pure type

---

[18]   E.g. R.E. Brown and J.P. Meier, *Antioch and Rome*, (New York:
Paulist Press 1983), p. 164. Meier's modern disdain for "mere secretaries"
intrudes when he asks of Clement's role: "Did *de facto* such a task make him
important (sic!), whence the later simplification that he was the bishop of
Rome?" Lampe clearly sees the "secretarial" functions of such presbyters as
contributing to their final emergence as the single bishop at Rome, see P.
Lampe, Die Stadtrömischen Christen in den ersten beiden Jahrhunderten, in
WUNT 2,18 (Tübingen: Mohr 1989), p. 334-345. See also H. Böhmer, Zur
altrömischen Bischofsliste, in *ZNW* 7 (1906), p. 333-339; P. Burke, The
Monarchical Episcopate at the End of the First Century, in *JES* 7 (1970), p.
499-518; E. Caspar, Die älteste römische Bischofsliste, in *SGK* 2 4 (1926).

of ministry legitimated in terms of the receiving and handing on of the apostolic tradition. Especially in the *Pastorals*, but in other instances too, the pseudonymous writer assumes the name of the Apostle in order to make the point that their ministry as leaders is primarily transmissive and not charismatic and prophetic. True "Timothy" possesses a χάρισμα but it is one transmitted through apostolic hands or the hands of fellow-presbyters. (*2 Tim.* 1,6 cf. *1 Tim.* 4,14) But it is through the ministry of ordination that he is so authorized to stand in the apostolic tradition. We must now examine further whether the device of pseudonymity pre-supposes an unqualifiedly transmissional view of Order that Schillebeeckx assumes.

We find the presence of an Order of ecclesiastical representa-tives implied by the literary device of apostolic pseudonymity in the New Testament epistles and elsewhere. Like Clement they could claim to be the official representatives of the faith of the community derived from the tradition of their founding apostle. Unlike Clement they wrote in the name of such an apostle as transmitters of the παραθήκη entrusted to them through him. As such, the pseudonymous epistles cannot be used as historical evidence for the existence of a pure presbyterian church Order before Ignatian mon-episcopacy. But as we shall now see in de-tail, neither can they be held to be in consequence evidence for a purely transmissional view of authorized ministry.

It is generally agreed that the Pastoral Epistles are deutero-Pauline just as *James* and 1 and *2 Peter* emanate from the post-apostolic age from churches who revere these apostolic names and claim their traditions as their own. But although the literary device of pseudonymity is shared by numerous works from the sub-apostolic period which occur both within and without the New Testament, the pseudonymity is not of the same kind in ev-ery case. Certainly one kind of pseudonymity was ruled out as reprehensible in Christian practice, namely the kind of romance represented by the *Acts of Paul and Thecla* which Tertullian mentions as forged in his own day by an unnamed presbyter, who claimed, apparently without much sympathy, that the pur-pose of his forgery was simply to honour Paul. (*De Bapt.* 17)

In one exceptional example, the weaving of historical romance is in evidence in New Testament pseudepigraphy, and that is in 2

Peter. The romantic backcloth is created of the apostle Peter's last will and testimony which condemns the heretics of the writer's own time. About to experience "the removal of my earthly abode, even as our Lord Jesus Christ revealed to me" (1,12-16), the pretended writer describes his author recalling the golden moment of his life which was the Transfiguration (1, 17-18), in two references in which he is clearly dependent upon both *Matthew* and *John* in their present form. (*Jn.* 18-19; *Mt.* 17,5)

In neither *1 Peter* nor in *James* are there any attempts to create such a historical background by this kind of writing of historical fiction.[19] In *James* we simply have the first verse to inform us that James is the writer to whom the contents are attributed, and that, since it was a "James" who had authority to address "the twelve tribes in the Diaspora," there is a very strong likelihood that he is meant to be identified as James the Lord's brother and first bishop of the church at Jerusalem. (*Acts* 21,18-24) In *1 Peter* all that we have to suggest such a pseudonymously created atmosphere is a list of names more reminiscent of Paul's biography rather than Peter's, namely Mark and Silanus. (5,12-14) It is a very important question therefore to ask what pseudonymity of this type is intended to achieve where there is no *motif* of the historical romance variety, with no alleged personal reminiscences to support the illusion of authenticity accompanying and fostered by the pseudonymity. The answer undoubtedly is that the pseudonymity registers that the writer stands in the apostolic tradition of which he is the interpreter. But the fundamental question is what is the character of his interpretive role?

The two letters of *Timothy* and *Titus* are different in this respect in that a scene in St. Paul's life is created by means of some very brief references and allusions which nevertheless are not embroidered to any great extent that would make them comparable with the historical romanticism of *2 Peter*. "Paul"

---

[19] M. Rist, Pseudepigraphy and Early Christian Literature, in D.E. Aune (ed.), *Studies in the New Testament and Early Christian Literature*, (Leiden: Brill 1972), p. 75-91, fails to distinguish different kinds of pseudepigrapha by the *a-priori* definition of this *genre* as an "attribution, designed to deceive, .. usually to some noted person of the past." Cf. B.M. Metzger, Literary Forgeries and Pseudonymous Pseudepigrapha, in *JBL* 91,1 (1972), p. 3-24.

requests "Timothy" to remain in Ephesus while he departs for
Macedonia, having exhorted him to put down something that
looks suspiciously like a late first century prototype of the
Marcionite heresy. (*1 Tim.* 1,1-3) We have a general reference to
Paul's problems with Asiatic Christians, to whom Onesiphorus
is hailed as the honourable exception whose diaconal service
ranges from both Ephesus and Rome. (*2 Tim.* 1,15-18) We hear
mention of Aquila, Priscilla, Mark, Titus, and Luke amongst
many others of the acquaintances and friends of the historical
Paul (*2 Tim.* 4,9-12,19), and of personal effects such as a cloak,
books, and parchments which Paul needs. (*2 Tim.* 4,13) How,
then, are we to understand this kind of pseudonymity if it is
neither historical romance, nor a straight statement of a church's
tradition under the name of its apostle?

If of course we were able to accept the Pauline authorship of
the *Pastorals*, or the Petrine authorship of *1 Peter*, there would
be no problems here for a traditional account of the threefold
Order and its apostolic origins in the form suggested in *1
Clement*. The clerical offices mentioned in the *Pastorals* are
deacons and *presbyter-episcopoi*.[20] In the event of the *Pastorals*
being genuinely Pauline, the non-existence of Ignatian bishops
would be consistent with what is derived hypothetically from
Clement's statement. We should simply say that there was no
need for bishops as an Order distinct from presbyters and
deacons whilst an Apostle was still present, but that such a
distinct Order was necessary as successors of Apostles after their
death.

The thesis of the Pauline authorship of the *Pastorals* is however difficult to sustain on a number of grounds, principally that
the writer's doctrine of the law has definitely failed to reflect the
complexity of Pauline theology on this subject. (*1 Tim.* 1,8-11)
But there are a number of considerations which must be taken
into account before we are lead to the conclusion that the
Pastorals constitute evidence for a presbyterian form of church

---

[20] Although πρεσβύτεροι are mentioned in a separate passage from that
which speaks of bishops (ἐπισκόποι) in *1 Tim.* 3,1-13, ἐπισκόποι and
πρεσβύτεροι are mentioned as though they were identical terms for the same
people in *Tit.* 1,5-9, cf. *1 Tim.* 1,8-11; 4,14; *2 Tim.* 1,6-8; *Tit.* 1,5-6; *1
Tim.* 1,18; 2,8; 4,11; 6,14; *Tit.* 3,8.

government in the immediate post-apostolic age of the seventies and eighties of the first century. We must decide principally what kind of literary *genre* such pseudonymous epistles are. *2 Peter* was the kind of document, we have argued, that could be purchased in the shops and read like a historical romance with an anti-heretical, edificatory theme. *1 Peter* and *James* were hardly such documents, since their contents were the traditional homiletics of their respective church traditions and well-known as such to all, with the result that the names of Peter and James neither deceived nor were intended to deceive, but rather were intended to attribute the developed and developing tradition to an ultimate apostolic foundation. But what of the *Pastorals* with their background of Paul's captivity and the lists of faithful, unfaithful companions and just plain enemies?

To begin with, I find persuasive the hypothesis of N.P. Harrison that this background is attributable, on grounds of vocabulary and syntax, to such details being surviving fragments of Paul's real letters, embedded by the pseudonymous author in his own text. But apart from the reference to books, a cloak, and parchment, which probably come from a personal letter quite out of place in a formal ecclesiastical letter, the remaining references are to persons and events well known within the collective memory of readers of the epistles, to many of whom what we would regard as their genuine written sources were well-known too. They are after all memories of those who injured the apostle in his mission, and so injured the Christian community too. What kind of person, therefore, we are entitled to ask, could write such a pseudonymous document in the name of the apostle and be entitled to not only respect for so doing but, more strongly, positive obedience in what he said?

It would I suppose be fashionable, in the light of the current charismatic climate within the contemporary Church, to say in answer to this question: "any Christian believer who felt moved by the Spirit to exhort the church to abide by the apostolic tradition." But there are two reasons for rejecting such an answer. Firstly, we have already seen how such a charismatic, Spirit-filled Seer would address the church from the *Apocalypse*. John writes not his own commands or those of an apostle in the tradition of his church but "what the Spirit says to the churches,"

tion of his church but "what the Spirit says to the churches," however much and in the background there may be recognition by a prophetic community like the prophets and teachers at Antioch. But in the second place the internal contents of the *Pastorals* rule out that kind of charismatic pattern of church Order.

The writer speaks to "Timothy" of "the χάρισμα of God which is in you through the imposition of my hands." Here is a church in which the gifts of the Spirit are given through the act of ordination in an established church Order. (*1 Tim.* 4,14; *2 Tim.* 1,6-8; *Tit.* 1,5-6) Nor, I submit, is it feasible to argue that its writer was unknown to the community in which it was written, as though it appeared suddenly out of no-where as an intentionally deceptive forgery. As I mentioned above, even the author of the intentionally forged *Acts of Paul and Thecla* was known to Tertullian as a quite general piece of knowledge, as general indeed as the Clementine authorship of the anonymous *Corinthians*. Given, then, the readers or hearers of the letter will know of the true identity of the author and accept his right to enunciate the tradition in terms of expressions such as "I command," "I charge," "I desire," (*1 Tim.* 1,18; 2,8; 4,11; 6,14; *Tit.* 3,8 etc.) and given that, in the familiar names of the Pauline characters, they will recognize figures in their own particular contemporary church situation and the problems that they are raising, such an author authoritatively commissioned to interpret and hand on the tradition will be regarded as a duly appointed minister for this task. Clement's letter writing, as we have seen, was a ministry which was "entrusted (ἐπιτέτραπται) to him."

But what will be the personal qualities and type of spirituality of this authorized, pseudonymous apostolic letter writer? On what grounds will his authority so to function be acknowledged? Schillebeeckx's answer was on the grounds that he was the possessor of the παραθήκη which he was transmitting. This is indeed part of the story, albeit only a part. If there was no remembered historical acknowledgement of Paul that he possessed such a role, he clearly, on the Harrison hypothesis, possesses some of Paul's actual and quite personal letters about cloaks, friends and enemies, etc. He has therefore some privileged historical contact with the παραθήκη, however tenuous, without which his

bishop without the διατάγματα and δόγματα, or the Seer of the *Apocalypse* without "the word of God and the testimony of Jesus."

But none of this is really enough for him to speak in the apostle's name. The churches of the *Pastorals* would never be satisfied with a mere transmitter, especially when what is transmitted is being radically developed and applied to the new ecclesiastical situation. The writer, like "Timothy," must have prophetic qualities too in terms of which such development of the δόγματα can be legitimated. The writer, like "Timothy," must "stir up" the χάρισμα that is within him through the imposition of hands. (2 *Tim.* 1,6) But we should not read into our image of what the writer, like "Timothy," will be like when he "stirs up" the χάρισμα of the Spirit assumptions derived from the insipid behaviour of contemporary evangelical preachers.

Our background documents in Ignatius and the Seer of the *Apocalypse* have shown us already what such a "stirring-up" of the Spirit would be like in the context of the first century. The pseudonymous letter writer's voice would change, to parody Ignatius, as he "cried with a great voice, the apostle's own voice" what he "knew not from human nature but what the Spirit proclaimed." (*Philad.* 7) His relation with the dead apostle will not be only and merely a personal as well as documentary link with the events of past, secular history, but there will be a perceived spiritual link like that of Ignatius. Ignatius claimed, as we have seen, to possess a more than human, spiritual habit of mind (συνήθεια) in common with Onesimus, bishop of Ephesus.

In Onesimus, he was able to see by means of the episcopal mystical vision which he shared with him, the spiritual qualities of the whole multitude of the Ephesian church of which their bishop is the sacred representative. Our authorized, pseudonymous letter writer thus may be held to have enjoyed his authority as a result of his people maintaining that he has this kind of mystical contact with the apostolic tradition, through his spiritual communion with the apostle himself and the faith of the community mystically present in him. When he "stirs-up" the gift within him, the accidents of the present vanish as they did with the Seer of of the *Apocalypse* no less than Ignatius. He is held to walk again in an eternal, eschatological "now," with the apostle and his companions, and to re-experience the saving acts by which, through enmity and conflict, the community was once historically founded. Those acts come to be relived again in a new form by the present community, which re-establishes their contact through such acts with salvation history, with the intervening events of secular history dissolved away in the prophetic vision of the church official.

We will pass over as purely speculative whether the writer in the apostle's name is perhaps an aged Timothy himself, who expounds to his late first century flock what Paul would have to say to them were he to have outlived the Neronian persecution, as though it were the Paul of his younger years articulating that tradition to himself. But what is not pure speculation is the character of the ministry of the presbyter-bishop, whose name, once it is admitted, will appear on later succession lists as a bishop of Ignatius' type. He is the authoritative letter writer who is more than a mere "secretary," but rather the representative to other churches of his own church's tradition. But his ministry cannot be characterized purely in terms of the transmission of the παραθήκη. He required the prophetic χάρισμα without which his testimony to the events of what is salvation and not secular history cannot be given. History and interpretation are indivisible so that ministerial succession and prophecy are equally so.

Let us now see how this fundamentally common pattern of ministry, in which the two themes of apostolic witness and prophetic charisma are inseparably combined, is found beyond Ignatius, the *Apocalypse,* the Pastoral Epistles, and in *Matthew.*

4. *Presiding Presbyters: Matthew*

In the figure of Peter in *Matthew,* we find the testimony to the saving events of history combined necessarily with their prophetic interpretation. We must now deal with the question as with what kind of figure Peter is to be identified in the Matthaean community. The critical text is the famous passage on Petrine primacy in *Mat.* 16,16-18.

As Meier has again pointed out, the power of the keys, of binding and loosing, is, when seen against its Rabbinic background, essentially the power to interpret the New Law authoritatively by binding some interpretations, but loosing or dismissing others. Meier sees Peter's authority therefore as apostolic in an essentially transmissive sense, interpreting Jesus' teaching in accordance with halakic rules of interpretation. His position is moreover juridical. He has power "to declare acts licit or illicit" in the light of the tradition." Meier thus continues:

> Matthew thus proclaims the Antiochene tradition of Peter as the bridge-figure, the moderate centre, to be the norm for the whole church, as opposed to those local churches, dissident groups, or sects which would appeal to a one-sided interpretation of the Pauline or Jamesian tradition as normative for the whole church.[21]

Thus Meier sees implications in *Matthew's* distinctive account of Caesarea Philippi for the writer's contemporary church.[22] Brown and Meier make a convincing case for *Matthew* in its compilation and composition as representing a reconciliation of traditions in potential conflict, as the previous quotation makes clear.[23] To this extent we are in agreement with Meier's thesis.

But as Meier is aware, a question now arises as to the extent to which the Peter who confesses Christ's Sonship, and is the rock on which the church is founded, represents an institutional figure in the Matthaean Antiochene church. Was it the justification of an actual ecclesiastical figure that lead both to the selection of the materials from the event at Caesarea Philippi, and their recasting into their present form? Meier curiously replies in the negative, seeing rather the Petrine figure as an idealization of the author's own imagination. The author is looking for an ideal, universal and authoritative interpreter of the Christian tradition, in order to deliver the church from the anarchic factionalism of the corporate

---

[21] Brown and Meier (1983) op. cit. p. 66-67.

[22] This particular version of Caesarea-Philippi is unique to *Matthew* and considerably adds to the Markan material common with *Luke*, cf. *Lk.* 9,18-21, and *Mk.* 8,27-30; See also H. Simonsen, The Gospel Literature as a Source for the History of Primitive Christianity, in *StTh* 37 (1983), p. 3-16.

[23] As such they would support Corwin's account of two distinct groups within Ignatius' church of Antioch which by this time had developed into Gnosticism on the Pauline extreme, and Judaism or Essenism on the Jamesian extreme, V. Corwin (1960) op. cit. chpt. 3; cf. L.W. Barnard, *Studies in the Apostolic Fathers and their Background,* (Oxford: Blackwell 1966); J. Smit Sibinga, Ignatius and Matthew, in *NT* 8 (1966), p. 262-283.

charismatic leadership of the various groups.[24] We have already, in Chapters 2 and 3, raised structuralist objections to such a reading of the development of the tradition, as if the various antinomies which exists in the sacred story of any community would necessarily require a kind of pre-existence in a pure social form before they became synthesized into a new community.

Meier's thesis represents an interesting variation on the disputed interpretation of the figure of Peter in *Matthew*. There are those who, on the one hand, argue that this gospel constitutes a defense of Petrine Primacy, and those on the other who argue that the figure of Peter represents the Matthaean community in its infidelity as well as fidelity in receiving and responding to the words of Jesus.[25] The problem with the former thesis is that it fails to come to terms with both the Peter who denies, and the church which appears to forbid, titles of ecclesiastical status. But what of the latter view?

Whether the actual corporate personality of the Matthaean community is in view, or Meier's idealized but as yet non-existent individual, there are a number of problems with which such an interpretation fails to come to terms. The condemnation of such a group as those who broadened their phylacteries and delighted in titles such as "teacher," "master" and "rabbi" on the one hand (*Mat.* 23,7-10,34), and of the group on the other hand who are false prophets performing miracles but not remaining faithful to Christ's teaching (*Mat.* 7,15-27; 24,11-12), was a condemnation which, in its present form, had application to actual groups within the Antiochene church in the eighties of the first century. But if this is the case regarding the peculiar Matthaean form of such discourses,[26] why therefore should not the emphasis and elaboration of the theme of Peter as the confessor and rock not also be directed as much in defense of a particu-

---

[24] Brown and Meier (1983) op. cit. p. 70-72.

[25] Bornkamm, Hummel, and Kähler represent the former point of view, whereas Strecker and Walker represent the latter. For a full bibliography and discussion see, J.D. Kingsbury, The Figure of St. Peter in Matthew's Gospel as a theological problem, in *JBL* 98 (1979), p. 67-83.

[26] Meier in other passages clearly admits this point, see Brown and Meier (1983) op. cit. p. 66.

lar institution as the former discourses were in attack of the groups that we have just mentioned?

Undoubtedly Meier's response is that, because Jesus refers to "my" church to be built on the rock of the Petrine tradition, a contrast is being drawn between conflicting local church-congregations and the universal Church. Thus Peter's activity as universal interpreter and harmonizer becomes very ideal indeed, to the point one might not unfairly say of being positively wistful. But in reality Meier's interpretation trades too much on this particular use of "my." The church of the first three centuries and indeed of all centuries before Luther was not an ideal abstraction but a concrete reality existing in time and space. Indeed so concrete is ecclesial reality that on the realistic, representative view Peter is far from ideal because he represents the actual community. (*Mat.* 14,30-1; cf. 8,25-6; 14,28-31; cf. 28,17 etc.)

The invariant use of ἐκκλησία in *Matthew* is of the church expressed as the local congregation, and not of the universal church abstracted from any particular local embodiment.[27] ἐκκλησία is used two further times outside this passage, in a single passage which deals with disputes within the Christian community. Any dispute is first to be considered by the parties themselves, and then, if no reconciliation is achieved, by two or three others. If they cannot resolve matters then: "tell it to the church (ἐκκλησία); and if he will not obey the church, let him be to you as the heathen and tax collector." (*Mat.* 18,17) The ἐκκλησία in this passage is clearly no ideal, universal ἐκκλησία, but an actual community existing with a geographical location in time and space, and able to pass sentence of excommunication.

It is not without significance that the second occurrence of the power to bind or loose occurs immediately following these words and that power is attributed to this adjudicating assembly (ἐκκλησία). (*Mat.* 18,18) If this second example of binding and loosing applies to the localized church, why should it not apply to the former? Admittedly we could see here a conflict between "episcopal" and "presbyterian" groups, but we only need do so on the assumption that the community as the interpreter of the tradition, or for that matter as the dispenser of absolution, is in-

---

[27] This is how Meier does in fact interpret them, ibid. p.56, 58.

consistent with an authorized representative doing such acts on the community's behalf and truly in union with it. Ignatius, as we saw in Chapter 3, believed in monepiscopacy, but at the period when he wrote it was still possible for him to regard the Roman community as a whole as exercising the bishop's office. Did the disparate church traditions embodied in the New Testament as a whole become one because unity was externally and artificially imposed upon them, or because there was within them a fundamental unity which produced by its own logic the resultant synthesis? If we affirm the latter, as does the present writer, the justification for the expression "my," signaling some ideal, universal church, thus disappears. The use of ἐκκλησία for "church" in *Matthew* is therefore an expression of the Order of the localized church.

If this is the case, the conclusion follows that the figure of Peter with the power of the keys exercised in union with the localized church is drawn in the Matthaean form because it had its counterpart in the author's contemporary church. But if this is so, we should note how absolutely consistent such an institutional figure would be with a minister who represents the particular traditions of the Christian community concerned in a unique way, as did our pseudonymous letter writer with both apostolic contact and the apostolic Spirit. Indeed the problem of a human figure representing the corporate community with nevertheless still distinguishable personal human features was precisely that which we saw in the case of the angel-bishops in the *Apocalypse*, and, we submit, soluble in the same way. Interestingly, Kingsbury came to a similar conclusion about the figure of Peter and its primacy, without claiming a church officer as bearing the community's corporate personality.

Such a figure has much in common with the authorized letter writer of Hermas *Vis.* 2 that we have postulated as the hander on, and interpreter of, the apostolic tradition because he is held to be uniquely representative of that tradition. Such a writer was no "mere secretary" especially when, unlike Clement, such people had the confidence of their personal authority to write in their own names, and to abandon the device of pseudonymity, although in the case of *1 Clement* the anonymous author wrote in the name of the church of Rome. Rather he is the rock on which the tradition is founded, and the interpreter who does not simply reflect but actively passes some interpretations and disallows others. He commands as much as he exhorts, just like the author of the *Pastorals* who saw in the ἐκκλησία— and the localized ἐκκλησία at that— "the pillar and ground of the truth."[28] And his authority is not so much of one who brings an apostolic witness from outside of the community into it, but rather that the community sees its apostolic witness and tradition articulated in what he says as their representative. Peter had a historical experience at Caesarea-Philippi, but what he saw went beyond mere empirical data, since it was about "what flesh and blood" could not reveal. The apostolic tradition cannot, therefore, be packaged in terms of a number of "objective" historical experiences, external to the faith of the community, and serving to corroborate independently that faith.

There is, however, one further figure in early Christian history that will repay some attention, in pursuance of our theme, and that is the figure of James the Lord's brother, according to tradition the first bishop of the church in Jerusalem. At first sight his example may seem to be at variance with the picture that we have so far built up of early Christian communities lead by representative figures incorporating the corporate personalities of their communities. That corporate personality was characterized as individually apostolic in some instances by pseudonymous letter writers writing in the name of an apostle, or apostolic figures like Peter in *Matthew* or the Beloved Disciple in *John* appearing in a community's sacred story with the same corporately characterizing intent. James appears like a traditional Jewish presbyter in the early records, surrounded by other presbyters in his early Christian synagogue. His is the authority of the teaching office handing on his παράδοσις, rather than the mystagogue and charismatic viewing the mysterious corporate personality of the Christian communities, as Ignatius did, and claiming office in consequence. Furthermore, he holds office, it has been held, not

---

[28] *1 Tim.* 3,15. The *Pastorals* at this point almost re-echo the Matthaean themes. Accusations against elders (presbyters) require two or three witnesses. (*1 Tim.* 5,19) The church is "the church of the living God," echoing Peter's "Thou art the Christ, the Son of the living God."

due to any particular mystagogical gifts but because of his blood-lineage with Christ.

Let us look at the role of James in the early church, therefore, in greater detail.

5. *James and the* παράδοσις

According to Dassmann, Ignatius was the inventor of monepiscopacy, and his reference to "bishops settled in the far parts of the earth" (*Eph.* 3,2) has lead commentators along a false trail. In consequence he rejects the two contenders for the place of single bishops before Ignatius, namely the angels of the churches in the *Apocalypse* and the position of James.[29] We have already argued against Dassmann regarding the former. But what of his argument that James is no true parallel to an Ignatian bishop but that his position was rather that of a caliph in a caliphate?

A "caliphate" is a system of government in which, as in the case of Mahomet and his heirs, authority is legitimated solely in terms of blood relationship with the charismatic founder of the ruling dynasty. James was the brother of Jesus and, following his martyrdom, according to Hegesippus, he is succeeded as bishop of Jerusalem by "Symeon the son of his uncle Clopas." (Eusebius *H.E.* 4,22) It can therefore seriously be asked to what extent Symeon's natural relationship through James to Christ can be described in such terms as "dynastic," and as inheriting the "blood of David" like the Maccabees.[30]

However, a clear distinction must be drawn between a situation in which (i) there is a formal requirement for office in terms of lineage and (ii) one in which lineage has simply helped a person to succeed. In the former case a blood line must be established in order to make an office legitimate so that the possession of blood-lineage is a necessary requirement In the latter it is

---

[29]   E. Dassmann, Zur Entstehung des Monepiskopats, in *JbAC* 17 (1974), p.8 1-83.

[30]   J. Colson, *Les fonctions Ecclésiales aux deux premiers Siècles*, (Paris: Desclée de Brouwer 1956), p. 117-9: ".. ces juifs convertis de Jérusalem avaient choisi.. celui qui était plus le proche par le sang du "Fils de David".. s'était continuée la "dynastie macchabéenne." Sans doute "la chair et le sang" trouvent encore leur compte dans une telle mentalitée."

simply the process of nepotism, and subconscious association of a charismatic leader with his blood relative, that has lead to the latter succeeding the former. The relationship in this case is a purely contingent one. For the distinction between James and an Ignatian bishop to hold on the grounds that the former was a caliph, therefore, it must be shown that the blood relationship between him and Jesus, and between him and his successors, was formally necessary for his holding office in sense (i). In other words the "caliphate" must be a real caliphate and not just a kind of metaphorical "caliphate," as when we call the Kennedies an American "dynasty." Here the caliphate is like that in sense (ii) since elections still have to be won before power is assumed, and other people, irrespective of their dynasty, are still entitled to stand.

Now the very text of Hegesippus under discussion, in which we have the account of how Symeon succeeded James his martyred cousin, the strong notion of caliphate as an indispensable blood relationship simply does not hold. While Symeon is unanimously elected, it is mentioned only incidentally that he was a cousin of Jesus. Eusebius' own earlier account (H.E. 3,11), admittedly secondary, says that Symeon was the son of Clopas mentioned in the gospel narrative, and that according to Hegesippus he was Joseph's brother. In this passage, the fact that Symeon was chosen as the most suitable (whatever that may mean), and not merely because of his blood-line, is corroborated by the fact that it is recorded that Thebouthis began the line of heretics out of disappointment that he had not been elected in succession to James. If the Jerusalem church had been ruled by a caliphate in a literal and strong sense, Thebouthis' candidature must have been ruled out from the start. Nor will it do to argue that the tradition of the caliphate has been overlaid by later concerns in Eusebius. Eusebius' concerns are identical to Hegesippus' apologetic ones[31]. Both were interested in catholic orthodoxy and eye witnesses, whether in terms of apostles or Christ's immediate family, in order to refute heretical claims.

---

[31] On Hegesippus primarily as an apologist, see N. Hyldahl, Hegesipps Hypomnemata, in StTh 14 (1960), p. 70-113. Cf. H.J. Lawler, Eusebiana, (London: Oxford University Press 1912).

Thus the kind of appeal made by Stauffer must fail to make its case and cannot go beyond a description, however detailed and well-documented, of patriarchal and nepotistic family and authority structures in the first two centuries, as the assumed background of James' "caliphate."[32] We need to find a "caliphate" in the stronger sense of necessary, as opposed to a merely powerful or convenient blood-line, for the comparison between James and an Ignatian bishop to fail.

The closest that Stauffer gets to my strong definition of "caliphate" is his allusion to the δεσπόσυνοι as related to the σωτήριον γένος in Eusebius (*H.E.* 1,7,14), and to three bishops in Seleucia on the Tigris in the third century who "nacheinander regiert, die ihren Stammbaum auf den Vater Jesu zurückführten."[33] Eusebius is actually alluding to Julius Africanus, *Ad Aristidem,* 5. But Stauffer trades too heavily on an allegedly concealed eschatological significance for σωτήριον γένος. He seeks to make this phrase equivalent to the "saving lineage" rather than simply to the "Saviour's lineage," thus endowing the blood-line itself with redemptive significance. And the existence of third century Seleucian bishops who made at that time their hereditary claim to such a succession which before their time had been valid without such a qualification surely supports my case rather than his.[34]

It is therefore vain to appeal to the reference of Polycrates of Ephesus in his letter to Victor of Rome in A.D. 193 to the seven bishops in his family, all dutifully following the Asiatic paschal practice, as evidence of an Asiatic caliphate.[35] Family influence and nepotism in a weak sense is fully consistent with episcopal qualifications which do not include a required blood relation in any strong, formal and necessary sense. It is equally vain to appeal to the δεσπόσυνοι in the fragment from Hegesippus.

---

[32] E. Stauffer, Zum Kalifat des Jacobus, in *ZRGG* 4 (1952), p. 193-214, who replied to von Campenhausen, Die Nachfolge des Jacobus, in *ZKG* 63 (1950-52). The most recent historical study assuming something like a caliphate view is M. Hengel, Jacobus der Herrenbruder– der erste Papst?" in *Glaube und Eschatologie, Festschrift für W.G. Kümmel zum 80 Geburstag,* (Tübingen: J.C. Mohr 1985), p. 71-104.

[33] Stauffer (1952) op. cit. p. 200.

[34] Ibid. p. 199-200.

[35] Eusebius *H.E.* 5,24,6 cf. Stauffer (1952) op. cit. p. 200.

Hegesippus had apologetic intentions in showing that Christianity made no political claims in recording the legend of Domitian's contemptuous dismissal of the poor, hand-hardened descendants of Christ, who admitted David's lineage but who professed a spiritual kingdom.[36]

Moreover, a closer examination of the earliest patristic evidence and other sources confirms our scepticism that the early church of Jerusalem was ruled by a caliphate. Josephus was, after all, the historian who lived and witnessed the events of Judaea first hand during the period A.D. 62-70, and who has something to say about James as head of the Jewish-Christian community. Josephus never connects James' primacy over the church at Jerusalem with a caliphate in the strong sense nor supports the later identification of both Levitical and Davidic lines necessary if James had been regarded as antitypical of the Maccabees. (Josephus *Ant.* 20,200) He does call James "the brother of Jesus," but nowhere associates James with the Levitical priesthood. Thus Josephus indirectly supports the contention of the writer to the Hebrews, ignored by Africanus in *Ad Aristidem,* that Jesus was of the tribe of Judah and could not therefore have been a levitical priest.

Moreover, had James' position been comparable with both Judas of Galilee and the Maccabees, as is so often claimed,[37] it is difficult to see how Josephus, by the time of his writing a friend of Rome and seeking to make the Zealots responsible for the Jewish war and not mainline Judaeism, could have been so sympathetic to James. The notion of a caliphate is, after all, bound up with political messianism. James' martyrdom, however, occurs, according to Josephus, between the death of Festus and the arrival of Cestius Florus. Ananus, the Sadducean high priest, is deposed by Agrippa II for the illegal stoning as the

---

[36] Eusebius *H.E.* 3,20 cf. Hydahl (1960), p. 87: "Die Fragen des Domitian an die Nachkommen Davids.. sind Fragen die nur innerhalb einer ganz bestimmten Problemstellung einen Sinn hatten, nämlich bei der Frage nach dem Verhältnis der Christen und der Kaisermacht zu einander."

[37] E.g. Stauffer (1952) op. cit. p. 119-200, 202, 206; S.C.F. Brandon, *Jesus and the Zealots*, (Manchester: University Press 1967), p. 28-32, 115-125; W. Telfer, *The Office of a Bishop,* (London: Darton, Longman, and Todd 1962), p. 11-12.

result of the protest of the "fair-minded" amongst the citizens. Any suggestion that James was a Davidic and priestly figure, whose authority derived from a caliphate based upon these two qualifications, would have made him far more akin to the Zealots in Josephus' eyes, and a definite *persona non grata* for his apologetic concerns regarding Rome.

At all events, Josephus relates that Ananus proceeded against him on a purely religious charge. James was stoned and not crucified, and the later would have been his fate, with Florus' consent, if charges could have been made to stick.[38] In this respect, Josephus' narrative must also count against the historical basis of Hegesippus' legend of the δεσπόσυνοι, which appears in any case to be a piece of contrived fiction designed to refute political charges against any Christian from the reign of Domitian onwards. Moreover, the further fragment advanced in support of James' sacerdotal position has been convincingly shown by Zuckschwerdt to point to exactly the opposite conclusion.[39] Hegesippus' description of James is not that of one who exercises priestly prerogatives, but rather of one who has taken a life-long Nazirite vow. The whole tenor of the James' legend is to suggest in fact anti-sacerdotal conceptions of holiness which underlay the narrative.[40]

Of course there was a later justification of the apostolic succession in which the chronology of the combined royal and Aaronic blood lines of the Maccabees, and its eschatological significance in Josephus' genealogical lists, played its part as a

---

[38] Brandon finds this passage most embarrassing to his case for the political messianism both of the historical Jesus and the Jacobean church, see Brandon (1967) op. cit. p. 119-121, where he tries to associate the present, allegedly corrupt text of Josephus with doubts about the *Testimonium Flavianum*, and possible christian insertions and editing. For a contrary view, see E. Schürer, *The History of the Jewish People in the Age of Jesus.* (ed.) G. Vermes, F. Millar, and M. Black, (Edinburgh: T. and T. Clarke 1979) vol. 1, p. 428-441.

[39] E. Zuckschwerdt, Das Naziräat des Herrenbruders Jakobus nach Hegesippus, in *ZNW* 68 (1977), p. 276-287.

[40] Ibid. p. 287: "Die Tradition des lebenslangen Nazirtums.. wurde durch den Gegensatz zu dieser priesterlichen Konzeption und durch die sich heraus ergebenden, im Laufe der Zeit zunehmend verschärften Antithesen, die Wiederspiegelungen geschichtlicher Spannungen und hieraus erwachsender Gegensätze zum priesterlich bestimmen."

suggestive model. Ehrhardt has convincingly shown the responsibility of Hippolytus for adopting this model in his *Chronicon*, which Eusebius took over in the *Praeparatio Evangelica*.[41] The later mentions fifteen bishops of the circumcision from James until the time of Hadrian, and the fifteen gentile bishops from the foundation of Aelia Capitolina until Narcissus. But his scheme is artificial and involves repeating in the case of the gentile-list the two identical names, in order to bring history into line with Daniel's apocalypse and eschatological events expected in the first years of the third century. And this was the very time at which Julius Africanus was anxious, as we have seen, despite *Hebrews*, to show that the two rival genealogies between *Matthew* and *Luke* mean that, like the Maccabees, Christ's descent is both regal and levitical.[42] We cannot, therefore, apply such late, second century concerns with sacral-political blood lineage to James the Just in the first century.

We have, then, established that the description of James as a kind of caliph was not primitive but a late, second century development. We saw that there is no evidence of a caliphate, in the strong sense of that term, but rather the reverse if one takes into account both the apologetic concerns of Hegesippus and, in his own way, Josephus, as well as the anti-sacerdotal, Nazirite features of the former's description. What, therefore, can we gather from the New Testament itself about the basis of the authority of James the Lord's brother over the church of Jerusalem?

6. *James and the New Testament*

In *Acts* it is implied that James becomes the prominent figure in the church of Jerusalem following the martyrdom of his namesake, James the apostle, at the hands of Herod Agrippa I in A.D. 45, and the departure of Peter "to another place." (*Acts* 12,1-3) In a passage fascinating for what it does not tell us about the constitutional evolution of primitive Christianity, Peter declares his miraculous escape from prison in the house of Mary

---

[41] A.A.J. Ehrhardt, *The Apostolic Tradition in the First Two Centuries of the Church*, (London: Lutterworth 1953), p. 46-61.
[42] Ibid. p. 58-59.

the mother of John Mark and her slave-girl Rhoda, which appears to be a house-church. He then instructs them to "make this announcement to James and the brothers (ἀπαγγείλατε Ἰακώβῳ καὶ τοῖς ἀδελφοῖς)," before his departure.[43]

Whether the Petrine house-congregation, described in terms of synagogal worship (ἱκανοὶ συνηθροισμένοι καὶ προσευχόμενοι) (Acts 12,12), can be regarded as a separate Petrine congregation from that of James, the latter from this point on in the narrative appears as the president of the Jerusalem church surrounded by his elders in a picture that has parallels in the synagogue. Throughout the subsequent story of Acts, though at first mentioned in the company of the apostles, James gradually emerges as the sole church leader in Jerusalem, like a later single bishop, or a contemporary Jewish ἀρχισυνάγωγος, surrounded by presbyters and deacons. (Acts 6,1-6; 15,2-4,6,13; 21,17-18)

In this respect the Paul of Acts likewise has his presbyters as a counterpart to those of James in the mother church, although the historicity of Acts on this point is frequently disputed on the grounds that presbyters are not mentioned in Paul's genuine letters. On the first missionary journey, even before the Council of Jerusalem, Paul and Barnabas are recorded as χειροτονήσαντες δὲ αὐτοῖς κατ' ἐκκλησίαν πρεσβυτέρους (14,23). It is these selfsame presbyters at Ephesus who gather at Paul's apostolic command at Miletus to hear his last will and testament, where they are also termed ἐπίσκοποι. (Acts 20,28) Whether indeed they were called πρεσβύτεροι in the Pauline churches, or whether Luke is not rendering ἐπίσκοποι better understood by his readers is debatable.[44] But it is at least arguable that the author of Luke-Acts is right when he regards them as functionally similar to each other despite the use of different terms within different

---

[43] The development of Jacobean primacy has been widely discussed, see e.g. Brandon (1967) op. cit. p. 161-166; Ehrhardt (1953) op. cit. p. 20-23; W. Telfer, The Office of a Bishop, (London: Darton, Longman, and Todd 1962), p. 5-14; Campenhausen (1969) op. cit. p. 20-23; Zollitsch (1974) op. cit. p. 40-65.

[44] πρεσβύτεροι as opposed to ἐπίσκοποι are not referred to in the genuine letters of Paul by contrast with the Pastorals. See Philip. 1,1 cf. Campenhausen (1969) op. cit. p. 78-85; Telfer (1962) op. cit. p. 33-9. R.E. Brown, Priest and Bishop: Biblical Reflections, (London: Geoffrey Chapman 1971) p. 68-70 ff. defends the existence of presbyters in Paul's churches.

groups of churches. The main difference in this regard between the Pauline churches and the church of Jacobean Jerusalem might be thought to be that in the former the presbyters or bishops were several, whereas in the latter a presbyter *par excellence* presided, like an Ignatian bishop, over other presbyters. But this would be to place too great a credence on *Luke's* distinction between apostles, of whom Paul is one, and others like James. As we shall see, Paul claimed to be both an apostle and the equal, not the superior, of James so that for Paul's communities, though in contrast with James he did not reside, there was one presiding figure too.

The Jacobean presbyters are associated with the apostles in *Acts*, particularly when the church of Jerusalem is described as issuing the so-called Apostolic Decrees. (*Acts* 15,2,4,6,22,23; 16,4) But as Campenhausen has shown, the limitation of the term "apostle" to the Twelve was a later development and imposed on the primitive tradition by the author of *Luke-Acts*.[45] In a moment we shall have to ask whether there may have been a closer identity of function between an "apostle" and "presbyter" in the early church where the former could be as numerous as the later, in the historical tradition which Luke took over and transformed in terms of his own historicism.

The primitive community, to which Paul's genuine letters bear witness, was one in which the term "apostle," at least in one of its senses, did refer to a witness of the resurrection, but their number was far larger than the Twelve. Paul's record of the resurrection experiences, which begin his account of the apostolic παράδοσις, groups in the same company both Peter and the Twelve, the five thousand brothers, and "all the apostles," and then Paul as joint witnesses of the resurrection. Apostolic witnesses to the resurrection clearly therefore outnumbered the Twelve. (*1 Cor.* 15,1-9) Paul does identify, therefore, the Twelve as a distinct group as he does the Lord's brothers, but they have the authority that they do neither from pre-resurrection, nor from family relationships, but from their part in the wider community of witnesses. We see in the Lukan tradition that develops the Twelve at the expense of the rest of the primi-

---

[45] Campenhausen (1969) op. cit. p. 14-16, and Campenhausen (1950-2) op. cit. p. 133 ff.

tive community of witnesses a parallel with that which we have observed taking place in other parts of the church with James and Christ's natural family.

But if neither natural blood-line nor membership of the Twelve were the sources of James' authority, but the fact of his membership of the community of witnesses, how does this relate to his or anyone else's position of authority in the organization of the primitive Christian synagogue? To this question we must now turn.

7. παράδοσις and the organization of the early Christian synagogue

In every Jewish synagogue there was a council of elders or πρεσβύτεροι, even though no one was appointed in the first century for the sole conduct of worship. Synagogues were at that time, in any case, "places of prayer" (*Acts* 16,11) so that questions of any lay/ordained distinction, appropriate to the Temple cultus, were quite out of place in their regard. The evidence for an ordained rabbinate before A.D. 70 has, not surprisingly, therefore, been disputed.[46] But there was an office of some relevance to our present discussion, namely that of ἀρχισυνάγωγος or "ruler of the synagogue."

Although there were administrative "rulers" whose leader was called γερουσιάρχης or "chief of the senate," the ἀρχισυνάγωγος had a quite different function from those who administered the general affairs of the congregation. The ἀρχισυνάγωγος, probably chosen from the presbyters, was the leader of worship, deciding who should read from the Torah scrolls or lead in prayer, and who was to be summoned to expound the text of the Torah. There was moreover a third officer in addition to the ἀρχισυνάγωγος and γερουσιάρχης, and this was the διάκονος. He signaled the beginning and end of the Sabbath with a trumpet,

---

[46] H.B. Swete, *Essays in the Early Church and Ministry*, (London: MacMillan 1918); C. Gore, *The Church and the Ministry, New Edition revised by C.H. Turner*, (London: S.P.C.K. 1919); A.A.J. Ehrhardt, Jewish and Christian Ordination, in *JEH* 5 (1954), p. 125-138; E. Lohse, *Die Ordination im Spätjudentum und im Neuen Testament*, (Göttingen: Vandenhoek und Reprecht 1951); G. Kretschmar, Die Ordination im Frühen Christentum, in *FZThPh* 22 (1975), p. 35-69.

carried the Torah scrolls into the congregation, and taught the children to read.[47]

Thus in the pre-Christian, Jewish synagogue we have the basis of the kind of church Order of which we find traces in *Acts*, centred on the figure of James the Lord's brother. Moreover, granted a late first or early second century date for *Acts*, and a colouring in terms of a later church Order, James does nevertheless also prefigure in the primary sources that are Paul's *1 Corinthians* and *Galatians*. In the later, James appears as the undoubted leader of the Jerusalem church along with Cephas and John. The three are described as "pillars," but Peter departs afterwards for Antioch and James is identified as the villain of the piece for refusing table fellowship with gentile Christians and thus, according to Paul, breaking a solemn agreement. (*Gal.* 2,1-4) As we hear of John no more, and Peter has clearly taken up residence in Antioch, James' leadership, according to the primary source of *Galatians*, is unquestionably as *Acts* so describes it.[48]

But how does the position of James as so described fit into the picture of the first century synagogue as we have briefly sketched it? At first sight he appears simply as the ἀρχισυνάγωγος of a group of elders of the kind of ἐκκλησία that is called "your synagogue" in the pseudonymous epistle of James. (*Jam.* 2,2). But not only the texts in *Acts, Galatians* and pseudonymous *James*, but also the latter tradition of the *Clementines* witness a predominance on the part of James that the ἀρχισυνάγωγος simply did not possess. This should not however deter us from the comparison, since what is critical is not simply what made such a primitive Christian congregation similar to its Jewish counterpart, but also what made it different. The critical difference is, I submit, in the form that the authority of tradition took in Judaism by contrast with that of Christianity, which in turn necessarily distinguishes both the nature of the authority and the function of the official concerned.

In the synagogue, before Judaism established the category of heresy and the mechanism for excommunication, any male could

---

[47] Schürer (1979) op. cit. vol. 2 p. 434-439.

[48] T. Holtz, Der Antiochienische Zwischenfall (Galater 2,11-14), in *NTS* 32 (1986), p. 344-361.

participate in any part of the worship under the general direction of the ἀρχισυνάγωγος. But this was possible only within Judaism because the revelation that existed there was in a written form. The scrolls of the Law and the Prophets could stand theoretically as the impersonal director and controller of what was said and done, notwithstanding the notion of an oral tradition which, in Judaism, arose only after A.D. 70. But although a Christian community still part of the Jewish synagogue might appeal to that impersonal, literary source when its literate members like Apollos or Paul stood up and showed how the law and the prophets pointed to Christ, there were as yet no written testimony to the saving events which fulfilled those documents. Instead there was an oral tradition. But an oral tradition, unlike definitively written forms of such tradition, cannot exist independently of the human bearers of that tradition, at least when it is rooted in certain historical events.

Paul is insistent that he has a παράδοσις, like James, and derived from the ἀποκάλυψις of the risen Christ. (*1 Cor.* 15,7-8) The Easter event of Christ risen, he says, "I received (παρέλαβον) not from man (παρ' ἄνθρωπου) but through Jesus Christ's revelation (δι' ἀποκαλύψεως)" (*Gal.* 1,11-12) His παράδοσις is therefore that which he "received" or "took over" (παρέλαβον), and which he "passes on" (παρέδωκα: *1 Cor.* 11,23; *2 Thes.* 2,15; 3,6), and these expressions have their aramaic equivalents in the teaching practice of rabbinic Judaism.[49] The παράδοσις is not confined to the Easter events alone, but also to the "night in which he was betrayed," and the words and acts appropriate to the communion liturgy (*1 Cor.* 11,23-25) and to Christ's moral teaching (*1 Cor.* 7,10,12,25). His παράδοσις does not rest on a purely spiritual, Easter or post-Easter ἀποκάλυψις. But his παράδοσις is an oral one, like the "gospel" which he likewise receives and passes on. (*Gal.* 1,11-12)

Thus the character of the παράδοσις that in *1 Cor.* 15,5-6 marks its bearer as possessing apostolic authority is an oral one. But since that tradition was rooted in the history of the spatio-temporally confined events of the life, death, and resurrection of

---

[49] G.G. Blum, *Tradition und Sukzession: Studien zum Normbegriff des Apostolischen von Paulus bis Irenäus*, (Berlin: Lutherisches Verlagshaus 1962), p. 32-35.

Jesus of Nazareth, there follows necessarily a specific mode of transmission. Those who were the historical eyewitnesses of such events, and subjects of such experiences, had to pass them on to others who were not present because they did not occupy the same spatio-temporal position in the history of those events. Those who were bearers of the tradition were necessarily placed in an authority relationship with those who received it by the very *oral* nature of that tradition. Even though there was no formal apostolic commission from the risen Christ in the form in which *Matthew*, for example, gives it (*Mat.* 28,16-20), the events of its historical origin, decisively if implicitly, both created and legitimated the ecclesiastical office of those who transmitted it.

The oral character of the παράδοσις, therefore, means that it is impossible to divorce "continuity of teaching" (Lehrkontinuität) from "continuity of office" (Amtskontinuität) that has become fashionable following Campenhausen and Blum.[50] As I mentioned above, Paul did not confine his παράδοσις to the Easter experience but included Maundy Thursday and Christ's earthly teaching, and this implies an historical experience which some had (like himself and James), but others could not have, and a resultant relationship of dependence and authority. Of course the παράδοσις, like the Gospel, in a sense "stood over" its human bearers. But without a written form, it is impossible to reify its existence apart from its human bearers.[51] In an oral form the authority of the παράδοσις, and the authority of its human bearers, were quite inseparable.

---

[50] H.von Campenhausen, Der Urchristliche Apostelbegriff, in *StTh* vol. 1 Fasc. I-II (1947), p. 112-114: "Auch für Paulus hängt das ganze Christentum an der Wirklichkeit und Gewissheit der Auferstehung und er fügt sich an diesem Punkt bewusst der älteren Überlieferung an. Aber anscheinend war er nicht enger verbunden, und darum müssen wir die herrschende Auffassung über die Begründung des Apostolats im Zeugentum mit einem Fragezeichen versehen." See also Campenhausen (1969) op. cit. p. 70-75; Blum (1962) op. cit. p. 80-85ff.

[51] W. Schmitals, Das Kirkliche Apostelamt. Eine Historische Untersuchung, in *FRLANT* n.f. 61, (1961) p. 43: ".. die Autorität des Apostels liegt nicht in dem Amt an sich, sondern in der Botschaft, die durch das Amt verkündigt wird."

Such an account does not mean of course that there were not disputes between different claimants to the παράδοσις. As we saw in Chapter 3, the ultra charismatic τῶν ὑπερλίαν ἀποσ-τόλων could also claim, in terms of the tradition of the Seventy Two preserved in *Luke*, that they were witnesses to the historical ministry of Jesus. Indeed, it is against them and the "false brethren" that Paul may be regarded as tightening the concept of apostolicity in terms of the procession of eyewitnesses in *1 Corinthians* 15. Nor do we deny that the term "apostle" can be extended by Paul to include the *Shaliah*/representatives of communities in which his oral *paradosis* has taken root so that they become almost proxies for its reified, written form. The Corinthians are "manifestly the letter of Christ ministered by us (ἐπιστολὴ Χριστοῦ διακονηθεῖσα ἀφ᾽ ἡμῶν), written not with ink but in the spirit of the living God.. on the fleshly tablets of your hearts." (*2 Cor.* 3,3)

Those who become associated with the Pauline παράδοσις, thus taken root in the community and written on hearts, such as Titus and his companions, achieve the status of "communicant" (κοινωνός) and "fellow-worker" (συνεργός), and so are numbered amongst the ἀπόστολοι ἐκκλησίων. (*2 Cor.* 8,23) We hear of other such associates of Paul such as "Andronikus and Junias," whose precise position in the Roman community are unknown but who are ἐπίσημοι ἐν τοῖς ἀποστόλοις. (*Rom.* 16,7) We must not, therefore, simply regard their role as community representatives in a Jewish sense, any more than we should simply regard παράδοσις in a Jewish sense. We need to look at what in terms of the conditions of the primitive communication of the Christian gospel made such concepts *different* as between Judaism and Christianity.

Whereas therefore in the Jewish synagogue the authority of the ἀρχισυνάγωγος or liturgical director could be considerably weaker because of the impersonal and reified authority of the Torah scrolls, in the Christian synagogue there were no scrolls embodying the παράδοσις of prophetic fulfilment. Instead there were people, whether present or absent, who bore that παρ-άδοσις in their persons and voices. The very oral character of the revelation thus created such persons who alone had the right to articulate and express it, as a result of a particular set of historical experiences. It is as a result of these conditions that we see in *Acts* the figure of James arising out of, and being distinguished from, the judaeo-christian presbyterate by which he is surrounded.

In the Christian synagogue, therefore, only someone who bore the oral παράδοσις because they had an historical experience of it in terms of the saving events could have the role of delivering it as Paul delivers it to the Corinthian charismatics in all their enormities. James, as one of the acknowledged bearers of the παράδοσις, is even called with Peter a "pillar" of the church by a Paul frankly resisting their authority in *Galatians*. (2,1-14) Later, in *Romans* and *Corinthians*, Paul seeks a measured reconciliation with that Jerusalem authority through the collection for the poor at Jerusalem in an act which has its analogy in the Temple tax paid by the Diaspora. The description of the bearers of the παράδοσις as "pillars" thus mirrors the Matthaean figure of Peter, which we analyzed earlier, as the "rock" on which the church is built,— the same church that was described in *1 Timothy* as "the pillar and ground of the truth." In the pseudonymous letter writer Paul's παράδοσις continues to live and grow in the community, as the charismatic gift that describes the experiences of history in terms that "flesh and blood" could not reveal.

Far from James' position therefore being unique and personal over the church of Jerusalem, as Paul's description of their common apostleship has shown, his authority is of a piece with both that of his contemporaries and that of his successors. In asserting his apostolic authority against the scandalous celebrations of the Eucharist, Paul constantly appeals to "the traditions (παράδοσεις) which I have passed on (παρέδωκα) to you." (*1 Cor.* 11,2) He acts initially like an ἀρχισύναγωγος organizing those who wish to speak, be they prophets, teachers, or interpreters. (*1 Cor.* 11,1-21; 14,26-40) Then as apostolic president he virtually orders the liturgy by which they are to celebrate the Eucharist on the grounds that "I received from (παρέλαβον) the Lord what I also delivered (παρέδωκα) to you." (*1 Cor.* 11,23) When exercising discipline, it is not simply that the community is to deliver to Satan the offender in Christ's name but rather, Paul says, "when you gather together and my spirit with you with the power of our Lord Jesus Christ." (*1 Cor.* 5,4-5) It is no disembodied παράδοσις, and certainly not a reified, written one, but Paul's παράδοσις that lives *viva voce* in his community. It is, as he says, "my spirit with you" that gives the community the authority to excommunicate on an ethical issue.

In this respect there is not a great deal to distinguish Paul and James, both of whom were witnesses to the resurrection, and bearers of a παράδοσις by virtue of which they exercised superintendence over their respective congregations. Their superintendence is like that of an ἀρχισύναγωγος, but where, with no objective and interpersonal written tradition to which they can appeal, and to which others can appeal against them, the oral authority of their παράδοσις rests with them alone. The difference between Paul and James is that the former traveled, whereas the latter, like a later Ignatian bishop, was stationary, so that the need for associates, συνέργοι or κοινώνοι, in handing on the tradition was not so pressing.

We have earlier in this chapter (section 3) sought to show how the primitive apostolic office came to be transmitted to a second generation of church leaders who were considered to have the παράδοσις (or like Timothy the παραθήκη), but who in the nature of the case could have no personal involvement of the saving events. Had the παράδοσις at that early stage achieved a determinate written form, like the later New Testament canon, then there could have been an Irenaean view of the transmission of apostolic office some one hundred years earlier. But the literary device of pseudonymity, as I interpreted it in section 3, reveals how alien, in the first and early second century, the concept of the παράδοσις, as a kind of title-deed or *depositum fidei* , really was that could be inertly handed on. The living voice of the apostle must still speak his παράδοσις and interact dynamically in the life of the living community rather than be read statically in dead records of a by-gone age. "Paul" or "James" or "Peter" continue to speak in and through the community, and the charismatic letter writer who represents its faith to the community, like an Ignatian bishop, rather than delivering it externally as a book of rules.

Thus the Christian communities, after the death of their apostolic founders, continued to prefer, in the words of Papias, "the

living and abiding voice" (τὰ τῆς ζώσης φῶνης καὶ μενούσ-
ης)⁵², and according to *1 John* to refer to "that which was from
the beginning, which we have heard, which we have seen with
our eyes, which we have contemplated (ἐθεασόμεθα), and our
hands have handled, concerning the word of life (τοῦ λόγου τῆς
ζωῆς)." (1,1) Significantly for our discussion, Eusebius
characteristically refers to his quotes from Papias as τοῦ
πρεσβύτερου Ἰωάννου παραδόσεις. (*H.E.* 3,9,7) Because there
was no objectively fixed, written medium into which the Pauline
παράδοσις could flow, the means of transmission was person-
to-person, by means of "the living and abiding voice." LeMaire
was therefore correct to see the seeds from which were to develop Irenaeus' later doctrine of the apostolic succession in such
relations between Paul and his fellow-workers, however distorted the Irenaean growth arguably was to become.⁵³

Finally, in another way, the position of the oral παράδοσις
legitimating both apostolic office and representative office in the
ongoing community after the death of the apostolic founder has
left its mark upon early Christian history. The New Testament
pseudepigrapha, as well as the extra-canonical material, in particular the *Clementines,* bear testimony to what we referred to in
Schillibeeckx's term as "a whole theology of ministry" which
antedates Irenaeus' jurisdictionally based theory of an apos-
tolic/episcopal succession. But we have endeavoured to show
that, contrary to Campenhausen and Blum, such legends such as
those from Hegesippus about James, cannot be explained simply
as a symbolic device for representing the coherence of apostolic
doctrine.

---

⁵² Eusebius H.E. 3,39,4 cf. U.H. Körtner, Papias of Hierapolis, in
FRLANT 133 (1983), p. 121-122: "Die Presbyter des Papias ja in einem
bestimmten Funktion, nämlich der Verteidigung der christlichen Wahrheit
und der Überlieferung apostolischen Lehren und Nachtrichten, wichtig sind."
J. Munck, Presbyters and Disciples of the Lord in Papias, in *HThR* 52
(1959), p. 223-243.
⁵³ For a full description of the names and ministerial descriptions of
Paul's companions (σύνδουλος, συνεργός etc.) see, A. Lemaire, Les
Ministères aux Origines de l'Église: Naissance de la triple hiérarchie:
évêques, prebytres, diacres, in *LeDiv* 68, chpt. 4. See also E.T. Merrill,
Essays in Early Church History, (London: MacMillan 1924).

The episcopal succession lists before Irenaeus do mean something, although hardly what he meant by them, since, as even Caspar originally pointed out, it is difficult to dismiss such lists as pure fabrications.[54] Blum is particularly hard pressed to dissociate Hegesippus' account of the dispute over James' successor from a succession of teachers rather than teachers. The story of the disputed Jacobean succession indicates for Hegesippus, or so he thinks, the validity of his theory of decline and corruption.[55] But as we have argued, the disjunction between continuity of teachers (Amtskontinuität) and continuity of teaching (Lehrkontinuität) cannot be sustained given the nature of the oral παράδοσις in primitive Christianity, as we have described it.

Let us now summarize where this chapter has taken us in our discussion.

8. *In conclusion*

We began by considering a fundamental objection to our concept of cultural episcopacy derived from the decrees of Vatican II. That objection stated that although the concept of the bishop as the sacral-representative of a culture in process of redemption was valid as far as it goes, in order to complete that validity historical succession with the successors of the apostles was also necessary.

In the course of our argument we have sought not so much to reject that objection wholesale, but considerably to modify it. If the objection assumes the form of an Irenaean succession from apostles to bishops with a designated act of ordination in the imposition of hands, then we would reject it as having no historical

---

[54] Campenhausen (1950-2) op. cit. p. 138 regards Hegesippus as the creator of a legend representing the true descent of orthodox teaching rather than of teachers, though finding it apologetically useful to identify both teaching and teacher with his contemporary, orthodox bishops. In support of Caspar, he continues: "Caspars an sich recht unwahrscheinliche Annahme, den ältesten Bischofslisten seien mehr oder weniger zuverlässige Listen, nichtamtliche Traditionsträger vorangegangen, könnte wenigstens hier Recht behalten." (p. 143)

[55] Blum (1962) op. cit. p. 82: "Hegesipp hatte keine Interesse an dieser Überlieferung als Beleg für seinen Diadochegedanken."

basis in early Christian history. If furthermore that objection involves a strong boundary maintenance between the *depositum fidei* entrusted to a minister from outside the community of faith, and the faith and life of the community itself, I would likewise reject the objection. I have endeavoured to show that in the nature of "the living and abiding" oral παράδοσις, having no definitive written form, no such strong boundary maintenance can exist. Paul's παράδοσις is "ministered" to the Corinthians but lives and grows in them, and retains the character of its historical origin and its bearer in so far as it remains identified with Paul's personality. The charismatic, pseudonymous letter writer, with a ministry like Clement's committed to him, thus represents the community's faith by writing with the community's corporate, apostolic personality. Like Ignatius, who had nevertheless necessarily to write to the Trallians in his own name, he could greet his correspondents ἐν ἀποστολικῷ χαρακτῆρι ("in the apostolic character").[56]

In unraveling this theme in the literature of the early church, we saw a common pattern emerging between the angel/bishops of the *Apocalypse*, Ignatius' bishops as bearers of the corporate personalities of their communities, and the representative letter writer like Clement or those who wrote pseudonymously in the names of Peter, James, Paul, or John. Each corporate apostolic personality stands for the Christian παράδοσις, in its various versions, differentiated both by its individual apostolic origin, and the life and culture of the particular community in which it took root. We saw too a similar function regarding corporate apostolic personality in the figure of Peter in *Matthew,* which paralleled the figure of John the Beloved Disciple in *John,* and discussed in Chapter 3. In our contemporary scene, therefore, whether our concern is with ethnic episcopates in a missionary situation, or mutual recognition of ministers in an ecumenical one, we should not be deterred by the fact that the cultural or subcultural growth of our late-medieval, Western παράδοσις might not be able to establish apostolic succession in an Irenaean sense.

---

[56] *Tral.* insc. cf. Schoedel (1985) op. cit. p. 137 who translates "in the apostolic literary style."

For similar reasons we took issue with Dassmann regarding the parallel between Ignatian bishops, the angels of the churches, and the figure of James, which he sought to deny. Dassmann was nevertheless aware that there was, in view of that denial, a real problem, namely the painlessness of the episcopal revolution in terms of the threefold Order that Ignatius had apparently instituted single-handedly, with no charismatic or presbyterian denial of bishops surviving in the historical record. The *Didache,* whose fate I fear has been to be progressively dated early in unknown periods because no later period will fit, will not help as an example of protest because it accepts the early stage of the revolution. In the contextless and undatable fragment that is *Did.* 15, ἐπισκόποι and διακόνοι are commended rather than condemned as adequate liturgical replacements for absent prophets.[57] Montanism, furthermore, never claimed to reassert a primitive church Order, but rather regarded itself as the new, perfect Age of the Spirit, replacing the less perfect Age of the Son to which the rite of episcopal absolution once validly applied but no longer did so.

Dassmann in consequence proposed, rather extraordinarily, to explain Ignatian church Order as arising from the triumph of a subordinationalist christology which Ignatius' represented, and which lead to all things being put into subjection to the Father-bishop. But Ignatius was more modalist than subordinationalist. (*Eph.* 1,1; *Rom.* 6,3) Furthermore, we have argued in Chapter 3 that Ignatius was not the supporter of a monarchical concept of episcopacy as Dassmann's explanation assumes.

Our own account of the ministry before Ignatius has endeavoured in this chapter to show how episcopacy according to Ignatius evolved from earlier, corporately representative views of ministry and παράδοσις found, amongst and along with

---

[57] The value of the *Didache* in this respect will be further reduced if it is to be understood, not as a full-blown church Order at all, but a list of piecemeal corrections of a variety of abuses, see G. Schöllgen, The *Didache* as Church Order, in *JbAC* 29 (1986) p. 5-26, cf. J.-P. Audet, *La Didachè: Instructions des Apôtres*, (Paris: Libraire Lecoffre 1958); A. Vööbus, *Liturgical Instructions in the Didache,* (Stockholm: Etze 1968); B. Layton, The Date, Sources, and Transmission of the *Didache,* in *HThR* 61 (1968), p. 343-348.

others, in James, pseudonymous letter writers, Clement, and the angels of the churches. In Chapters 2 and 3 moreover, we sought to give a sociological and cultural account of that revolution, which, we argued, interestingly paralleled modern developments in ecumenical dialogue. We regarded the threefold typology (as opposed to "hierarchy") of bishop, presbyters, and deacons as marking the development of a cultural identity distinct from that of the Jewish synagogue in terms of that typology as collective representations of the collective consciousness. As liturgical representatives of the Christian sacred story, they made concrete the communities central values and beliefs, and so were the community's collective representations, symbolizing the community's cultural identity, and effecting what they symbolized. We understood in a structuralist dimension the development of both Order and its sacred story as overcoming antinomies in new syntheses, and we saw similar tendencies, in Chapter 2, to be mirrored in current ecumenical discussions. It will be our task in the next chapter to offer some explanation of why, given the corporate and representative thrust of the typology of Order in Ignatius, jurisdictional episcopacy with a purely transmissional view of doctrine was to emerge in the early middle ages.

CHAPTER FIVE

JURISDICTIONAL EPISCOPACY

The rise of geographical jurisdiction.

The argument of our first chapter was that our traditional jurisdictional and geographically based concept of *episcope* was a truncated one. It was truncated in important aspects that were being brought to our notice through the expressed desires of such cultural groups as the Aboriginal and Islander peoples of Australia, like the Maoris of New Zealand, to have cultural bishops with an episcopal ministry to members of their own culture, regardless of territorial jurisdiction. Its defectiveness was also being brought to our notice in terms of ecumenical dialogue and schemes of re-union which presuppose different episcopates occupying at least for a time the same geographical area, and by the episcopalian prejudice that such episcopates could only be temporary, since geographical jurisdiction must be ultimately the criterion to be satisfied.

In our second chapter, we sought to develop an alternative concept of episcopacy that we argued to be a cultural one, namely that the bishop, as the focal point of the unity of the redeemed community, was, in a sacramental sense, a representative to God of a redeemed culture. Any human representation and celebration of redemption in terms of a redeemed community had an inseparable cultural form. Culture at a purely human level is an inseparable part of the history of our humanity which, by definition, requires a spatio-temporal location. But it is also inseparable at the level of God's redemptive activity in Christ, since grace perfects nature and does not destroy it.

In our third and fourth chapters, in support of our thesis, we sought to delineate patterns of ministry and Order in the experience of the early church, before the rise of jurisdictional episcopacy, which illuminated our cultural theme. We sought to show how for Ignatius bishops were very much ikons of the corporate and redeemed personalities of their communities, and how such corporate and representative themes ran through early notions of the apostolic παράδοσις as represented by Peter and the Beloved Disciple in *Matthew* and *John*, and by Paul, Peter, and James in early Christian pseudepigrapha. We associated our literary and theological account with an anthropological account in Chapters 2 and 3, in which we used a sociological model, based upon Durkheim's structuralism and the later-Wittgenstein, to account for the rise of the threefold Order in its Ignatian form, and its subsequent unquestioned and, until the twelfth century, uncontested dominance in Christendom.

It is our task now to show how these representational and cultural themes became suppressed in the post-Ignatian situation, and a different, jurisdictional view of episcopacy emerged. Our explanation will be partly theological and historical, and partly sociological, and proceed as heretofore at both levels.

1. Post Ignatian episcope

In the course of the late second and early third century the Ignatian concept of *episcope* experienced the change mentioned in the last chapter in which, crudely speaking, the bishop as the representative of the *paradosis*, incarnated in the various churches in its various cultural forms, was transformed at the level of theological reflection into the bishop as the representative of the *paradosis* to the church. From Irenaeus onwards, the idea of the *ecclesia docens,* as distinct from the *ecclesia discens*, receives its theological articulation. Ignatius of course might be said to have commenced this transformation in localizing the sacral- representative *episcope* of apostolic times, extending over the "twelve tribes of Israel" (as in *James* or *1 Peter*), or "the gentiles" (as in *Galatians* and *Romans*), to geographical areas of the size of Hellenistic city states in which Ignatius claimed theological grounds for there being one bishop alone. But the challenge of Gnosticism in the form of a number of fully developed heresies created, and, arguably, distorted the relationship between the one geographically located bishop and the *paradosis*.

The problem which both Irenaeus and Tertullian faced was that of a Gnosticism in its various and conflicting forms which was organized into churches making claims to a similar framework of ecclesiastical Order as the catholic church. Their churches too had bishops, priests, and deacons.[1] They also claimed an arcane tradition going back to the apostles and quite independent from that of the catholic church. (Irenaeus *Adv. Haer.* 3,3,1) But the assertion of such a secret tradition inevitably made Christian identity problematic in terms of different forms of the living, oral *paradosis*, surviving in, and creating, church Order in terms of apostolic corporate personality, and validating its ministerial representatives in the way that I have described. When the gnostics claimed not only the secret tradition of the "good news" of psychologically conceived salvation, but that their tradition had been passed down quite concretely by actual apostolic bearers, then the great church was also compelled to reify its *paradosis* as well in terms of such a story of named persons going back to a named apostle.

One way of answering them was, of course, to point out that the very literary form of the Gnostic Gospels such as that of the *Gospel of Thomas*, gave away the game and revealed the contemporary and recent composition of what they contained.[2] That literary form described the doctrines which the work contained as having been communicated by Jesus secretly to certain apostles, and then handed down through a select group of enlightened followers. Only by such a device could what was patently new and hitherto unheard of in the catholic tradition be made plausible as part of the original but as yet undisclosed faith.

The credibility of such a response, however, in the ears of twentieth century critics, rings rather hollowly. All three synoptic gospels mention for example the interpretation of the parables as communicated to the disciples alone, (*Mat.* 13,10-13; *Mk.* 4,10-12; *Lk.* 8,9-10) and thus bear witness to a catholic claim to authority on the basis of a secret tradition. Moreover, the definition of orthodoxy cannot be settled in so straightforward a way in view of the contestable, though arguably common, Wisdom tradition of sayings of Jesus shared by both *Matthew* and *Luke*,

---

[1] Tertullian in *De Praes. Haer.* 41 seems ambiguous on this point, where it is not clear whether those mentioned were formally ordained, or simply were simply assigned *ad hoc* functions.

[2] R.M. Grant with D.N. Freedman, *The Secret Sayings of Jesus*, (London: Fontana 1960), p. 112.

in their common, Q tradition, and thus reflecting strands of testimony to the historical Jesus, parallel with the *Gospel of Thomas*.[3]

A second way was to apply to them the test of "consanguinity" with catholic doctrine. Tertullian at one point having made the apostolic succession the primary test for correctness of doctrines, goes on to articulate a second test in the following words:

> This is the test which can be demanded from those churches which cannot historically claim as a founder either an apostle or an apostolic man because they were founded later and even still today. They should be regarded no less as apostolic churches when they agree in the same faith because of a kinship in doctrine (*pro consanguinitate doctrinae*). Thus all the heretics are challenged by our churches to submit to both kinds of test and must show the one by which they can think that they are apostolic. But so much are they not apostolic nor can they provide evidence for what they are not that they are not received into the peace and communion by churches that are in either way apostolic on the grounds that they are in neither way apostolic due to the diversity of their deposit (*ob diversitatem sacramenti*).
>
> (*De Praes. Haer.* 32)

Thus we see how by Tertullian's time what was originally one test, consanguinity in succession, has become two.

The notion of *consanguinitas*, in this connection, can fruitfully be compared with that feature of human discourse to which the later Wittgenstein drew attention, and which we described in detail in Chapter 2. Particular instances of ideas, practices, beliefs, etc. can be and are legitimately classified as part of a single conceptual family, not because of any exhaustively defined or indeed definable features, but by a variety of links and interconnections. The churches that bore and indeed incarnated in their corporate personalities the *paradosis* in its Jacobean, Petrine, Pauline, and Johannine forms, under the conditions and in the

---

[3] For a fascinating though controversial thesis along these lines see H. Koestler, ΓΝΩΜΑΙ ΔΙΑΦΟΡΟΙ the origin and nature of diversification in the history of the early church, in *HThR* 58 (1965), p. 290-306. See also W. Bauer, Rechtgläubligkeit und Ketzerei im ältesten Christentum, in *BZHT* 10, (Tübingen: Mohr 1964), F.W. Norris, Ignatius, Polycarp, and 1 Clement: Walter Bauer reconsidered, in *VCh* 30 (1976), p. 23-44, and H.E.W. Turner, *The Pattern of Christian Truth*, (Oxford: Bampton Lectures 1954).

terms that I described in Chapter 4, had no exhaustively defin-able *depositum fidei* such that tight conceptual equivalents could be established.

Granted that they were of the at least philosophically defensi-ble opinion that, although Christianity can assume a variety of forms, not just anything can count arbitrarily as an instance of Christianity, nevertheless what could so count was at that time ecumenically diverse. What we have argued to have united the church in the mutual recognition by representative persons such as the bishops of the various churches was a consanguinity of faith maintained by the various cultural groupings, and repre-sented in their respective bishops who embodied the apostolic *paradosis* because they represented their people who did the same. Ignatius claimed, like the Matthaean figure of Peter, the mystical vision which flesh and blood had not revealed to him of the faith of a whole local Christian community in their bishop. And it was, as we saw, the common perspective of the churches of Asia Minor as revealed by the *Apocalypse*, and indeed repre-sentative letter writers whether pseudonymous or, like Clement, writing in his own name.

But now, in view of Irenaeus' reformation, the detection of family resemblance in the diversity of doctrinal forms and ex-pressions that constituted one group catholic, and the lack of family resemblance between this and other diverse doctrinal forms called "Gnostic," gives way to what I have called the "field marshal's baton" view of the *paradosis*.[4] Bishops no longer reveal the consanguinity of their Orders by displaying the consanguinity of the faith of their people whom they sacramen-tally represent. Rather they now exhibit their lineal descent from the apostles or apostolic men which gives them jurisdiction over their people by a rite of ordination which Ignatius had never mentioned.

But in view of the gnostic claim to possess a superior, written tradition kept secret from the psychics, the church has now to reify its *depositum fidei*, with, from Irenaeus' time, four gospels

---

[4] Such a view of validity is called "a relay race theory of Orders" in N. Lash, *His Presence in the World*, (London: Sheed and Ward 1968), p. 190. See also the discussion on general problems of mutual recognition, idem p. 190-199 ff.

(*Adv. Haer.* 3,11,8) and a number of other writings, which it took until Athanasius' *Festal Letter* (AD 340) to settle finally. There must not only be an exhaustively defined group of men in terms of the apostolic succession lists, but an exhaustively defined set of dogmas interlocking into a comprehensive doctrinal system agreed by the various episcopal apostolic successors possessed of the charism of interpretation. (Irenaeus, *Adv. Haer.* 3,3,3-4) The *paradosis* must have a fixed and written form. There must now be reification in the form of an "evangelical stability" (*evangelia haec firmitas*). The "doctrine of the apostles" (*doctrina apostolorum*) must be "clear and stable" (*manifesta et firma*). (3,11,7)

Irenaeus might wish that, despite the reification of the *paradosis* as "our faith (*in fide nostra*) which, taken possession of by the church (*quam perceptam ab ecclesia*), we guard," what is now "a kind of deposit " (*quoddam depositum*) might, through the Spirit, renew (*iuvenescere*) both itself and the the church as the vessel in which it is contained. (*Adv. Haer.* 3,24,1) He does at one point appear to hedge his bets on the necessity of a written tradition. He says: "Had not the apostles even left us their writings (*si neque apostoli quidem scripturas reliquissent nobis*), ought we not to follow the arrangement of their tradition (*nonne opportebat ordinem sequi traditionis*), which they committed to those to whom they committed churches?" (*Adv. Haer.* 3,4,1) Papias' "living and abiding voice" of the *paradosis* was thus no longer shared between ministerial representative and the community in which it took root. It is possessed by "those to whom they committed churches," namely bishops in the apostolic succession. Moreover, it is not the *paradosis*, the *traditio* that they possess as such. It must instead be *ordinem traditionis*, "the methodical arrangement of tradition." Ironically enough, the reification of the *paradosis* in the form of our present New Testament ill-fitted the process of systematization that was now envisaged. A historical and critical approach to the text, as developed in the last four centuries, readily reveals the distortions which take place when the reified oral Petrine, Johannine, Jacobean, and Pauline *paradosis* is not allowed to speak with its own culturally varied voices of distinct traditions in a relationship of *consanguinitas* or family resemblance. The reification into a system that tells a uniform and totally complete dogmatic story at the expense of that variety and distinctiveness produced a distorted dogmatic edifice.

It might also be thought that the test of consanguinity has been even further overlaid, by the identification of *paradosis* with episcopal jurisdiction, come the time of Tertullian's theological successor, Cyprian. Writing in a church divided by the Novatianist schism as well as by several heresies, he emphasizes the unity of the church through the mutual intercommunion of the one valid bishop in every place, who alone can succeed his predecessor. Furthermore, the bishop locally incarnates the *episcopatus*, the episcopal college with which he is joined, to which, and for the sake of which, obedience is required from clergy and laity alike. Ignatius' threefold typology is thus undergoing radical change. Thus the cultural diversity of the the various bishops, and the traditions which they represent, may be thought to have been obscured by Cyprian's apparent desire for a quite monolithic unity. As Cyprian says:

> This unity we ought especially as bishops who preside in the church to maintain firmly and to defend. Thus we shall recommend the episcopate itself as one and indivisible...The episcopate is one of which each part is held together in a solid form by the individual bishops...Thus the church of the Lord directs its rays of light spread through the whole world. However the light is one which is shed everywhere, nor is the unity of its physical form divided from it...Whoever separates himself from the church and is joined to an adulteress is removed from what has been promised to the church and he does not attain to the gifts of Christ who has left the church of Christ.
>
> (*De Cath. Ec. Unitat.* 4-6)

But this tendency to suppress diversity in a monolithic unity never succeeds in completely overlaying the earlier, Ignatian sacral and representational dimension of the episcopate.

Re-echoing Ignatius Cyprian does say that not the hierarchy alone constitutes the church but that the church is "a people united to its bishop (*sacerdoti*) and a flock joined to its own shepherd." He then continues:

> Wherefore you ought to recognize that the bishop is in the church and the church is in the bishop; and they flatter themselves in vain

who while they have no peace with God's bishops (*sacerdotibus*),
creep around and believe that they have secret communion with certain people, when the church which is the one catholic church, is not
divided, but is everywhere mutually connected and bound together
by the glue of bishops (*sacerdotum*) in mutual union.

(*Ep.* 66,8)

Thus the Ignatian notion of the people being "in their bishop" is
retained by Cyprian, even though the cultural diversity represented in that union is eliminated by his quest for a monolithic
unity. We thus find the force of Tertullian's earlier test for
catholicity in consanguinity highly diminished. "Consanguinity"
admitted of identification of a common catholic faith in a diversity bounded by a family resemblance. There is a shift in
Cyprian towards the notion of the episcopal "glue" purely in
juridical terms however much the Petrine primacy was, in contrast with individual bishops, one of honour rather than formal
jurisdiction.

In Cyprian, as in Irenaeus, the *paradosis* has become, so to
speak, a kind of field marshal's baton to be waved by the *ecclesia docens* over the *ecclesia discens*. In such a context the
bishop, it might be thought, albeit endowed with the prophetic
charism, becomes the external transmitter of the faith *to* the
community rather than the representative of the faith *of* the community. We shall see that such initial thoughts, making the
church of the second and third centuries similar in attitudes to
that of the 19th Century Rome of Pius IX, is too simple, though
we have found that such an aspect did tend to push into the
background a continuing representational theme which nevertheless still made its presence felt in the understanding of Order in
the early church. Tertullian's *consanguinitas* was to influence
Augustine.

We have, then, in this section described the first movements
from representational and cultural in the direction of jurisdictional understanding of episcopacy in terms of a shift from *consanguinitas* and *paradosis* towards exhaustively defined and
systematized dogma of which the apostolic/episcopal succession
was a social expression. We shall have more to say of such developments in connection with Augustine, the Gregorian reforms, and the European Reformation later in this chapter, and

of a sociological model in terms of which this change can be understood. So far we have understood the change from an historical and theological perspective in so far as we have argued that it was Gnosticism's claim to a written, reified but hitherto secret *paradosis* that lead to the catholic church's reifying response.

Let us now examine a second reason for why Ignatian representative episcopacy was replaced by a jurisdictional one, in terms of the theology of martyrdom and its sacerdotal denial in the course of the third century. We shall focus upon the changes which we can see in the third-century *Didascalia Apostolorum* to the Ignatian theology of the threefold typology.

2. *The Didascalia Apostolorum and the theology of martyrdom*

In the course of the third century, the primitive Ignatian picture of the threefold typology, and the representative view of the early ministry which we have argued that he shared with other early writers and communities, was challenged and superseded from a highly unlikely quarter. The events of the Decian (A.D. 249) and Valerian (A.D. 257) persecutions in North Africa, which intertwine with Cyprian's biography, reveal a popular theology of martyrdom which challenged the position of the ordained ministry. It will be interesting for our purposes to inquire in detail why this occurred.[5]

Ignatian bishops, like John's angels of the churches, or the letter writers, pseudonymous or otherwise, wrote as the representatives of the corporate life of the church which is the Body of Christ. But the experience of the martyrdom of the few, and the phenomenon of large numbers of apostates in the persecutions which arose in the course of the third century onwards, convinced many that there was a group of people that were more than representatives of the community in its failures as well as its successes. There was a group that instead represented the Body of Christ in a way that others could not do, who bore in their tortured bodies the sufferings of Christ more abundantly than others. That group was, of course, the martyrs. They repre-

---

[5] W.H.C. Frend, *Martyrdom and Persecution in the Early Church*, (Oxford: Blackwell 1965), p. 406-429.

sented not the faith and life *of* their communities, but the sufferings and glory of Christ *to* their communities. They could not of course represent the corporate life of those who were apostates.

But Christ, especially present with the scars of his cross in the confessor in the hour of his trial, could channel his forgiveness through the martyr. The catechumen who was a confessor needed no baptism in water to engraft him into the Body of Christ. Of that there was no dispute, as Hippolytus shows. (*Ap. Trad.* 19,2; cf. *Didasc.* 5,9 4-6 (Syriac))[6] But whether the status of confessor could go proxy for ordination, so that a confessor could grant absolution, was more contestable, particularly in view of the scandalous and theatrical practices of many confessors in absolving wholesale, or issuing writs of absolution which went on the market for sale. (Tertullian *De Fuga* 12 and 13; Cyprian *Ep.* 55,14; *De Laps.* 27)

The church hierarchy had to respond to this popular movement by insisting on the powers of the clergy alone to absolve, as evidenced in the career of Cyprian.[7] But in doing so, they were themselves placed in the position from which the confessors had thus been displaced. We shall now see that this western development also takes place in the eastern *Didascalia Apostolorum*, to be dated early to mid third century.

The *Didascalia Apostolorum* is a product of Ignatius' Syria in which references to Ignatius' view of church Order are to be found and, at a superficial level, apparent similarities.[8] The early third century date may be deduced from the fact that the *Didascalia*, in contrast with the *Constitutions* in which work its Greek text is embedded, mentions no minor Orders other than subdeacon, whose existence Eusebius testifies at Rome towards

---

[6] All references are taken from F.X. Funk, *Didascalia et Constitutiones Apostolorum*, (Turin: Bottega d'Erasmo 1979). The Latin is preferred to the Greek when in agreement with the translation of the Syriac in R. Hugh Connolly, *Didascalia Apostolorum: The Syriac Version Translated and accompanied by the Verona Latin Fragments*, (Oxford: Clarendon 1929).

[7] W.H.C. Frend, *The Rise of Christianity*, (London: Darton, Longman, and Todd 1984), p. 405-413.

[8] For one such highly superficial comparison, see A. McArthur, The office of a Bishop in the Ignatian Epistles and in the *Didascalia Apostolorum* compared, in *StudPat* IV (Berlin 1961) *TU* 79, p. 298-304.

the end of that century, and Cyprian in the course of the 250s.[9] Furthermore, the theology of martyrdom that I outline in the previous paragraph is alluded to directly by the Didascaliast, when he says:

> For let him that is condemned in the name of the Lord God be esteemed by you as a holy martyr, and angel of God or God on earth, even one that is spiritually clothed with the Holy Spirit of God; for through him you see the Lord our Saviour inasmuch as he has been found worthy of the incorruptible crown, and has renewed again the witness of his passion.
>
> (5,1,2)

Indeed, it is not without significance to the radical change in the Ignatian theology of Order in which the Didascaliast is taking part that the Greek of the Constitutionalist, writing a century later, obscures this third century theology of martyrdom to which the Syriac and Funk's Latin translation testify. Apart from this passage, however, the rest of Book V consists mainly of exhortations to assist and provide for the confessors, and nothing of any putative sacramental role that they may possess.

When however the Didascaliast describes the role of clerics, we find him applying directly to them the themes of the theology of martyrdom, namely "imitation" (μίμησις) of the sufferings of Christ in a non-martyrological context. The Didascaliast exhorts the bishop as a pastor to be of such a character that "he will be able to constrain his disciples also and encourage them by his good manners to be imitators of his good works" (διὰ τῆς ἀ–ναστροφῆς αὐτοῦ προτρέψασθαι τῶν ἰδίων αὐτοῦ ποιημάτων μιμητὰς ἀξίους γενηθῆναι). (*Didasc.* 2,6,5) Christ forgave the woman taken in adultery. "In him our saviour, king and God, O bishops, you must have your aim (pattern) and be imitators of him (σκοπὸν ὑμᾶς ἔχειν δεῖ τούτου μιμητὰς εἶναι). (2,24,7)

They are to become imitators of Christ in taking away sin through the "binding and loosing" of the penitential discipline (μιμηταὶ γὰρ ἔστε Χριστοῦ... οὕτως καὶ ὑμᾶς τοῦ λαοῦ τὰς

---

[9] For a full discussion of the dating, see F.X. Funk, *Die Apostolischen Konstitutionen: ein literar-historische Untersuchung*, (Frankfurt/Main: Minerva GmbH 1970), p. 49-55 ff.; J.C.J. Sanders, Autor de la Didascalie, in *A Tribute to Arthur Vööbus*, Ed. R.A. Fisher, (Chicago: Lutheran School of Theology 1977), p. 47-54.

ἁμαρτίας ἐξιδιοποιεῖσθαι χρή). (2,25,9) Bishops, deacons, and deaconesses, in laying down their lives in service for the church, become also, like the martyrs, μιμητάς of Christ's service and suffering, *quia imitatores eius sumus et locum Christi sortiti*, in a place where the Constitutionalist's Greek is very loose. (3,19,4) In the exhortation to martyrdom, having rehearsed the incidents from Christ's passion he says, according to the Syriac though not the Constitutionalist's Greek : "Let us therefore, who are his disciples, be also his imitators. For if he bore and endured all things for us , even to the sufferings (of his passion), how much more ought we, for our own sakes, to be patient when we suffer." (5,6,10)

We may furthermore bring out the character of the Didascaliast's revolution by contrasting him this respect with Ignatius.[10] The theme of μίμησις in Ignatius is by contrast primarily martyrological. Whereas the Didascalian bishop imitates Christ by taking away the people's sins in absolution, in Ignatius "imitation" is closely allied with sharing Christ's suffering in martyrdom. Ignatius describes the Ephesians as μιμηταὶ ὄντες θεοῦ because they are "inflamed" by God's blood as they see him on his way to martyrdom. (*Eph.* 1,1) They are to pray for the world in general (ὑπὲρ τῶν ἀλλῶν δὲ ἀνθρωπῶν) that, in facing the world, they may be μιμηταὶ κυρίου in his injury (ἀδικηθῇ) and rejection (ἀθετηθῇ). (*Eph.*10,1-3) The Romans are to allow him to be μιμητὴν εἶναι πάθους τοῦ θεοῦ μου. (*Rom.* 6,3)

The Didascaliast, on the other hand, prefers to apply the term to the clergy in the context of purity and giving of absolution. Indeed the Constitutionalist, in his addition to the Didascalian text, remedies this paucity of references to μίμησις in the book on martyrs. When the Didascaliast simply pronounces blessed someone arrested trying to give help to imprisoned martyrs, the Constitutionalist adds: ὅτι κοινωνὸς μαρτύρων ἐγένετο καὶ

[10] For the definitive discussion of Ignatius' concept of martyrdom, see K. Bommes, Weizen Gottes, Untersuchungen zur Theologie des Martyriums bei Ignatius von Antiochien, in *Theoph.* 27, (Köln-Bonn: Hanstein 1976); Th. Preiss, La Mystique de l'imitation de Christ et de l'unité chez Ignace d'Antioche, in *Rev HPhR* 18 (1938), p. 197-241; W.M. Swartley, The Imitatio Christi in the Ignatian Letters, in *VCh* 27 (1973), p. 81-103.

μιμητὴς τῶν τοῦ Χριστοῦ παθημάτων, (5,2,3) though "imitators" does occur once in the Syriac text of 5,6,10 in application to the martyrs.[11]

Just as the bishops in the *Didascalia* have Christ for their aim or pattern (σκόπος), so also they must as bishops (ἐπισκόπους) be patterns aimed at (σκοπούς) by the laity. (2,6,7 and 2,25,11) The bishop is to be a "pattern of righteousness" (τῆς δικαιοσύνης σκοπὸν). (2,17,6) They must beware of imperiling their people through schism by becoming σκοποὶ ἀπωλείας. (6,4,2). In the sense of being imitators, therefore, the bishops in the *Didascalia* become the mediators between God in Christ and the laity subject to them. Because they exemplify Christ, the people can make them their pattern. Because they forgive sins in God's place they can become "mediators between God and the faithful (οἱ μεσίται θεοῦ καὶ πιστῶν)." (2,25,7) In order to absolve from sin they must be pure from sin, (2,1,8; 2,11,1) and in the act of absolution they imitate or become patterns of Christ's passion:

> For you are imitators (μιμηταὶ) of Christ, just as (καὶ ὡς) he himself "bore the sins of all of you" so also (οὕτως καὶ) you ought to make away with (ἐξιδιοποεῖσθαι) the sins of the people.
>
> (2,25,9)

The martyrs likewise are found pure because they imitate Christ's passion. (5,8,1)

The bishop as high-priest is "minister of the word and mediator between God and you" (λόγου διάκονος μέσιτης θεοῦ καὶ ὑμῶν). (2,26,4) In administering the penitential discipline, they must not become "mediators of unjust judgment" (ἀδίκου κρίσεως μεσίται). (2,48,3) Thus in the *Didascalia* the bishop is the representative of God in Christ to the laity subject to them. So we observe the course of the *Didascalia* the development of a theology of Order from μάρτυς to μίμησις and then to μεσίτης as a consequence of which Ignatius' theology of Order in terms of representation of a community in process of redemption is transformed into a theology of Order as mediating redemption to

---

[11] For an earlier version of my comparison here, see A. Brent, The Relations between Ignatius and the *Didascalia*, in *SecCent*, 8, 3 (1991), p. 129-156.

an unredeemed community. The Didascaliast in Syria is participating in the movement that was to assign to the clergy alone the prerogatives claimed on behalf of the confessors regarding the right to pronounce absolution, by appropriating to them the μίμησις of the martyr. For Ignatius originally it had been "Jesus Christ alone who releases you from every bond (ὃς λύσει ἀφ' ὑμῶν πάντα δέσμον)." (*Philad.* 8,1)

In consequence of the Didascaliast's recasting of Ignatian theology, it is not surprising that he can no longer understand προκαθημένος εἰς τύπον in Ignatius' original sense. The Didascaliast, in understanding the church and its clerical Orders, almost always uses the word τύπος as referring to the antitype which is prefigured in the Old Testament type, and as seen in the Old Testament cultus in the Tent of Meeting.

The predominant meaning of τύπος in the relevant *Didascalia* passage is what later became known as the "anti-type" of an Old Testament "type."[12] Now as the backcloth to his claims about the clerical "type" figures, there lies the Tent of Witness in the desert in the Old Testament. Those who ministered in the Tent of Witness (οἱ λευῖται λειτουργοῦντες τῇ σκηνῇ τοῦ μαρτουρίου) were ministering in what was a general type of the church (ἥτις ἦν τύπος τῆς ἐκκλησίας κατὰ πάντα). (2,2,25) The bishops are therefore today to their people the levitical priests who stand, not in the Holy Tent, but in the holy catholic church, and who stand before God (ὑμεῖς οὖν σήμερον ὦ ἐπίσκοποι ἐστε τῷ λαῷ ὑμῶν ἱερεῖς, λευῖται οἱ λειτουργοῦντες τῇ ἱερᾳ σκηνῇ, τῇ ἁγίᾳ καθολικῇ ἐκκλησίᾳ καὶ παρεστῶτες κυρίου θεοῦ ἡμῶν). (2,25,7)

In the passage immediately following, the laity are informed that "the then sacrifices are the present prayers, supplications and thanksgivings" (αἱ τότε θυσίαι νύν εὐχίαι καὶ δεήσεις καὶ εὐχαριστίαι) and "the then first fruits and tenths and offerings and gifts are now the offerings offered through the bishops to the Lord God" (αἱ τότε ἀπαρχαὶ καὶ δεκάται καὶ ἀφαιρέματα καὶ δῶρα νύν προσφεραὶ αἱ διὰ τῶν ἐπισκόπων προσφερόμεναι τῷ κυρίῳ τῷ θεῷ). The bishops are the high-priests

---

[12] John Damascene *Hom.* 5. There is however no consistency and sometimes ἀντίτυπος is used e.g. of Abraham offering Isaac as the antitype of the type to come, see e.g. Gregory Nazianzen *Orat.* 28,18.

(ἀρχιερεῖς), the presbyters are the priests (ἱερεῖς), and the deacons, widows and orphans of the present are the levites of old (οἱ λευῖται ὑμῶν οἱ νύν διάκονοι καὶ αἱ χῆραι καὶ οἱ ὀρφανοί ὑμῶν). (2,26,2)

Thus τύπος in its "typological" sense is fulfilled in the account that the Didascaliast thus gives in terms of the Tent of Witness ἥτις ἦν τύπος τῆς ἐκκλησίας κατὰ πάντα. But now follows the passage in which each of the Orders is described as a τύπος in different senses depending on the Order in question:

1. The bishop presides (προκαθεζέσθω) "as a type of" (Syriac b-duktâ; Latin in typum; Greek τετιμημένος) God.

2. The deacon "stands beside" the bishop (παριστάσθω) "as a type of" (Syriac b-duktâ ; Latin in typum; Greek ὡς χριστὸς) of Christ.

3. The deaconess is to be honoured (τετιμήσθω) "as a type of" (Syriac b-duktâ; Latin in typum; Greek εἰς τύπον) "of the Holy Spirit."

4.The presbyters are "to be thought of" (νενομίσθωσαν) "as a type of" (Syriac b-duktâ; Latin in typum; Greek ὡς τύπον) "of the apostles."

5.The widows and orphans are "to be thought of" (νενομίσθωσαν) "as a type of" (Syriac b-duktâ; Latin in typum; Greek ὡς τύπον) "the altar" (τοῦ θυσιασηρίου). (2,26,4-8)

Now in no sense can God, Christ, or the apostles of whom bishops, priests, and deacons are "types" (1,2, and 4) be found in the Old Testament description of the Tent of Meeting as the Didascaliast describes it. He has already registered their "types" in the typological sense of τύπος in terms of high-priests, priests and levites. He has suddenly and quite unreflectively therefore inserted into his text the use of τύπος in a quite different sense, namely that of the Orders as types or representatives of a transcendent church Order incarnated in the community as Ignatius originally understood the term. Yet he shows scant recognition that the word has this sense as he simply and unreflectively introduces it into his discussion.

The Didascaliast has therefore adopted unreflectively a commonplace of his church tradition, derived from Ignatius of Antioch, alongside his own, quite different understanding of τύπος. Indeed the very Orders which the Didascaliast adds to

Ignatius' bishops, priests and deacons are those which can best fit into his Tent of Meeting typology, and τύπος in their case alone has any chance of fitting this word in sense (ii). Though the levites are οἱ νῦν διάκονοι, αἱ χῆραι καὶ ὀρφανοὶ ὑμῶν, the widows and orphans can be the antitype of the altar in the Tent of Meeting too as they receive like the altar the offerings. And, although the point is much weaker, the pillar of the cloud in the Tent of Witness, though not mentioned specifically by the Didascaliast, could be the type of the Holy Spirit fulfilled in the deaconess. As we have seen, in this sense of "type" the bishops stand for the high-priests and not in the place of God.

But for Ignatius' three Orders, there were no typological equivalents in such an Old Testament context. Indeed, when he speaks of θύσιαστηριον, he is not thinking in Old Testament terms, but is reminding us rather of the vision of the heavenly church in the *Apocalypse*, which is realized for Ignatius in the present liturgical community. The present church gathers as a choir or chorus around the heavenly altar, the counterpart of the "one altar" being the "one bishop" rather than the Didascaliast's "widows and orphans." (*Philad.* 4,1)[13] His τύπος refers, as we argued in Chapter 3, to "representation" of a transcendent and heavenly church Order incarnated in the community extended in time and history.

As a result, the Didascaliast account of the bishop as the representative of the Fatherhood of God now radically diverges from Ignatius. The Didascaliast exhorts the bishop to be pure in his works and "to know your place (τόπον, *ba-dmutâ*, *locum tuum*) as set in the likeness of (ὡς θεοῦ τύπον ἔχων, *b-duktâ*, *observans similitudinem Dei*) God." Formally here, on this second occasion, the bishop does represent God in the Ignatian sense of τύπος, but the aspect of God which he so represents is expressed in thoroughly non-Ignatian imagery. The bishop sits in his place in the church building (ἐν ἐκκλησίᾳ καθέζου), exuding God's authority to judge sinners, and with the power of binding and

---

[13] *Eph.* 5,2; *Mag.* 7,2; *Philad.* 4,1 cf. *Apoc.* 4,4; 6,9; 7,11-14; 8,3-6 etc. Schoedel (1985) op. cit. p. 55 points out that early Christian writers deny that the τραπέζα was an altar (Minucius Felix, *Octavius* 32,1; Origen *Contra Celsum* 8,17). See also Padberg (1963) op. cit. p. 338. Polycarp does use widow as a type of the altar in *Phil.* 4,3.

loosing associated with the penitential discipline emerging in the early third century, and in this sense he is a τύπος. (*Didasc.* 2,11,1-2) He has to be pure in his dealings with his penitents, not respecting persons, not dealing lightly with the wealthy, not re-admitting the hypocritical and impious in order to keep the church from defilement so that it is God's purity that he "represents." (2,6-10) In both taking away sin and being pure, as we have seen, he has become the clericalized proxy of the martyr figure.

We saw in Chapter 3 that in Ignatius the bishop, as τύπον πα–τρός, (*Tral.* 3,1) is pre-eminent at the Eucharist in a joint pre-eminence with the two other (τύποι), and perhaps too for the Johannine reason that "it is my Father who gives you the bread from heaven to eat." (p. 92 above) It was therefore in virtue of his eucharistic, not his baptismal role as in the case of the Didascaliast, that the bishop wears the representative image of God's fatherhood. According to the Didascaliast, the bishops are fathers because they "loosed you from your sins, regenerated you through water" (διὰ ὕδατος ἀναγεννήσας ὑμᾶς) and "fed you with the milk of the word" (τῷ λόγῳ γαλακτοτροφήσαντ–ας). (2,33,2) The semitic euphemism of "water" for the male semen, which seems to us so crude, is clearly here in view. Tribute in terms of firstfruits, tenths, and part-offerings are due to the bishop as king, but also as one's father for whose nourish-ment his children must provide. (2,34,5)

Thus we find in the case of the Didascaliast's image of father-hood the closest connection with liturgical usage in Ignatius, even though the significant difference is that the former envis-ages the baptismal liturgy, whilst the latter has the Eucharist in mind. Yet the "image" is no τύπος in Ignatius' sense, but a bare metaphor, whether it be of baptism as paternal impregnation, or of the bishop's financial share as filial support. Such an image further reinforces against Ignatius the concept of the hierarchy as mediating to the community an external grace. It is as a result, then, of a radical reorientation produced by the third-century theology of martyrdom that Ignatius' threefold-typology is re-placed by a threefold hierarchy, and the non Ignatian concept of "monarchical" episcopacy is born. For a brief account of the extent to which this is now true let us compare the *Didascalia* with Ignatius on the subject of ecclesiastical obedience.

3. The creation of the "monarchical" episcopate

Just as the martyr was called "God on earth" in the passage quoted above, so is now the bishop also. In *Didasc.* 2,26,4 the bishop is called "high-priest" (ἀρχιερεύς), "teacher and father after God" (οὗτος διδάσκαλος, οὗτος μετὰ θεόν πατὴρ), "ruler and leader, mighty king and God after God" (οὗτος ἄρχων, καὶ ἡγούμενος ὑμῶν, οὗτος ὑμῶν βασιλεὺς, δύναστης, οὗτος θεὸς μετὰ θεόν). As they are considered rulers and kings, so the laity are to bring them their material offerings as tributes (δασμοὺς) in order to support both them and their dependents. (2,34,1) In this respect they stand as recipients The bishop's family must all be his subjects (ὑπήκοοι πάντες εἰσὶν αὐτῷ), because otherwise those outside his house will not be subject to him (ὑποταγήσονται). (2,2,3-4)

According to Ignatius, the laity must be "subject" (ὑποτασσόμενοι) to the bishop too. But presbyters and deacons never enjoy with them that same subject status that they do in the *Didascalia,* with the result that the episcopate for Ignatius is not "monarchical" in the Didascalian sense. The Ephesians are to be "joined together in one subjection" (ἐν μιᾷ ὑποταγῇ κατηρτισμένοι). But the submission is to the presbyters as well as the bishops (ὑποτασσόμενοι τῷ ἐπισκόπῳ καὶ τῷ πρεσβυτερίῳ). (*Eph.* 2,2) In *Magnesians* and in *Trallians* the verb ὑποτάσσειν is used again for bishops and presbyters together. (*Mag.* 2,1; *Tral.* 2,1-2; 13,2) In *Mag.* 13,2, subjection to the bishop is unqualified by the addition of one or both of the other two Orders, but here the qualification is even more stronger because submission is also to be "to each other" (ὑποτάγητε τῷ ἐπισκόπῳ καὶ ἀλλήλοις). Moreover, in *Pol.* 6,1 even the deacons are included in this submission to bishops and presbyters (τῶν ὑποτασσομένων ἐπισκόπῳ, πρεσβυτέροις, διακόνοις), although the required response from the laity towards the deacons is usually put less strongly than "subjection." The bishop does not therefore rule alone in the way that he does in the *Didascalia*.

A particularly frequent word used by Ignatius regarding the appropriate attitude towards the deacons is the concept of "respect" or "reverence" (ἐντρέπεσθαι). Here too we shall see a difference in the use of this same term in the *Didascalia*. In *Smyr.* 8,1, the bishop and presbyters are to be "followed" (ἀκολουθεῖτε), whereas the deacons are to be "respected" (ἐντρέπεσθε). But there is no distinction here in what is owed to clerical rank since ἐντρέπεσθαι is also applied towards bishops and presbyters.[14]

Yet in the *Didascalia* ἐντρέπεσθαι is reserved only for the bishop amongst the clerical ranks. Whilst it is true that a wife is exhorted to "reverence" (ἐντράπηθι) her husband (1,8,2), and the bishop is not to "reverence" the wealthy (μήτε πλούσιον ἐν-τρεπόμενος *neque revereatur dives*) (2,5,1), the word is never applied in a clerical context to presbyters and deacons. The bishop's children are to reverence him together with other people generally (εὐλαβούμενοι καὶ ἐντρεπόμενοι αὐτόν). (2,2,3) Furthermore, in the very context which would give him the opportunity to invite reverence for the deacons as well, the Didascaliast according to the Latin version with which the Syriac agrees, chooses his words so as to avoid doing so. "Widows must be pious, subject (*subditas*) to the bishops and deacons, reverencing and respecting and fearing the bishop as God (*reverentes et trementes et metuentes episcopum sicut deum*)." (3,8,1)[15] Thus ἐντρέπεσθαι has become the Didascaliast's preferred attitude towards the bishop in contrast to Ignatius who applies it to all three Orders, as we have seen.

Thus it is a misnomer to call Ignatius' concept of episcopacy "monarchical."[16] It is the three Orders conjointly that are the

---

[14] *Tral.* 3,1; 3,2; *Mag.* 3,1 : πᾶσαν ἐντροπην αὐτῷ ἀπονέμειν.

[15] Connolly (1929) op. cit. p. 138-139. The Constitutionalist's Greek is a very free rendering here, and says what the Didascaliast refuses to say, see Funk (1979) op. cit. p. 197.

[16] H.J. Vogt, Ignatius von Antiochien über den Bischof und seine Gemeinde, in *ThQ* 158 (1978), p. 18-19, and R. Padberg, Das Amtsverständnis in der Ignatius Briefe, in *ThG* 62 (1972), p. 51. Cf. E. Dassmann, Zur Entstehung des Monepiskopats, in *JbAC* 17 (1974), p. 74-90, and Rius-Camps (1980) op. cit. p. 220-235. Dassmann overlooks the fact that Ignatian obedience is to the threefold Order in unity. In attributing monepiscopacy to Ignatius' alleged subordinationism, he has also overlooked the predominant modalist character of the former's theology, see *Eph.* 1,1; *Mag.* 7,2; *Rom.* 3,3; 6,3.

objects of ὑποτάσσεσθαι or ἐντρέπεσθαι. He never orders presbyters or deacons to obey one another as he so orders the laity.
The nearest that he ever comes to so doing is when he claims that
it is fitting that the Trallians, especially the presbyters, "refresh"
(ἀναψύχειν) the bishop. (Tral. 12,2) Moreover, as we have
seen, in all but one instance obedience is not to the bishop alone
but to the bishop in union with the presbytery and the deacons.[17]

So natural is the mutual interrelations of the three Orders and
the mutual interdependence of their functions that such obedience
does not have to be required. Furthermore, the interrelationship
between the laity and the hierarchy is not described in monarchical terms. The model of authority for which Ignatius looks is the
internal authority of the choir, symphony or chorus, moving according to its own self-governing rules, rather than an authority
of external imposition. (Eph.4,1-2; Philad.1,2) This partly explains the paradox of instructing the churches to do what he is
convinced that they are doing anyway.[18] Ignatius thus considers
the harmonious interrelationship of the threefold Order as the
natural expression— which needs no commandment— of the
true church as it represents the unity of the Godhead. In Eph.
1,1-2 the much loved character (πολυαγαπήτον ὄνομα) they
possess is "by a just nature" (φύσει δικαίᾳ) which makes their
labour "congenital" or "suited to them" (συγγενικόν ἔργον).

In the Didascalia the deacons have ceased to be an Order of
equal rank. Unlike in Ignatius, they are in subjection to the
bishop. The deacons are ὑπηρέται through which the people,
who are commanded not to "crowd the ruler" (ἐνοχλείτωσαν τῷ
ἄρχοντι), are to approach their bishop. They can be more open
in their requests to the deacons (διὰ τῶν διακόνων πρὸς οὓς
πλέον παρρησιαζέσθωσαν). Their desires are communicated
"through the deacon" (διὰ τοῦ διακόνου) but people only re-

---

[17] Eph. 2; Tral. 1,1; 3,2; 7,13; Rom. 2,1; Smyr. 4,1. Philad. inscr.
Smyr. 8,1 in the light of which 8,2 should be read. Cf. also Philad. 8,1
where the penitent returns εἰς ἑνότητα θεοῦ καὶ συνέδριον τοῦ ἐπισκόπου i.e. to the presbyterate as well as to the bishop.
[18] Eph. 4,1; 8,1; Tral. 2,2; Rom. 2,1; Smyr. 4,1. Cf. Schoedel (1985)
op. cit. 51 who regards it, I believe mistakenly, as a formula reflecting the
general diplomatic background of Hellenistic letters.

ceive their requests at the bishop's discretion (οὕτω κατὰ τὸ δοκοῦν ἐκείνῳ ἐπιτελείτωσαν). (*Didasc.* 2,28,6)

Thus in comparison with the threefold Order in Ignatius, each rank of which is equal in honour to the other but different in function, the deacons of the *Didascalia* are totally subject the bishop. The deacons no longer "please" the bishop, as they once did the bishop of Antioch, in his phrase τῶν διακόνων τῶν ἐ-μοὶ γλυκυτάτων, even though to Ignatius as bishop the deacon Zotion was still τοῦ συνδούλου μου, (*Mag.* 2) as the deacons collectively are συνδοῦλοι.[19] Instead they have become the episcopal servants (τοῦ ἐπισκόπου ὑπηρέται), instead of ἐκκλη-σίας θεοῦ ὑπηρέται.[20] The deacon is "hearing and mouth, heart and soul" of the bishop. (*Didasc.* 2,44,4) The deacon is to refer pastoral matters, which in the *Didascalia* are usually either charity distribution or assessment of penance, totally to the bishop, as Christ to the Father, though he is to "judge what he can" (ἀλλ' ὅσα δύναται, εὐθυνέτω δι' ἑαυτοῦ). The remaining issues the bishop is to decide (τὰ δὲ ὑπέρογκα ὁ ἐπισκόπος κρινέτω). (2,44,3) With the *Didascalia*, therefore, and not with Ignatius, monarchical episcopacy was born.

Thus we see how Ignatian representative *episcope* has undergone a radical revolution in the course of the third century under pressure of the theology of martyrdom. That revolution, in conjunction with the reification of the *paradosis* after Irenaeus, submerged the concept of representative episcopacy. That concept was to be finally obliterated in the aftermath of a further "sea change," in the reforms of Gregory VII which, as we shall shortly see, established jurisdictional episcopacy in the form that

---

[19] *Rom.* 2,2; 9,1; *Philad.* 4; 10,1; *Smyr.* 11,1; 12,2. It is Rius-Camps (1980) op. cit. p. 34-38 who propounds the thesis that the alleged forger did not know *Romans* and who thought Ignatius was a deacon, but cf. Schoedel (1985) op. cit. p. 46, and Joly (1978) p. 124, who also points out that Rius-Camps supposes too late a date for the interpolator to make such a mistake possible: "Avec l'interpolateur, nous serions pratiquement à l'époque de Jules l'Africaine et d'Origène qui voient en Ignace le deuxième évêque d'Antioche après Pierre." See also Hammond Bammel (1982) op. cit. p. 68-69; 88-89.

[20] *Tral.* 2,3. In *Pol.* 6,1 the people are generally addressed as "God's stewards, assistants, and servants." (οἰκονόμοι καὶ πάρεδροι καὶ ὑπηρέται).

episcopally governed churches, on either side of the Reformation, were to inherit it.

But before we proceed to the Gregorian reforms, we must note certain features of the early medieval period that served to keep alive certain representative themes in the church's tradition regarding the sacrament of Order.

4. *Representative themes in the early medieval period*

There were, however, a number of factors which prevented a totally jurisdictional understanding of Order such as was to surface later, with Gregory VII from A.D. 1073 onwards. The first of these was the influence of Augustine who found the jurisdictional argument of Cyprian of no use against the entrenched national church of North Africa which was Donatist. The second factor we shall see to have been the prevalent ethos and customary practice regarding *episcope* in the church of the third and fourth century was never in line with such jurisdictional theological interpretations of its significance. And the third we shall locate in the universal absence before the time of Gregory VII, and in the ensuing centuries, of any political jurisdiction conceived unambiguously in terms of an essentially territorial and geographical domain.

The jurisdictional argument of Cyprian would have largely justified the Donatist church of North Africa against the minority catholic group with which Augustine, on his return as a convert from Manicheeism, found himself in communion. Against the security of the majority church of the North African nation, bolstered by a succession of Donatist bishops going back to the breach between Majorinus and the catholic Caecilian in A.D. 313, Augustine made his famous claim: "The judgment of the wide world stands sure (*Securus iudicat orbis terrarum.*)." (*Ep.* 49) Thus he denied a Donatist, jurisdictional claim, not with reference to a rival jurisdiction alone, but with reference to the judgment of the different, catholic dioceses who could not recognize a consanguinity or family-resemblance between their collection of catholic traditions and those of the Donatists.

Not of course that such schismatics could in any sense be regarded as heretics. What was at fault was their ethos that in puritanical isolation from the world caused them to "croak like frogs in the marshes, "we are the only Christians."'" (*Narr. in Psa.* 95,11) Moreover, the test of that catholicity was not a simple legalistic and jurisdictional recognition. Augustine recognizes that in certain doctrinal areas at least, the *consensus fidelium* or the *dogma populare* is the test of doctrinal validity. For example, the necessity and efficacy of baptism for salvation, particularly for babies, is justified with reference to what is agreed on by "all catholic ears and all catholic hearts" (*De Pecc. Mer. et Rem.* 1,24) which "have experience of the authority of the Gospel, or rather are constrained by the most concordant unison (*conspiratione*) of faith of all Christian people."[21] There was clearly no field-marshal's-baton-view of the *paradosis* here, but an articulation of a living *paradosis* in the bosom of the mystical Body of Christ, which the bishops represented rather than informed.

So much for our first exception to the post Irenaean, predominant reification of the *paradosis*, and the persistence of a post Didascalian, monarchical and jurisdictional model of church Order. If at the theological level the experience of the dialogue with Donatism had convinced Augustine of the shortcomings of a too Cyprianic insistence on a juridically and monarchically considered model of catholic Order, there were nevertheless other factors that prevented the triumph before the eleventh century of such a model. Our second exception is to be found, therefore, in the actual customary arrangements for the election and ordination or consecration of the clergy, and the accompanying feeling within the church about such arrangements that a Cyprianic emphasis never succeeded in articulating with any justice. Let us now briefly consider the character of such customary arrangements.

At first sight someone who was anxious to argue that geographical and territorial jurisdiction was the *esse* of the sacrament of Order might be encouraged by some examples which are often cited from this period. It is possible to invoke at this point a general rule in the prɜ-Nicene Church that forbade the appointment

---

[21] *Ep.* 194,31. Other examples in Augustine are: no rebaptizing of heretics, the necessity of grace, and the canonicity of the biblical books. For a full list of such references, see Y. Congar, *Lay People in the Church,* (London: Geoffrey Chapman 1965), p. 466.

of two bishops in any one city. Cyprian argued in A.D. 252 to Cornelius that there should be but "one bishop (high priest) in the Church at any one time, and one bishop in Christ's place." (*Ep.* 59) Ignatius, as we have seen, had assumed one bishop per city-state community, on similar grounds, namely that there was one church and one eucharistic sacrifice. (*Smyr.* 8,1) With Cyprian and Ignatius many other Fathers could be quoted, but suffice it to be said that this ancient rule was to be confirmed by canon 8 of the ecumenical Council of Nicaea in A.D. 325. Furthermore, when the Christian emperor Constantius in A.D. 357 proposed to the Romans that they have as their bishops both Felix and Liberius as co-partners, clergy and people unanimously agreed to reject the motion with the cry: "One God, one Christ, one Bishop." (Theodoret *H.E.* 2,14)

It would, however, be wrong to jump to the conclusion that the insistence on territorial considerations were responsible for this position of the pre-Nicene church. In regarding the requirements of the pre-Nicene Fathers as territorial ones, we are, therefore, seeing the situation through the eyes of our post medieval, Western cultural heritage. The requirement of Ignatius, Cyprian, and Nicaea that there be one bishop was not, in its primary focus, a territorial requirement, but a requirement that the Christian people remain part of the catholic church. Through the catholic culture, we might say in the light of our earlier theological argument, the incarnation was being genuinely extended, as opposed to pagan, heretical and schismatic cultures such as those of the docetists (Ignatius), or the Novatians (Cyprian and Nicaea), in which the catholic church judged that Christ as *logos* had no true extended incarnation.

The catholic bishop in this case was the one bishop, not of the one territory, but the one true people of God as opposed to his false pagan or heretical people. That we think in territorial terms regarding jurisdiction in these cases shows therefore that our thinking may be unduly influenced by the post medieval, modern political doctrine that sovereignty is a case of supreme jurisdiction over everyone who lives within a given geographical area. But as Congar has shown, the jurisdictional understanding of episcopacy was the creation of the medieval reform movement represented by the Pontificate of Gregory VII.[22] It was to be a view fostered by the post- reformation rise of the modern, nation state in which sovereignty was conceived in terms of jurisdiction over territory. In Chapter 1 we argued that not only does such a geographical and jurisdictional notion impede realization of ethnic episcopates, but that it is also a similar obstacle in the path to ecumenical reconciliation with non-episcopal communions. We shall now explore in greater detail the substance of our charge as we seek to unravel now, not merely the continuance into the early medieval period of Didascalian, monarchical *episcope*, but its transformation into an *episcope* defined as essentially geographical as well as jurisdictional. Thus we come to the third factor mentioned at the beginning of this section, namely the absence of an unambiguous, territorial concept of *episcope* before the rise of the modern state.

Medieval kings generally considered themselves as kings of peoples rather than of geographical territories. In England William I, Henry I and Richard I took the title "king of the English" (*rex Anglorum*), even though they might add "duke of Normandy" (*dux Normanniae*). The term "king of England" (*rex Angliae*) only dates from Henry II and his successors. Louis of France still has the title "king of the French" (*rex Francorum*) as late as A.D. 1264.

So moreover did early medieval bishops regard themselves as bishops of peoples. In the early missionary situation in England, we find that Aidan was bishop of the "race of the Angles" (*gens Anglorum*) and resided in the monastery of Lindisfarne.[23] On the other hand Cedd was consecrated bishop of the east Saxons (*Orientalium Saxonum*)[24], whereas Chad was bishop of "the race of the Mercians and people of Lindsey (*gens Merciorum simul et Lindisfarorum*)."[25] Boniface, moreover, although he was

---

[22] Y. Congar, *L'Église de Saint Augustine à L'Époque Moderne*, (Paris: Les Éditions du Cerf), p. 99-109, and A. Brent, The Investiture Controversy: An Issue in Sacramental Theology? in *EThL* 65 4 (1987), p. 59-89.

[23] Bede, *H.E.* III,3. I am grateful for many details in this paragraph to the suggestions of the distinguished Augustine scholar, Mr G. Bonner of Durham University.

[24] Ibid. III,22.

[25] Ibid. IV,3.

consecrated in A.D. 722 and given the pallium in 732, was without a geographically locatable See until 747. While it is true that Boniface finally went to ground at Mainz in that year as Chad had done at Lichfield, it is nevertheless significant that the territorial location was incidental to a consecration whose focus was clearly cultural, and focused upon a people rather than a defined geographical territory.

It is important nevertheless to note how a static, medieval society inevitably concealed from us this cultural character of either secular or episcopal jurisdiction, since the number of people who traveled from country to country as from diocese to diocese would inevitably be small. Identification of peoples in terms of a culture and in terms of occupancy of territory would have been equivalent, particularly when the cultures in question were not seeking to live side by side so much as to obliterate each other. We think of territorial identity as constituting nationality when for the medieval mind it was race and culture. Thus the very real group identity, not in geographical but in social and cultural terms leading to a sense of loyalty and belonging to culturally representative kings and bishops and their particular traditions would, paradoxically, not have been as alien to the medieval as to the modern mind, forged in the Western ideology of the nation state.[26]

There are, it is true, few examples of cultures living side by side within geographical areas since peoples tended to occupy one geographical tract and simply annihilate any rival cultural tradition as happened during the barbarian invasions in early medieval Europe. But we do have one notable example of cultural pluralism. Where by agreement different European Christian cultural groups were to occupy the same territory, as in Jerusalem and its environs after the crusades, it was never envisaged by medieval political thinkers that the same jurisdiction should cover all peoples within the same territory. Rather, as the *Assizes of Jerusalem* makes clear, what laws one followed would very much depend on one's cultural tradition, and diocesan jurisdiction would undoubtedly have reflected secular juris-

---

[26] For the creation of the modern concept of the sovereign state in territorial terms, and its historical origin, see G.R. Elton, *England under the Tudors*, (London: Methuen 1974), chpt. 7.

diction in this respect.[27] The medieval view of episcopacy has far more in common in this respect with the cultural and representative rather than territorial concept.

But even if we look to the early, more orderly life of the early Christian empire before the early medieval reconstruction following the barbarian chaos, we do find features of early episcopacy that suggest developments in cultural rather than in territorial directions. It is well known that canon 15 of the Council of Nicaea appears to prohibit absolutely the translation of a bishop from the diocese of his consecration to another.[28] This prohibition was not merely directed against political interference from the predominantly Arian court at Nicomedia of the kind that drove Athanasius into his various exiles. It reflected also how a bishop was considered fundamentally the representative of the cultural traditions, heritage, doctrine, and life of the people of the diocese to those outside of his diocese.

Thus his formation from his earliest years amongst the people of whom he was to be the bishop was regarded as of so vital an importance, as was his consecration in his own diocese and the subsequent "letters of communion" (ἐπιστολαὶ κοινωνικαὶ) proclaiming his (and their) faith and life to the episcopal *collegium* of the catholic world. Consecration by at least three neighbouring bishops was part of this general process of mutual recognition of faith and doctrine between whole Christian communities.[29]

---

[27] Jean d'Ibelin, *Assisizes of the High Court,* (Ed. Bcugnot 1841), i and iii. "Jean d'Ibelin tells us that when Godfrey of Bouillon had been elected as the head of the newly conquered state of Jerusalem, he... appointed a certain number of wise men to inquire of those who were in Jerusalem what were the customs of their various countries... he then with their counsel and consent selected such of the customs as seemed good to him, ... the Kings of Jerusalem, with the same advice and consent, added from time to time other Assizes and altered old ones, after inquiring of those who came to the Holy Land about their customs and usages, and how several times the Kings of Jerusalem sent to other countries to inquire directly about their customs." R.W. and A.J. Carlyle, *A History of Medieval Political Theory in the West,* (London: Blackwood 1928), p. 43-44.

[28] Socrates *E.H.* 7,36.

[29] Cyprian *Ep.* 67 and 172; Gregory Nazianzen *Ep.* 101. In Eusebius *H.E.* 7,3, where Domnus is consecrated in place of Paul of Samosata, the Council of Antioch instructs all bishops to write to him for such letters.

We see therefore that the acceptance of the newly consecrated bishop was very much the acceptance of the faith, life, and culture of the people of his diocese that he represented externally. We have in this monograph seen how such a theme is as early as Ignatius who in Onesimus, bishop of Ephesus, saw and received into his communion a whole people. We have, therefore, in the course of our argument so far, established a point that is of major importance for our development of the concept of a cultural episcopate. Far from the territorial and jurisdictional concept of *episcope* being part of the essential character of the episcopate as it has come down to us, the focus on the possession of territory rather than the focus on representing a distinct culture and people is post- medieval and therefore very recent in Christian history.

Thus we have seen that the jurisdictional strand in the justification of *episcope* that comes into theology with Irenaeus remained only one strand, however much it might be emphasized by Cyprian. Tertullian had emphasized "consanguinity" too, and Augustine had emphasized catholicity understood in terms of a *consensus* or *conspiratio* between the clergy and laity. Such a representative, alternative strand to the jurisdictional was, moreover, part of the pattern presupposed both in the church by practices and principles regarding non-translation of bishops, and in the state regarding the focus of sovereignty in peoples rather than in territories.

But this being the case, it must now be asked when and how, historically, the sacral and representational theme came to be fully submerged, and the jurisdictional one to preponderate? We shall locate the emergence of the unqualified jurisdictional model of the church's Order in the theological reflection on the reforms of Gregory VII in the eleventh century, which also saw the beginnings of movements towards the idea of the sovereignty of the state being geographical. Such movements were, of course, to reach their final form in the emergence of the nation states in the wake of the sixteenth century Reformation exemplified in the work of Thomas Cromwell in England from A.D. 1531-1538. But in the eleventh century, with the renaissance of Roman

---

Basil of Caesarea replies to Ambrose's encyclical on his consecration in *Ep.* 197.

jurisprudence, jurisdictional motiffs are found in the discussion both of secular politics and ecclesiastical Order.

5. *Gregory VII and the triumph of the jurisdictional concept*

According to Congar, there occurred in the eleventh century a radical shift from a representational and sacramental view of what constituted church Order to primarily a jurisdictional one.[30] For this change of perspective, the year A.D. 1045 becomes critical for it was in this year that pope Leo IX tried to impose his theory upon the Eastern Orthodox church and thus precipitated a schism. From this date, in the Western church, the juridical began to displace the representative and mystical view of Order which, as we have seen, continued in synthesis since the age of Cyprian and Augustine.[31] Basically, the Carologinian concept of church and state as one *congregatio fidelium*, with the sovereign minister of state in some way sacred and within the church, now gives way to a concept of the church outside the state, and constituted by a hierarchically constructed clerical Order with public and juridical rights against the state. This juridical ecclesiology was developing in the West in the place of an ecclesiology expressed in terms of sacramental mystery.[32]

We can see in such a context the famous decree of Nicholas II in A.D. 1059, which replaced the election of the bishop of Rome by clergy and people, and placed such an election in the hands of the Cardinal priests. No longer could the bishop be seen as the mystical representative of the faith and life of his people, but rather was now the fully-fledged representative of the *paradosis* to his people. My only quarrel with Congar on this score is that

---

[30] I am grateful to Professor Nicholas Lash for having pointed out to me the significance of Congar's work for my thesis, in particular, Y. Congar, *L'Église de Saint Augustine à l'époque moderne*, (Freiburg: Herder 1970).

[31] Congar (1970) op. cit. p. 99-101. See e.g. p. 100: "Il n'est pas faux de situer ici un fait spécifique de l'histoire des doctrines ecclésiologiques: les deux part de l'Église vont suivre chacune sa propre voie, presque dans l'ignorance de l'autre."

[32] "Une ecclésiologie juridique, consistant surtout en thèse de droit public ecclésiatique, et qui sera pout autant une ecclésiologie cléricale, va se développer, en Occident, d'abord et longtemps à côte d'une ecclésiologie mystérique ou sacramentelle, puis à sa place..." ibid. p. 101.

far from initiating this change, the Gregorians rather completed it.

As we have seen, the revolution in reality began when Irenaeus and his age reified the *paradosis*, and the Didascaliast and his altered the basis of Order in Ignatius from sacramental representation to sacramental mediation. It would be a mistake in this context to interpret Nicholas II's act as a reaction against imperial pressure on, and interference in, the election of the pope or other bishops. Rather the act reflected a positive and new ecclesiology. But it was an ecclesiology representing a long, Irenaean and Didascalian antithesis within the western tradition now negating critically its thesis. The authority to bind and loose given in *Mat.* 16,19 was no longer regarded as beginning, in Peter, the episcopate and priesthood to be found generally throughout the church, but rather of "the founding in Peter and his successors of the total monarchical power of binding and loosing." Whatever he has as pope bound no other bishop could now loose. Christ had made no man an exception, he had withdrawn nothing from Peter's power.[33]

That the power of binding and loosing was now no longer regarded as of the same nature as that possessed by the other bishops can been seen in the change of title ascribed to the Roman pontiff by writers on the papal side of the Investiture Controversy, in contrast to their predecessors in the century before. The *Decretum* of Burchard of Worms (*circa* A.D. 1010), for example, has a first book entitled "On the Primacy of the Church" (*De Primatu Ecclesiae*) which is concerned with Pseudo- Anicletus on the *Ordo Sacerdotalis*. Here the pope is described as "bishop of the first See" (*primae sedis episcopus)* and not "prince of priests" or "high priest" (*princeps sacerdotum, summus sacerdos*). When however we come to the writers who support Gregory, we find the position has radically changed. Anselm of Lucca (A.D. 1083) entitles one of his tracts "On the Power and Primacy of the Apostolic See." Although

---

[33] Ibid. p. 103: "Mais Grégoire, tout comme ses prédécesseurs, entend le texte de Mt. 16,19, non du commencement, en Pierre, de l'épiscopat et du sacerdoce, mais l'institution, en Pierre et en ses successeurs, du pouvoir monarchique et total de lier et de délier: *Quodcumque ligaveris...* = *nullum excepit, nihil ab eius potestate subtraxit...*"

Deusdedit (A.D. 1084) may make the pope subject to the Cardinals in certain decisions, and they may not follow him into heresy, nevertheless such limitations are normal in any monarchy with a senate of advisers.[34]

Accordingly, from a juridical primacy over bishops with whom he is sacramentally equal, the pope now emerged with judicial powers justified in terms of a juridical ecclesiology which quite nullified the the patristic and sacramental understanding of Order. That jurisdictional ecclesiology made the gift of binding and loosing the exclusive prerogative of the Holy See to the extent that, increasingly, papal legates could now overrule local archbishops. As Congar says:

> In the ecclesiastical order all power derives from the pope. With the Gregorians, the earlier theme according to which Peter had been the *origo* (source) of the *ordo sacerdotalis* (the sacerdotal Order) of the whole church is transposed in favour of the Roman church; as the pope he is *a quo omnis ecclesiastica potestas procedit* (from whom all ecclesiastical power proceeds)....There is over the church entirely one "jurisdiction" (*potestas*) of the episcopal type but superior to that of the local bishop. Many texts of the Gregorians express the entire church in terms of an immense diocese in which...the pope institutes those called his vicars...that is to say those who participate in his jurisdiction without the possession of his plenitude.[35]

It is in connection with such a jurisdictional interpretation of Order that we can now interpret the often hailed reforms of Gregory against simony and fornication, the later being a grotesque characterization of the requirement of clerical celibacy. Often Gregory is regarded as hypocritical for only requiring the deposition of those who received their bishoprics through simony if he disagreed with the politics of the vendor. But we should regard the whole question of simony in the context of an ecclesiology that located the only security for the validity of Orders in the papal jurisdiction, and not in any sacramental act of a consecrating or ordaining bishops.

Even though a man might be ordained or consecrated with the appropriate matter and form, according to the customary rites of the church, and by the proper episcopal minister of the sacra-

---

[34]   Ibid. p. 107-109.
[35]   Ibid. p. 105.

ment, a man's Orders could still be invalid. They could be invalidated by a defect of intention on the part of the ordinand shown in the reception, or the attempted reception, of the Holy Spirit for money. In feudal society, as the lay claim to invest with the ring and the staff now being hotly disputed showed, one could be neither consecrated nor ordained without receiving property in the form of granaries, vineyards, villages as well as those of cathedral and church buildings. In any consecration or ordination, therefore, there was always the possibility of a simonaical intention thwarting the intention to do what the church does, irrespective of all being done according to the traditional form and matter of the church. The ordinand's only security became, therefore, not the sacramental validity of his ordination which could now always be questioned with the accusation of simony, but that he was ordained according to a jurisdiction and a power given by the pope from the fullness of his power (*plenitudo potestatis*).[36]

It was of course from this time that not only the transmission of the ring and the staff, but that of other instruments related to priests, deacons, subdeacons, readers, acolytes and doorkeepers began to assume an importance in many instances equal to the imposition of hands. Such instruments and their transmission were part and parcel of the ceremonies of the delegation of jurisdiction now becoming increasingly sacramentalized. In fact, there was now, given the new papal thesis, very little distinction to be made between the sacrament of Order and rights of jurisdiction. Indeed, the form of priestly Ordination accompanying the *traditio instrumentorum* of the full chalice and paten made this point unambiguously. In one's ordination one was being given a jurisdictional power, a *potestas* to offer the eucharistic

---

[36] Congar (1970) op. cit. p. 104: "... si cet ordre se traduit principalement par l'institution papale, on comprend... que la réforme tienne essentiellement à suivre l'autorité du pape, que la fermeté indéfectible de l'Église romaine fonde la sécurité de l'ordre sacramentel et que Grégoire admette ou rejette la validité d'ordinations entachées de simonie, selon que l'intéressé se soumet ou résiste à son autorité. Tout est fondé sur cette pierre..."

for the living and the dead, rather than the symbolic and representative function of re-realizing the fruits of calvary.[37]

We see therefore historically from Gregory VII onwards a jurisdictional view of Order which distorted the sacramental and representative character of Order found in one strand of the Fathers. We shall need to return to this theme when we come in our next and final chapter, where we complete our consideration of the ecumenical implications of our proposed theological response to the claim of such groups as antipodean indigenous peoples for culturally rather than geographically based bishops. Suffice it to say that the church has yet to recover an essentially sacramental view of Order thus overlaid by the jurisdictional triumph which dates from the eleventh century.

As we shall see in our next and final chapter when we discuss the ecumenical implications of our discussion, a primarily jurisdictional view of episcopacy was to prevail in the English Reformation, which was fought by both Anglicans, and what by then had become Roman Catholics alike, in purely jurisdictional terms. The specific attack on Anglican Orders as sacramentally invalid was of far more recent origin. Even as late as the 1830s Palmer then on the Anglican side, and Wiseman in Rome's defense, were still arguing the validity or invalidity of Anglican Orders primarily in jurisdictional terms.[38]

For the moment, however, having given a historical explanation of how what I have argued to have been the essential, sacramental and representative character of *episcope* has become distorted into a purely jurisdictional one, I should now like to explore a sociological account of why this has taken place. In many respects this sociological account will be even more critical than the historical one.

Our historical account has shown us what the sacramental and representational understanding of *episcope* was in terms of the

---

[37] For a more detailed discussion of these and the following points, see A. Brent, The Investiture Controversy— an issue in Sacramental Theology? in *EThL* 63,1 (1987), p. 59-89.

[38] W. Palmer, *The Apostolical Jurisdiction and Succession of Episcopacy in the British Churches Vindicated*, (London: Rivington 1840), and N. Wiseman, *A Letter on Unity addressed to the Earl of Shrewsbury*, (London 1841).

Ignatian bishop bearing the corporate personality of his community, as the sacred representative of a redeemed community. We have also seen how similar, representative patterns of thinking about ministry were shared with Ignatius by the *Apocalypse*, by letter writers representative of the faith and life of their community who, if they write pseudonymously, bear the faith and life of their community as a corporate personality that bears an individually apostolic form, whether Pauline, Petrine, Jacobean, or Johannine. Our historical account has further shown us how, in Tertullian and Augustine, the bishop's teaching authority is such because he represents the *conspiratio* or *consensus* of all the faithful people of God, and represents the faith of a community that has family-resemblance or *consanguinitas* with other communities who hold more directly the apostolic tradition. But our historical account so far has lacked any explanation as to why church Order, so expressed and originally represented sacrally as an incarnation in a specifically cultural form, became overlaid by a jurisdictional and territorial view of *episcope* associated with a reified *depositum fidei*.

Our historical account has nevertheless given us some clues. Bishops, like kings, were bishops of peoples and not of territories, but the nature of the cultural expression of the faith that they taught was obscured because multi-culturalism was not yet a sociological possibility. The distinction between territorially and culturally identifiable peoples was somewhat academic, when only one culture was permissible for a people in occupation of a territory and all others were to be obliterated. It is in societal form that we can, therefore, now proceed to locate the barriers to the development of a fully-fledged concept of the church as incarnation in a culture, however much the grounds for such a development existed in the circumstances of the development of New Testament and the reflections of the Fathers, as we have shown.

6. *Cultural pluralism and models of social solidarity*

We can I believe give a convincing sociological account for why a fully-fledged concept of cultural episcopacy failed to emerged from the theology of the church as the extension of the incarnation, with sacral-representative bishops, in the nature of the societies in which Christian theology received its original and historical articulation. In Chapter 2 we outlined a structural/-functionalist model of social solidarity, for which we were greatly indebted to Durkheim. The model which we outlined there was one in which a distinct cultural identity was achieved by a society's concretizing its central value system or collective consciousness in the form of collective representations.

We saw however that such collective representations consisted of words and concepts as well as artifacts, persons, and things, which could not be reified as Durkheim, and even more so, Tylor, had done before him. Artifacts, persons and things derived their meaning from a universe of discourse which inter-wove with them so as to give them comprehensive meaning. We proposed understanding this interweaving of discourse with arti-facts, persons, and things in terms of what the later-Wittgenstein described as a "form of life," and the development of culture as form of life in terms of a structuralist account of the evolution and development of a sacred story. We have already described (in Chapter 3) how such a model is seen to function as an expla-nation of the rise of the threefold Order in Ignatius. Moreover, we used the Wittgensteinian notion of family resemblance to show how translation and inter-cultural dialogue, and with it new syntheses in terms of sacred stories, could grow. At the close of Chapter 2 we applied the sociological model thus con-structed to some examples taken from the literature of contempo-rary ecumenism.

It is now time for us to develop our model somewhat further in order to explain the social phenomenon that we are now de-scribing. How does it come about that there is a shift from repre-sentation to jurisdiction, and similarly a shift from intercultural and inter community dialogue in terms of conceptual webs of family resemblances to one in which there must be a total and exhaustively definable dogmatic system which closes dialogue by imposing its own terms of understanding?

We have not so far told Durkheim's whole story, nor our phe-nomenological re-interpretation of it. No language, and therefore no human social system, could function by evolving generally concepts that were exhaustively defined, closed classes. If there were some exhaustive paradigm of a table, for example, the concept could have no function in any human communication system, since we would not be able to encompass new or unusual instances into a known scheme. Nevertheless some kinds of social order endeavour with some of its key moral and theological concepts to produce exhaustively defined paradigms. We have just claimed an instance of such societies as the post Irenaean and post Cyprianic churches which which began reifying the primitive *paradosis,* and so denied community of belief with other versions of that *paradosis* in terms of *consanguinitas* or family-resemblance.

A development of our phenomelogically Durkheimian sociology will enable us to characterize the different cognitive stances of these two different kinds of social order, though we should never forget that such models are formally ideal and that actual societies contain mixed forms at a sub-cultural level. Durkheim distinguished two kinds of social solidarity, one characteristic of industrial societies that he termed "organic," and one characteristic of pre-industrial societies that he termed "mechanical." In the context of our present discussion, given that the threefold Order developed, as we have suggested in Chapter 3, as collective representations which created the uniqueness of a Christian sub-culture capable of self-identification, the pre-industrial social context in which that sub-culture arose meant inevitably that its social cohesion would be what Durkheim described as "mechanical." In other words, the concept of cultural episcopacy, implying as its social backcloth a situation of multi-culturalism, could not develop within the context of a society whose principle of social cohesion was that of mechanical solidarity.[39]

"Mechanical" solidarity describes the principle of social cohesion in which society hangs together by everyone behaving in extremely similar ways, as exemplified by identity of dress, a common agricultural or pastoral occupation, etc. "Organic" solidarity describes the principle of social cohesion in which society hangs together by every member behaving differently. Indeed,

---

[39] For a full discussion and critique of Durkheim's social theory, see S. Lukes, *Emile Durkheim: His Life and Work,* (London: Penguin 1973); A. Brent, *Philosophy and Educational Foundations,* (London: Allen and Unwin 1983), p. 256-280; and R. Aron, *Main Currents in Sociological Thought,* (London: Penguin 1970), vol. 2.

the division of labour, observed in an industrial society, is the product of this principle of cohesion in which we all specialize in producing quite different goods and services which we exchange through the monetary medium.[40]

As a result of these differences, systems of law are different between mechanical and organic forms of social solidarity. Under mechanical solidarity there is little difference between the criminal and the civil law, and between customary morality and punitive law. Under organic solidarity, such distinctions are clearly maintained and legislation tends to become consensual rather than coercive, as laws make it possible for different groups of people to enter contractual relations with one another if they choose to do so. Under mechanical solidarity too, as Bernstein ans his associates have argued,[41] the classification and framing of bodies of knowledge in educational institutions is also different from that exhibited in an "organic" context. Mechanical solidarity produces subject oriented curricula in which one subject is insulated against another by the imposition of a strong "frame," which I have characterized here in terms of a distorted logical strategy that seeks to define exhaustively key concepts and investigative procedures. Under organic solidarity, the "framing" and "boundary maintenance" between different kinds of inquiry ("subjects") is considerably diminished, and the integration of bodies of knowledge takes place in seeking the kinds of solutions such as we find typified by a variety of technologies. I am suggesting here that, whether in a denominational or in a cultural context, different approaches to bodies of religious doctrine differ as between a social context where solidarity

---

[40] As Durkheim believed that social development, like social facts, were *sui generis,* it would be a mistake to say that the division of labor produced organic society rather than the reverse. The shift from mechanical to organic solidarity was produced by the social facts of population increase accompanied by what he described as "moral density." See Brent (1983) op. cit. p. 273; 278-279.

[41] B. Berstein, R.S. Peters, and L. Elvin, Ritual in Education, in *Philosophical Transactions of the Royal Society of London*, Series B vol. 251 no 772 (1966); B. Berstein, Open School, Open Society, in *New Society*, Sept. 14 (1967); B. Berstein, On the Classification and Framing of Educational Knowledge, in M.F.D. Young, *Knowledge and Control*, (London: Collier Macmillan 1971), p. 47-69.

is mechanical, and one where it is organic. In contrast with the kinds of analysis and inquiry that have arisen within theological inquiry in the increasingly "organic" social context of the last two hundred years stand those which arose in a mechanical context in the age of Irenaeus, and were completed in the age of Gregory VII and its aftermath.

Even more basic, however, is the difference of character between the central value system, which Durkheim called the "collective consciousness," in the two kinds of societies. Under mechanical solidarity the collective consciousness extends throughout the social group and is able to give specific and quite concrete directions governing every aspect of life and behaviour. This is possible when social solidarity requires close and quite absolute conformity to identical patterns of behaviour. But under organic solidarity, because society hangs together by individuals behaving with those differences of which the industrial division of labour is but one example, the collective consciousness is no longer able to prescribe precise and concrete maxims governing all the particular situations of life. After all, if everyone follows different occupations, then occupational and professional norms and values cannot be identical for every citizen. The "collective consciousness" becomes generalized and ceases to pervade every area of life and production. Instead it becomes contracted and confined to a number of non-specific, and non-concrete general and abstract norms and values which must nevertheless be of sufficient force in a healthy organic society to prevent social disequilibrium and disintegration.

It was under such a social condition of mechanical solidarity that we saw taking place the reification of the *paradosis* in the age of Irenaeus, and the ensuing destruction of the concept of the bishop as representative of the *paradosis* living and abiding in the life of the community. The ministry of Clement of Rome could not be allowed to remain conceived as that of a "mere" secretary, however much the later might speak with his community's voice, without using his own name, with a ministry "committed" to him. The bishop representing the central value system as a collective representation, under conditions of mechanical solidarity, became the bearer of a reified system of authority, external to the community, and organizing exhaustively all areas of its life.

The social disequilibrium, which Durkheim called *anomia* or *anomie,* is, on the other hand, endemic in organic societies.[42] In organic societies, the very principle of social cohesion, being the very different patterns of social behaviour as between different social and occupational groups, is what can cause breakdown in the social order. Though one's role as a teacher, miner, farmer etc is clear, one's role as a citizen and what constitutes social morality can no longer be spelled out in concrete and specific terms. The more general and abstract nature of values arising from the constriction of the collective consciousness means that the different social groups can easily lose their grasp upon such general and abstract norms so that social order lapses into "normlessness" or *anomia.*

It is my argument that, under conditions of mechanical solidarity, however much the basis for a theology of cultural *episcope* was present, such a concept could not develop. The sacral-representational concept of episcopacy was indelibly stamped on Christian tradition in Ignatius and in Tertullian. Yet the consciousness of the cultural expression of the faith of the redeemed community, which was quite inseparable from what was expressed, was inevitably lost on a community whose principle of social cohesion was mechanical. In such a community, cultural differences had to be suppressed, glossed over, or ignored otherwise there could be no community,— no social entity at all.

In such a community, the possibility of a diversity of orthodox positions, with the diversity explained in terms of cultural incarnations of theological expression, is ruled out. In making such a statement I must emphasize that I am not taking an extreme position in which the taking seriously of a cultural dimension to the expression of faith requires a cultural relativism in an epistemological sense.[43] The position which I am taking simply involves

---

[42] Durkheim described breakdown of social order as seen objectively and from the outside as *anomia.* Seen from the inside and felt and perceived by the individual as a debilitating and alienating effect this became *anomie.* See Brent (1983) op. cit. 229, 258, 261-262, and 282.

[43] Even a seminal writer in the sociology of knowledge such as Berger finally rejected an extreme, culturally relative position in discussing all theo-

being able to say that, whilst Arianism was unquestionably heresy, Monophysitism, for example, was a phenomenon more explicable in terms of cultural forms which made the disputants end up talking at cross purposes.[44]

Under mechanical solidarity the collective consciousness or central value system must consist of specific and concrete rules and principles which regulate all areas of thought and activity. The early Christian communities, with their different cultural incarnations of the ministry of the Word and Sacraments, were not initially subject to the conditions of mechanical solidarity in so far as they represented social developments that were at that time in a highly fluid state regarding cultural identitiy. Once, however, those different and fluid cultural incarnations coallesced, in the course of the ecumenical dialogue of the second century, into a distinctive cultural identity in the form of the great church of the age of Irenaeus, as in Asia Minor with Ignatius they had done some years previously, the community thus created was subject to the conditions of mechanical solidarity in all their rigour.

Whilst the church practiced theology in a societal context governed by mechanical solidarity, that theology was inevitably dogmatic and practiced as a tightly closed deductive system rather like canon law. As such it supported the jurisdictional view of Order rather than the sacral-representative, though the former's final form was only to emerge with Gregory VII. Such a view of Order went well with a theological logic that proceeded by identifying exhaustively definable equivalents which follow syllogistically, and, therefore, almost tautologously from one another.[45] Such a societal context was, moreover, increasingly exemplified in the social and historical currents that forged the ideology of the nation-state, in which individual national

---

logical concepts and issues. See P. Berger, *The Social Reality of Religion,* (London: Penguin 1973), Appendix II, p. 181-190, and *A Rumor of Angels,* (London: Pengiun 1971).

[44] F. Young, *From Nicaea to Chalcedon,* (London: SCM 1983), p. 178-265; G.L. Prestige, *Fathers and Heretics. Six Studies in Dogmatic Faith with Prologue and Epilogue,* (London: Macmillan 1958).

[45] For an explanation and discussion of the logic of "family resemblance" analysis as opposed to exhaustive definition in terms of closed class universals, see Brent (1983) op. cit. chpts 8-10.

churches would constitute the source of an exhaustively defined and all extensive central value system, regulating behaviour in minute detail throughout the societies in question, and brooking no rival alternatives under threat of the destruction of mechanically based social solidarity. Such were the societies of the European Reformation which by slow degrees followed the Gregorian reforms.

The detection of valid doctrinal developments in terms of what Tertullian called "consanguinity" (*consanguinitas*)[46] and family-resemblance was impossible under the conditions of knowledge imposed by mechanical solidarity. All that was possible under such conditions were syllogistic deductions from an exhaustively defined and closed conceptual system constituted by the collective consciousness of a society whose solidarity was mechanical. Consanguinity, and the ability to draw inferences in terms of family-resemblances, required a different social structure than that available in the medieval and post medieval era. Such a method of inference depended upon a collective consciousness organized in terms of a set of generalized and abstract concepts that we have seen to be a feature of organic and not mechanical solidarity.[47]

Moreover, the concept of organic rather than mechanical solidarity is more suited to the ecumenism of the current dialogue between separated Christian communions. In seeking to reconstruct a society in terms of one holy catholic and apostolic

---

[46] Tertullian, *De Praes. Haer.* 32 where "family resemblance" (*consanguinitas*) between the doctrine of a particular church and the apostolic tradition can constitute the mark of validity, irrespective of evidence for the original establishment of that church by an apostle or his companion.

[47] The transition from syllogistic models of development to what I call here "family resemblance" ones is becoming a commonplace in the post Vatican II Roman Catholic Church. It was foreshadowed in 1845, in J.H. Newman, *The Development of Christian Doctrine*, (Westminister: Christian Classics 1968). I have sought to show the radical disjunction in this respect between Newman's theological method, and the senior theologian in the church of Newman's conversion, J. Perrone, in A. Brent, Newman's Conversion, the Via Media, and the myth of the Romeward Movement, in *DR* 345 (1983), p. 261-280; Newman and Perrone: Irreconcilable Theses on Development, in *DR* 349 (1984), p. 276-289; and, The Hermesian Dimension to the Newman-Perrone Dialogue, in *EThL* 61 1 (1985), p. 73-99.

church, broken and fragmented by the Reformation, we can seek either a mechanical or an organic solution. The mechanical solution would be that of one communion submitting to another, and reconstructing a dogmatic theology which produced an ironclad system of canon law, regulating in an exhaustively defined and concrete way every belief and practice of the reunited church. But the organic solution I believe to be the truly catholic solution, and one which connects well with our sacramental and representational theme.

Such a solution sees the varieties of belief and tradition in all their differences as the key to reconstructing our lost unity, and that very variety as producing the real unifying force. We see in what the sects have broken off and exclusively emphasized to the exclusion of all else that which the church has lost or failed to represent adequately. Far the admission of unity in diversity representing a breakdown of Order and a fragmentation of unity, such an approach to catholicity represents a truly organically as opposed to mechanically understood principle of re-union. The broken fragments of the apostolic *paradosis* finds in our contemporary situation its sacral and representative focal point in a multiform and multicultural expression of *episcope*. The present denominational differences of those holding the apostolic faith, as defined in the Councils and Fathers of the first six centuries, constitute the present divisions which ecumenism is seeking to overcome. But in a broader sense, ecumenism can be understood as seeking to recover the various cultural voices of the oral *paradosis* before the reification of the age of Irenaeus. We saw this process at work in particular in the generalization of open-textured concepts evidenced in ecumenical dialogue and exemplified in Chapter 2.

It is at this point that a sacramental theology for ecumenism makes contact with my cultural argument for indigenous bishops in Australia and New Zealand. Under a sociological theory of organic solidarity, there is no difference in kind, though there may be of degree, between sub-cultures within society and cultural differences between societies. My account therefore argues at a theoretical level the need for denominations or sub-cultures to be brought together through the mutual recognition that these are cultural incarnations of the apostolic faith. The mechanism for that reunion must moreover be through the mutual recognition of representative episcopates whose theological *raison d'etre* must be understood as sacramental and cultural-representational, and not in jurisdictional and territorial terms.

In our concluding chapter, we shall comment more specifically on the ecumenical dimensions of cultural episcopacy, and how the concept can act as a dynamic force for reintegration into one holy catholic church in place of a disintegrating, territorial and jurisdictional concept. Let us summarize where this chapter has taken us so far.

7. *Summary and Conclusion*

We have shown that there is a clear development between Ignatius' theological argument for the threefold Order as representative of a redeemed community's union with God, the angel-representatives to whom the author of the *Apocalypse* wrote, and "secretaries" like Clement or the anonymous writers of pseudonymous apostolic letters. We saw a clear continuity between the figure of Peter in *Matthew*, and Ignatius' mysticism in which the whole multitude of the gathered church could be seen in its bishop, and the theology of the *paradosis* that lives in the faith of the community of which the bishop is the representative. We saw moreover the clear implication that the *paradosis* has a cultural form symbolic of a culture's redemption, in the way in which Ignatian bishops wear the corporate personality of their churches like the angel bishops of the *Apocalypse*, letter writers like Clement write anonymously by virtue of their committed ministry in the name of whole communities, and pseudonymous writers wear the collective personality of their communities personalized as that of a named apostle.

We traced how from Irenaeus' time the threefold Order was justified predominantly in terms of the transmission of the *paradosis* granting jurisdiction, although we presented evidence for the survival of the alternative, sacramental and representational view of Order in such writers as Tertullian on *consanguinitas*, and Augustine on the *conspiratio fidelium et pastorum*. We argued earlier (Chapter 2) that the modern, *ARCIC* position on the *consensus fidelium* as a test for doctrinal validity is reflected in such a cultural, sacral and representational view of Order. We drew attention to the way in which, before the modern, territorial concept of the modern state in terms of territorial sovereignty, bishops like kings were primarily bishops of peoples and not of geographically defined domains.

A full development of an exclusively jurisdictional view of *episcope* was late medieval. Following Congar we argued that the representative dimension, previously present and exemplified both by the practices surrounding ordination and in Tertullian and Augustine's view of tradition and succession, to have been finally repressed in the events of the Investiture Controversy, and in the radical shift of ecclesiological perspective accomplished in that controversy. Here the jurisdictional view of an Irenaeus or Cyprian, recognized by the Fathers as one strand of validity, became the sole criterion. We also argued that the cultural element in the *sensus fidelium* had even before remained to some degree embryonic since the societal mechanism of social solidarity was, in Durkheimian terms, mechanical and not organic. Only in terms of the latter can a concept of cultural *episcope* achieve a full development, and, in consequence, only in terms of the latter can the possibility be established of a united church in terms of unity in diversity, together with a multi-cultural expression of that unity. It will be our object in our final chapter to give a more concrete account of how cultural *episcope* can function as a means of reintegration and reconciliation.

We must now explore the contemporary and ecumenical implications for our argument.

CHAPTER SIX

ECUMENICAL DIMENSIONS

Ecumenical implications for cultural episcope

This book has sought to explore the theological foundations on which to develop a theological concept of cultural *episcope*. I have sought to argue that our present territorial and jurisdictional approach to episcopacy, itself in its pure form a late medieval creation, has distorted vital strands in the New Testament and early patristic understanding of bishops as representatives of redeemed cultural and historical traditions. Though my treatment of this subject has been fundamentally academic, the contemporary pressure on theologians to re-examine *episcope* from such a standpoint has come undoubtedly from the collapse of the traditional concept, both at a theoretical level in terms of the critical study of the the historical development of church Order in late New Testament and early patristic times, and from three practical concerns which that theoretical collapse have served to accentuate. Those three practical concerns are as follows.

The first is the missionary dimension to the problem of intercultural communication, in which doctrine, liturgy, and Order seem so inextricably interwoven into either Western European, or, for that matter, Eastern European cultural traditions and forms of thought so as to render the communication of the gospel problematic in other cultures whether of the southern Mediterranean, or the Near and Far East, or in Africa, or amongst the indigenous peoples of Australasia. We have taken, as one specific example of our general, ecumenical problem regarding church Order, and steps towards its solution, the current, Australasian developments towards ethnic bishops who will exercise *episcope* over any member of their cultural group across traditional diocesan jurisdictions, irrespective of geographical location.

The second problem is that of how we proceed beyond ecumenical dialogue and basic doctrinal agreement to mutual recognition of Orders. In Chapters 1 and 2 I sketched some of the sociological issues involved, and sought to show how a theology of Order in terms of cultural representation rather than jurisdiction could help to positively resolve, rather than to perpetuate, the ecumenical crisis represented by our continuing denominational divisions. Here I will briefly sketch in more concrete terms what would be involved in using a model of cultural *episcope* in understanding the process of reconciliation.

The third problem is more parochially Anglican, and that is the question of the situation in the Anglican dioceses throughout the world regarding the piecemeal consecration of women priests and bishops where individual dioceses would wish them. I will briefly sketch how it is the incapacities of the jurisdictional and territorial model that itself will contribute to the inevitable schism, whereas a cultural model could both reduce the practical effects of such schism, and allow, with a greater degree of mutual self-respect, dialogue to continue.

Let us begin with the Australasian situation, from which I originally began my reflection, only to find that it was but one example of a more general breakdown in the traditional, post Irenaean and post Gregorian concept of episcopal Order.

1. Cultural Episcopates in the contemporary Australasian scene

The request for Aboriginal and Islander cultural episcopates received their impetus from the Aotearoa model to be seen operating with the Maoris in New Zealand. In New Zealand the bishop of Aotearoa is genuinely cultural, and is the bishop of all Maoris regardless of the territorial boundaries of the New Zealand, Anglican dioceses. But a claim for similar indigenous episcopates in Australia were to reveal not simply the inadequacy of our theology of Order to produce such changes, but the very constrictions of our *territorial* concept of jurisdiction in practice, as it is embodied in our canon law. In May 1984 the Anglican Diocese of North Queensland, meeting in Synod, proposed the consecration, with effect from Australia's bicentennial year of 1988, national Aboriginal and Islander bishops exercising episcopal oversight over all members of their cultural groups within Australia, in pursuance of our developments and modifications of the Aotearoa model.

But the due process of discrete consultation was to reveal how hazardous the success of such a proposal would be, given the kinds of jurisdiction possible within our existing framework of canon law, particularly at the level of the Synod of the national church which was to meet in August 1985. Most certainly the comments of the Anglican Church of Australia's Doctrine Commission on the paper which formed the first draft of this book revealed an inability in an Australian context to regard *episcope* in any other terms than those of *territorial* jurisdiction. Furthermore the author did not find the experience of the discussion of the aforementioned paper, referred to that commission by the Australian Primate, in any way intellectually enlightening.

The North Queensland Synod of May 1985 made a modified proposal which was to succeed with the General Synod of the Anglican Church of Australia in August of that year. We used the present canonical provisions for making an assistant bishop to create a cultural bishop with responsibility for Aboriginal peoples within our diocese, on the understanding that other dioceses will enable such a bishop to be more than simply one of our assistant bishops. The bishops of our neighbouring dioceses, the bishop of Carpentaria and the bishop of the Northern Territory, were subsequently the first diocesans to agree to receive our cultural bishop within their jurisdictions in order to perform his episcopal ministry when invited to do so by groups of his own culture. The then bishop of of North Queensland, the Rt.Revd. H.J. Lewis, fully reciprocated these arrangements by agreeing that an assistant bishop for Islander peoples, to be consecrated in Carpentaria, would be accepted on the same basis within the jurisdiction of the See of North Queensland. Thus we have agreed to proceed tentatively and experimentally with our concept, and to allow it to grow by the natural force of its own gradual acceptance and development.

In proceeding in this way, we have sought, whilst remaining true to our initial convictions, to respect with integrity the susceptibilities of the National Church, and to be guided by the the outcome of the consultation conducted by our then Primate,

Archbishop John Grindrod. But it is our view that such a proposal is supported by a theology of cultural episcopacy of the
kind that I have sought to develop in this monograph. There is
however a very real danger in adopting such an approach which
arises out of the very tentative and experimental nature of what
we are proposing within the existing canonical framework of the
Assistant Bishops Canon (1966) of the Anglican Church of
Australia. The danger is that our cultural bishops, having arisen
in the matrix of our existing canonical framework, will be imprisoned there and simply not be allowed to fulfil the promise of
becoming genuinely *cultural* bishops. A lot will depend on the
personal qualities of the men themselves, in additional to the
sacramental grace of their consecration, but a lot will depend also
in our being prepared to explore and recover the lost themes in
the Church's theology of the sacrament of Order to which this
book has endeavoured to point.

Having been consecrated with a view to performing a uniquely
episcopal and cultural ministry to their own cultures, it would
have been a disaster if such a ministry had not been sought from
them by members of their cultural groups outside their territorial
jurisdiction. In that event, they would have remained but mere
assistant bishops. They may, of course, still do so. Those who
were subsequently consecrated, namely the Rt. Revd. Arthur
Malcolm, to whom this work is dedicated, and the Rt. Revd.
Kwami Dai, are, in formal canonical terms, merely assistant
bishops to the See bishops of their respective dioceses of North
Queensland and Carpentaria. But they have both began to function as more than assistant bishops to their respective geographical and jurisdictional diocesans.

The reality of the position in Australian society of both bishops is one that belies their formal status of subservience awarded
by their canonical status of "assistants." At the visit of his holiness Pope John Paul II at Alice Springs, and in the official bicentennial celebrations in Canberra, they were certainly regarded
as representatives of their peoples. At those ceremonies, they
stood as representatives of their peoples in a liturgical act of
mutual reconciliation and mutual forgiveness for past wrongs.
Moreover, there is evidence of feelings of a strong religious
affinity with these bishops on the part of lay members of their

cultures which cuts across the denominational differences imported originally by Northern European missionaries. On them personally will depend therefore whether they can win further acceptance by their tact, their sensitivity and pastoral awareness, and above all by the exercise of the apostolic grace of the episcopate exercised in this new, cultural form.

But secondly the concept will need to be supported and fostered by other dioceses themselves beyond North Queensland, Carpentaria, and the Northern Territory. A very grave responsibility rests on the remaining dioceses of the Anglican church to encourage and foster the acceptance of cultural episcopacy within the relevant cultural groups in their midst, and to do nothing to hinder the access of such bishops to such cultural groups seeking their episcopal ministrations. Otherwise a very grave responsibility will rest upon them of preventing the assistant bishops from growing into what we argued that they should be, namely genuine cultural bishops, and we will incur the very grave fault as a church of having strangled at birth the very clearly expressed aspirations of our indigenous peoples. If the Anglican communion becomes responsible for such a failure, it will be, I am sure, not so much deliberate, but a failure to see the connection between the importance that it attributes to the enculturalization of the gospel, and the enculturalization of Order.

We saw in Chapter 1 that the most glaring example of that failure was the 1988 Lambeth Conference, whose pre-conference material was the Report of the Inter-Anglican Theological and Doctrinal Commission, entitled *For the Sake of the Kingdom* , which properly emphasized the enculturalization of the Gospel.[1] The Final Report of the Lambeth Conference however, whilst emphasizing this theme, felt it necessary to record the traditional Anglican position that two bishops with overlapping territories was a potential source of disunity, but to which exception could be made in certain, limited pastoral exigencies.[2]

---

[1] Inter-Anglican Theological and Doctrinal Commission, *For the Sake of the Kingdom*, (London: Anglican Consultative Council 1986), p. 34, 44-47, 49.
[2] The Lambeth Conference 1988, *The Truth Shall Make You Free: Reports, Resolutions, and Pastoral Letters from the Bishops*, (London:

It has been the object of this monograph to demonstrate that the concept of cultural *episcope* cannot be so limited, particularly in view of antithetical themes in patristic tradition which survived the Irenaean revolution, though perhaps not the Gregorian.

It is not without relevance to our thesis to reflect on how indeed post Gregorian is the Anglican view of episcopacy reflected in the reluctance of a succession of Lambeth Conferences to regard *episcope* in any other terms than geographical ones. If we read the works of immediate, post-Reformation controversialists regarded the validity of Anglican Orders, we find that the issue is argued out on both sides on jurisdictional lines. While *Apostolicae Curae* in 1895 may have made an alleged defect of form and intention critical, such considerations only arose relatively late in the controversy amongst the contemporaries of the 18th Century Gallican, the Abbe Couraiyer.[3] The earlier fabrication of the Nag's Head fable, moreover, had its origin around 1605.[4] Undoubtedly the original focus of the debate was whether two bishops could be validly bishops where only one had been given, and only one could be given, lawful juris-diction.

The argument then proceeded within the parameters that we have seen, in Chapter 5, to have been set by Gregory VII. Although the issue of identity of doctrine between past and present bishops were raised, and passages from the New Testament and Fathers exchanged on both sides, the prominent and critical issue was whether or not "lawful" jurisdiction could only be given by the Pope. On such grounds, regardless of validity of matter, form, intention, and the rite used, Bonner insisted that Horn his reformed successor could not be a real bishop.[5]

That this was the original and prime objection to Anglican Orders can be seen in Jewel's *Apology,* in the passage where he

---

Anglican Consultative Council 1988), Ecumenical Relations sect. 38-40, cf. 41-42 with the final compromise of 43. See also chapter 1.

[3] P.F. Couraiyer, *A Disertation on the Validity of the Ordinations of the English,* (Oxford: Parker 1844), originally published March 14th, 1742, see also the *Memoire of the Abbé Renaudot,* idem p. 27-28.

[4] Ibid. p. 43-45.

[5] J.J. Hughes, *Absolutely Null and Utterly Void,* (London: Sheed and Ward 1968), p. 16-18. Cf. F. Clarke, *The Eucharistic Sacrifice and the Reformation,* (Devon: Augustine Publishing House 1980).

replies to Harding.[6] Harding claimed that the Church of England was "without priests made with lawful laying on of hands."[7] What he means by "lawful" becomes clear when he says that "St. Peter's chair is to the New Law that which Moses' chair was to the Old Law."[8] Jewel then replies:

> We deny not the consecration of three bishops. We deny not the confirmation of the Metropolitan. We ourselves are consecrated and so confirmed. The matter that lieth between us is this: "Whether through the whole Church of Christ no man may be allowed for a bishop without the confirmation of the Pope?[9]

There then follows a long list of the Fathers on whether or not or not the bishop of Rome possessed jurisdiction over England or not.[10]

There is therefore a direct apologetical line between the first 16th Century and final 19th Century defenses of the Church of England in Gregorian and jurisdictional terms. Such defenses in their final form were made by Palmer in the mid nineteenth century to Wiseman. They involved demonstrating that there were bishops in England before the Italian Mission of Gregory Ist so that Papal jurisdiction was a usurped jurisdiction.[11]

There is moreover a direct link between such apologetic, and the reluctance of the Anglican Diocese of Sydney to admit the cultural bishop of Aotearoa to minister to Maoris there on the ground that any soul within the domain of his territorial jurisdiction ought only receive the ministrations of the lawful, territorial bishop. Indeed, the Report on Ordination of that same diocese regards the presbyter as head of the local congregation as the supreme interpreter of the apostolic faith, and the bishop's role as supplying purely the appropriate "lawful authority" for the

---

[6] J. Jewel, Apologia Ecclesiae Anglicanae, in *The Works of John Jewel: The Third Portion*, (Cambridge: Parker Society 1848).

[7] Ibid. p. 320.

[8] Ibid. p. 325.

[9] Ibid. p. 320.

[10] Ibid. p. 331. See also Fulke's reply to Stapleton in *Fulke's Answers*, (Cambridge: Parker Society 1848), p. 1-27.

[11] W. Palmer, *The Apostolical Jurisdiction and Succession of the Episcopacy in the British Churches Vindicated*, (London: Rivington 1840).

presbyter's appointment.[12] The ghost of Gregory VII could indeed smile wrilely as he watches a highly protestant diocese interpret the New Testament in terms of categories of his own medieval devising!

Let us make no mistake, therefore, about how potentially radical a cultural and representative concept of episcopacy is. For although so far in the Anglican diocese of North Queensland we have chosen to realize our proposal just about within the confines of our existing canon law structures for the creation of assistant bishops, the concept itself contains the seeds of possible developments which will challenge our traditional theological formulations regarding the nature of episcopacy, and regarding which the 1988 Lambeth Conference was perhaps understandably nervous. This should not however disturb us. Already the traditional, Anglican concept of jurisdiction has undergone a somewhat conservative modification since the creation of suffragan bishops in the last century in England, and an even more radical one in such an example as bishops to the armed forces in many parts of the world. Already within the geographical area of dioceses, whether Anglican or Catholic, there are chapels of the armed forces with chaplains who owe their canonical obedience to another episcopal jurisdiction than that of the See bishop of the geographical territory. But it would be plainly absurd to think that such examples could even be approximately equivalent in what they presuppose theologically to a cultural episcopate in which the bishop represents, in a deeply spiritual and sacramental sense, a people and their inseparable culture. But we saw in Chapter 1, however, that although Rome remains wedded to the geographical model of *episcope* regarding the bishops *in partibus infidelium*, Vatican II granted equal status to Eastern rite bishops, to be found also in North America, who are in our sense cultural bishops.

But in all my reflections on this specific issue, I have been impressed throughout that its resolution in cultural terms has wider ecumenical implications too. I am convinced that I have not simply been wrestling with the problem of integrating into the life of the church of one particular group of indigenous people,

---

[12] Archbishop J. Robinson, Ds M. Rogers, and others, *Ordination*, (Sydney: Anglican Ir formation Office 1978).

in one denomination in one part of the world. The problem of re-integration is identical with the problem of the proper and fully sacramental means of reuniting the divided church of the twenti-eth century. And what stands in the way of that reintegration is a truncated theology of *episcope* held by the albeit majority epis-copalian group of Roman Catholics, Orthodox and Anglicans, and which makes the essence of that concept one of territorial jurisdiction. In the light of this, assistant bishops can never be regarded as "real" bishops, and they can never for example sit in the House of Bishops in an Anglican General Synod, because they have no jurisdiction. It will be clear that I believe that such a setting of jurisdiction against a sacramental ordering frankly ab-surd.

But let us now turn to the second practical example which I presaged at the beginning of this chapter, namely ecumenical reconciliation and how the sacral and representative view of cul-tural *episcope* propounded in this book will overcome the very ecumenical divisions that the jurisdictional view is perpetuating.

2. *Cultural episcope and ecumenical reconciliation*

Having established the fact of our imprisonment in episcopacy defined in terms of territorial jurisdiction, whether Roman or Anglican, it is now time to show how my cultural and represen-tative thesis points the way out of that imprisonment.

In this section we wish to draw the implications for such a theology in terms of our ecumenical dialogue with non-episcopal churches in a way that will show a parallelism of significance for the dialogue that is establishing cultural episcopates for the Aboriginal and Torres Straits Islander Peoples.

There were examples of two bishops over a given jurisdiction in the early church such as the proposal to end the Meletian schism. Meletius proposed to Paulinus that the holy gospels be laid on the bishop's throne instead of one of them sitting there, and that they would be joint shepherds until either one of them died. Subsequent to the death of the survivor, one catholic suc-cessor would be consecrated in the usual way. A similar pro-

posal was made by the catholics and Augustine to the Donatists
at Carthage in order to try to end their schism.[13]

There is a parallel between Meletius' proposal and the liturgical reception of the Pope at Canterbury Cathedral in 1982.
Neither he nor the Archbishop of Canterbury occupied the chair
of St. Augustine on that occasion, but an illuminated ancient
codex of the gospels. And this example shows quite graphically
how the mechanism for healing our disunity will be through the
acceptance of two or more bishops mutually recognizing that,
though they are representatives of distinct Christian traditions,
nevertheless they are both representatives of the catholic and
apostolic faith, even though they and their flocks occupy the
same territorial boundaries. Both communities come to see in
each other's life, doctrine and orders that there are found there
valid extensions of the incarnation that are the mark of the true
church.

But what of non-episcopal churches in this regard as they seek
reconciliation with the historic episcopate as the ancient focus of
the Church's unity? They too will eventually therefore be asking
episcopal communions to consecrate those of their ministers
who, like the President of the Methodist Conference or the
Moderator of the General Assembly of the Church of Scotland,
are endeavouring to fulfil episcopal functions. Many episcopalians may believe that such consecrations are indispensable to
the recovery of our lost unity because the episcopate, or rather
the three-fold Order of bishops, priests, and deacons, constitute
the *esse* of the church. In such an eventuality, of course, we
would once again, as the ill-fated schemes for reunion have suggested, be faced with more than one episcopal representative in
one geographical location in communion with one another as
with Paulinus and Meletius, or earlier with Polycarp and Victor.
But we should not let our grounds for asserting the indispensability for such consecrations pass without drawing out their relation to the central, cultural and representational argument of
this paper.

---

[13] Theodoret, *E.H.* 5. The significance of the Meletian schism should not
be overlooked. It marked the first schism between East and West in
Ambrose's time (381), when the Council of Constantinople supported the
Meletians, whilst the Council of Aquileia supported the Paulinists.

Our grounds have nothing to do with validity as traditionally conceived. Our concept of episcopacy is an instrument of ecumenical healing rather than one which judges the schisms of past history. We recognize that the broken unity of the church at the Reformation, and subsequently, was the result of the church's loss of catholicity so that in schism lost features of the Church's life and doctrine came to be emphasized, albeit in a fragmented and truncated form. Christ's body which is the church, being broken by our disunity, exhibits therefore a broken catholicity, in which Christ the incarnate *logos* cannot be born into the church as the extension of his incarnation as he wills to be born. As through our ecumenical endeavours we are seeking to restore that broken catholicity by gathering together the broken fragments of our devotion and witness into one whole Body of Christ, so we are giving a new and enriched content to those invariant formal features of the church that are the threefold Order of bishops, priests, and deacons, and making them what they ought to be in the unity of the catholic faith. But how does a concept of cultural episcopacy function as an instrument of reconciliation on such a view of catholicity?

Our theology of cultural episcopacy assists us to see how we should regard the liturgical arrangements bringing to an end our divisions. Were episcopalians to simply say to non-episcopal churches that their bishops will, after re-union, ordain all future sacred ministers as they would conditionally ordain their present ones, they would simply be asking for submission and no real re-union. Non-episcopal churches must have the power themselves for their own self-respect to create their own serving deacons and sacrificing priests, without being dependent on what they would regard as another church with other traditions. So undoubtedly those who ordain in what are at present non-episcopal bodies would receive consecration at the hands of episcopalian bishops, as episcopalians would receive recognition from them in a liturgical act of mutual reconciliation. Their assemblies and conferences would, therefore, in that eventuality have the same role in nominating for the episcopate as have Anglican Synods outside England. But the justification for these arrangements is not principally the desire to avoid pique and human pride, however understandable. It is a cultural argument.[14]

By so consecrating bishops for them episcopalians would be recognizing that the differently expressed traditions of non-episcopal churches bear the marks of the extension of the incarnation which is Christ formed in them. It is, however, the incarnation in a culture expressed in that culture's own style of proclamation, devotion, and liturgy. By consecrating those who represented those cultures we would be reclaiming that of Christ which is incarnated in them and which we are without. Such a church yet to be born will therefore consist of bishops as they were in the ancient catholic church, namely representatives of their people to those outside their dioceses. But their dioceses will be culturally based in terms of different historical traditions, like those catholic churches of the Eastern rite, and not territorially so.

From a sociological perspective, the breakup of church unity at the Reformation can be understood in terms of those social currents which created a pluralistic society. It is arguable that, unless our thinking regarding ecumenical relations takes account of those social currents, and acknowledges what it has become fashionable to describe as a "tolerable pluralism," then our changed social structures will defeat moves towards unity. Once again, our model of cultural episcopacy will assist in coming to terms with the kind of social structure which distinguishes the modern from the medieval world. In Chapter 2 and Chapter 5 we explored a possible Durkheimian model of social solidarity which would explain and positively license such a change. We saw that the classical concept of jurisdictional and geographical episcopacy presupposed a way in which individuals were integrated with social wholes through what Durkheim described as mechanical solidarity. That kind of principle of social integration will clearly be disfunctional in industrial and post-industrial societies which presuppose different, organic patterns of social integration. We saw moreover, that a cultural model for *episcope*

---

[14] For a brief discussion of the problems of intercommunion, see N. Lash, *His Presence in the World*, (London: Sheed and Ward 1968), p.190-199 ff. See also N. Lash and J. Rhymer (Ed.), *The Christian Priesthood: 9th Downside Symposium*, (London: Darton, Longman and Todd 1970).

assumed far more the cognitive and epistemological stances of a society integrated organically.

And thus our discussion leads us to our third practical application for the concept of cultural *episcope*, namely the situation between the Anglican dioceses created by the decisions of some dioceses to proceed piecemeal with the ordination of women to the presbyterate and episcopate, without others who are refusing so to act.

3. *Cultural episcope and the ordination of women*

The classical, jurisdictional and territorial concept of episcopacy is in a high state of disintegration within the Anglican communion in yet a third area, namely the ordination of women. The mutual recognition of Orders between the dioceses, on which the whole notion of "communion" and "fellowship" or *koinonia* rests, is threatened by the action of dioceses and provinces of the Anglican communion, lead by the divided and small Episcopal church of the United States, to ordain unilaterally and without achieving first any general consensus within the communion as a whole. This situation I consider to be highly regrettable[15], as I have commented elsewhere, particularly since such unilateral action must in Rome's eyes appear to falsify all that our theologians appeared to agree with them them in what was said about *koinonia* in ARCIC's *Final Report*. But the problem does not stop there. Within dioceses there are parishes who feel that they are not "with their bishop" on this issue. Are they to go into schism on this issue and to join such bodies as the Anglican Catholic Church of Canada or the U.S.A, or its offshoots in Australia and New Zealand or elsewhere?

Predictably this issue has generated more heat than light, and the current level of the discussion on both sides often is reminiscent of a medieval heresy hunt. The spiritual Franciscans of the middle ages, for example, were burned because, in disavowing the ownership of material possessions as necessary to salvation, they were held quite falsely to be also disavowing the incarna-

---

[15] A. Brent, The Crisis of Authority in the Anglican Communion, in D. Wetherell, *Women Priests in Australia, the Anglican Crisis*, (Melbourne: Spectrum 1987), p. 1-20.

tion. So any opponent of the ordination of women, despite his or her protest to the contrary, is likely equally falsely to be regarded as in favour of sexual discrimination in other areas of economic and professional life. The alarming ecumenical dimension to the debate, and one which the present writer finds himself in great sympathy with, is best expressed by the Catholic Cardinal Archbishop of Westminster. Basil Hume has frequently asserted that the Anglican communion cannot on the one hand claim that it accepts the conclusions of ARCIC on authority, namely that *koinonia* means that we do nothing apart that we cannot agree to do together, and then proceed to decide an issue as fundamental as ordination in a unilateral way.

But in many ways the current talk of "schism" in dread tones, with rending of hearts about being unable to gather at the one altar, is curiously bizarre. In our present ecumenical situation, we quite frequently gather for prayer with those whose Orders we cannot in conscience recognize, and have discussions on such things as the Lima *Statement* and *Liturgy*. At key moments in the ecclesiastical year we enjoy together non-Eucharist worship. Monastic Orders, whether Anglican, Orthodox, or Roman have a great and ecumenically mixed following regarding retreats which are popular.

Now if a parish or group of parishes opt out of the territorial jurisdiction of their diocesan and look for another as his rival, what they immediately do is to seek membership of the local council of churches, and re-enter the area of ecumenical dialogue. Furthermore, those who remain with their bishop can hardly with reason maintain their anger with those who have refused to recognize their bishop's ordinations and left, and who are thereby out of communion with them and under another bishop. They do, after all, regularly enjoy a limited fellowship with some churches who do not recognize their Orders, and with others whose Orders in turn they do not formally recognize themselves. Furthermore, they yearn to extend dialogue and fellowship more fully to the Eucharist on the ecumenical occasions and in the ecumenical ventures such as I mentioned in the last paragraph.

The obstacle, once again, is the territorial and jurisdictional model of episcopacy that we have inherited from the middle

ages, with its presupposition of a mechanical form of social integration. We can only hold together by everyone behaving the
same, recognizing identical and specific values and substantive
norms, etc. The central value system must pervade all areas of
life and activity. As a result, the two thirds majority must beat
into conformity the one third minority or force it to split off,
leaving it without a valid bishops since there can only be one
valid bishop per geographical territory.

On the view of cultural *episcope* as I have argued it in this
monograph, I can see something sad but hardly horrendous in a
group of parishes in these circumstances seeking another bishop
whom they see reflecting their traditions, values, way of life,
and style of devotion and spirituality. Rather than expulsion
from their parish properties, it would seem far more wholesome,
and far more facilitative of ultimate reconciliation to allow them
their own cultural bishop.

In such circumstances, rather than a schism taking place that
isolates the two communities between the walls of two exhaustively defined collective consciousnesses mutually insulated
against each other, the dialogue can remain open, and at a reasonably ecumenical hearing distance. The community can feel
that it is being recognized in the mutual and continuing dialogue
of representative episcopal persons. "Their whole multitude" can
be seen in their bishop being valued in a dialogue of mutual respect, albeit one that falls short of full communion, just as that of
Trallians was in bishop Polybius. The divided Anglican communion in this way can seek dynamically reintegration within a
common, Christian form of life that is characterized by organic
solidarity, and the social functioning of cultural *episcope* as we
have described it in this monograph.

4. *In conclusion*

We have seen in this chapter that our argument for *episcope* and
its cultural representation is a quite general one, and does not
treat Australia's indigenous peoples, or those of anywhere else,
as a special case. I have, moreover, argued that the 1988
Lambeth Conference was quite wrong to have done this. My
quite general argument has been that any distinctively Christian
culture, however personally antipathetic we may be towards its

appearance, even one that is contra feminist, should be represented by a distinct cultural episcopate for almost identical reasons to those for which non-episcopal churches will be given their own bishops in ecumenical re-union.

We have shown in justification of our thesis that the doctrine of the church as the extension of the incarnation implies a doctrine of church Order as displaying and expressing itself as such through what Ignatius of Antioch saw as representative τύποι of a community's common-life. We saw that Order was not so much imposed by dominical ordinance, for which there is no historical warrant, but by the growth of Christian, cultural self-identity in terms of what Durkheim called the collective representations of the collective consciousness. Though the Logos-Spirit is given to the whole community through the apostles, and the whole community thus re-expresses the light, life, glory, healing, forgiveness and judgment of Christ's incarnation, that re-expression takes place through Order which properly called sacramental because it is part of the process by which the Word is made Flesh in the church which is the Body of Christ. In fact for such a process the word "re-express" is wholly inadequate. It is inadequate because it is not simply the revelation given that is re-expressed, but the relationship of the one to whom it is given to the one who reveals it.

The Church which has received the Spirit from the apostles must therefore express not only what it has received, and what that which it had received in turn reveals, but also its union with the apostolic *paradosis* in what they have given and revealed. That *paradosis*, we argued, had originally, in the New Testament and early Fathers, an individualistically apostolic form, whether Johannine, Petrine, Jacobean, or Pauline, which was to some extent distorted by the post-Irenaean and post Gregorian revolutions.

A more traditional, sacramental concept than that of representation is re-presentation.[16] In the eucharistic sacrifice, according to the medieval mind, the words and acts of the priest both represent the offering made once and for all upon the altar of the cross, but also, in another sense, "re-present" that offering to the

---

[16] See Lash (1968) op.cit. p. 58-63 ff.

Father by spreading it forth to him in *anamnesis*. So the Church, receiving of the Spirit through the Apostles, and united with the triune God incarnate in Jesus of Nazareth, is represented and re-presented by the τύποι of her sacred ministers. In a word, the sacred ministry represents the total sacramental fact of the incarnation that constitutes the church as the extension of the incarnation. The fundamental defect in the medieval view was that the whole eucharistic action was seen to be something done for the people by an almost magically conceived transaction between the individual priest and God. By stressing the representative role of what in Ignatian terms was the threefold typology, I have endeavoured, with insights derived from Schillebeeckx, sought to show (in Chapter 2) the connection of the whole people of God in the eucharistic act, and to delineate its social and cultural dimensions.

At the conclusion of this book, I would like to make a statement which is more of a plea than an argument. It is a plea not only to the Anglican communion but to the whole Western Church, whether located either territorially or culturally in the eastern or western Mediterranean. It is a plea to learn the lesson of the Donatist experience.

Newman, as is well known, finding in 1844 that there was little to distinguish his argument for Anglicanism from that for Donatism in the fourth century, converted to Rome. In so doing, he alas applied a similar Donatist vision to what he found there also. But what precisely do I mean by the Donatist vision?

Augustine from his consecration as Bishop of Hippo (A.D. 395) until the Collatio of Carthage (A.D. 410) was an inveterate foe of the Donatist church. In looking at the subject of Anglican attitudes and what they should be to cultural episcopacy, it may be illuminating to ask why Augustine was so opposed to them. The Donatist Church was highly orthodox, as least to the extent that the pre-Nicene Fathers defined orthodoxy, and its differences with the catholic church were solely ones of the apparent laxity of the latter to the lapsed in time of persecution, and its lack of discipline over its communicants in time of peace. It had an impeccable line of of bishops that went back in unbroken succession to the apostles through Cyprian, whose episcopate had witnessed the beginnings of a breach, which was only to become actual at the consecration of a rival bishop to Caecilian after A.D.313. Thus it had valid orders and orthodox doctrine, and even a liturgy which was not that different from the liturgy of the catholic church.

In all this it was not unlike, in many respects, the present Anglican communion, according to some of its defenders. It was undoubtedly the largest Christian group in North Africa, certainly larger than the minuscule catholic church whose bishops nevertheless enjoyed communion with the remaining dioceses of the Mediterranean world. It represented Christianity according to the culture and tradition of that one group of nations in its great universities and magnificent basilicas. It stood for apostolic truth and Order against corrupting catholic influences against which it defended itself, albeit in days before Roman casuistry was to attack the validity of the Orders of such churches, and before the Bishop of Rome assumed the kinds of pretensions that a few of the later occupants of that See were perhaps guilty.

Certainly the Donatist Church of North Africa would not have welcomed the bishop of Rome should he ever have deigned to visit that province, any more than Marcus Loane as Archbishop of Sydney was willing to welcome the Pope. Then what, according to Augustine did it lack? It lacked a catholic vision that could embrace all mankind beyond the particular limitations of its historical and cultural origins in a small group of North African nations. And here a potential and dangerous similarity might, if we are not careful, be drawn not only with the Anglican communion, but with the whole Western Church.

In a nutshell, the Donatist symbol of the church represented its truncated vision of Christian truth. The characteristic symbol of the Donatists was the ark of Noah. What are the implications about the character of a church with an obsession with such a symbol? It is a church that is content with the doctrine that so very few can be saved. It is a church that sees its mission in building carefully its defenses against the wrath of God that is to come. It is a self-protective church, making itself and its members warm, dry, well-fed and secure, with limited space for anyone else in its well-protected bark. It is a comfortable and small self-satisfied group, well content with its own salvation, as the mass of the nations of mankind wend their remorseless and hell-bent way towards the floods of divine judgment and destruction. If the church is an ark, then one can pitch it within and without against the storms of this world, and one can slam shut the doors against all who try to enter. Augustine claimed that such a church was not so much judging as being judged by the Christian experience of a wider humanity beyond its narrow historical and cultural confines that it so biggotedly condemned.

But it is not to the Anglican communion alone that the Donatist example and Augustine's reply is pertinent. It applies to the whole Western Church whether Anglican, Catholic, Orthodox or Reformed. It is significant from the point of view of the present Australian location in the Pacific region to ponder how our thinking in terms of theology, history, or the presentation of the gospel is confined by the cultural experience of the Mediterranean civilization in which the Word was historically made flesh.

We speak of the "Western Church" by which we mean the western European Church of Northern and Southern Europe, of Canterbury, Rome and so forth. We speak of the "Eastern" church by which we mean the Orthodox communion of Greece, Eastern Europe, and Russia, Asia Minor, the Near East, which at this geographical distance on any realistic estimation would make it little more than the eastern European church. And the success of our missionary activity in Far Eastern and Asian cultures, whether that activity be Anglican, Roman, Orthodox, or Reformed, appears very related to the problem of how to express the Word made flesh in the thought forms and authority structures of one set of cultures to another quite different set of cultures to which they appear quite alien.

To the gospel as proclaimed by the heirs of our Mediterranean civilization, and the attitudes of cultural and religious superiority that goes with it, Augustine's strictures against the attitudes and piety of the Donatists surely apply. "Close up your ark, pitch it within and without, bolt fast the doors, but know that the world finds you wanting, and the judgment of the wide world stands sure."

If history teaches us anything about the nature of the Anglican communion it is surely that positive and determined action often takes a painfully long time to follow our initial grasp of what

God is revealing to us regarding the nature of the church, its Orders of ministry, and their role in the salvation of mankind. The issue of cultural episcopacy in which the Australian church has now hesitantly embarked is no exception. The century after Cranmer's death saw the slow evolution within the Anglican consciousness of the extent to which the attacks of Roman controversialists had misrepresented the true nature of the Anglican episcopate. The Anglican consciousness was formed during that period in the twin crucibles of puritan attacks upon our Ordinal and subsequent schisms on the one hand, and the judicial murder of Archbishop Laud (1645) on the other, by a presbyterian Parliament which had no knowledge of, nor would have respected if it had, the later doctrine of the Separation of Powers.

In such a crucible as this the Anglican consciousness finally assumed the fully developed form in which it made this unequivocal assertion. Our bishops were not "parliamentary bishops," those irrelevant and insipid creatures of the secular and civil power, but the heirs and successors of the apostles in life, doctrine, Order, and tradition, and that it was to such sources and not to appointment by the state that they owed their spiritual authority in the church of God. It has of course taken us more than a century of critical historical and theological study to convince us that the "apostolic succession," like the "apostolic doctrine," had not the straightforwardly legitimating function that Irenaeus claimed for it, and so to escape the bewitchment of the Irenaean reification of the *paradosis*.

But though informed by such a consciousness, did those bishops now consecrate bishops in the church of God throughout the world wherever a nascent church was to be found, irrespective of where the authority of the British state ran or did not run? The truth is that before Manning and others founded the Colonial Bishoprics Fund in 1841, there were only six colonial bishops throughout the vast British Empire. It had taken the fully formed Anglican consciousness some two centuries to express itself in action. It is essential we do not become pulverized into a similar inactivity in the present case.

If we do become so pulverized, it will be the transmission of the gospel and the administration of the sacraments that will suffer, and with it the representative ministry, developing from the shared experience of salvation of the whole people of God and for the salvation of mankind. We have witnessed in the twentieth century how the missionary triumphalism of the nineteenth century has given way to the black despair of the twentieth, as the extension of the church throughout the world has continually encountered difficulties the farther both regionally and culturally the gospel tries to advance beyond the Mediterranean European and near Eastern cultures where the church first came into being.

We can of course apply eurocentric categories and assume that this must be because Asian and Far Eastern peoples and their cultures are inherently more perverse, and their vision more jaundiced, than European and near Eastern ones. Or we can trace our major failure to communicate Christ's gospel, in word and liturgical act, to the alien character of our thought forms, as well as cultural expressions and artifacts within such cultures. It is because the second must surely be the case that, together with that other Western, liturgically-based church, the church of Rome, we are now seeking that process known to liturgical scholars as the "indigenization of liturgy." Here liturgy is allowed to take on the form of the culture which celebrates it, as we believe Order must be allowed also so to do.

We believe that in liturgy the word is not simply made word, but rather the word is made flesh. It is made flesh in the process of taking on the cultural forms in which it is being expressed. But the word is made flesh in a far deeper and sacramental sense than this bare statement suggests. The church is the extension of the incarnation and, when the church is extended across cultural frontiers, it must be allowed to express that extension in cultural terms. The church as the extension of the incarnation thus becomes the extension of the incarnation in a culture, and the ministerial ikons of its common life will bear the image of that life in a cultural form.

The Real Presence of Christ in the world is for all human cultures and not simply those around the Mediterranean ocean. Let us, I pray, not be judged as unequal to this task for which I have sought, no doubt hopelessly inadequately, to provide some of the historical, sociological and theological resources.

SELECT BIBLIOGRAPHY

1. *Texts*

Audet J.-P., *La Didaché: Instructions des Apôtres*, (Paris: Libraire Lecoffre 1958).

Bardy G., Eusèbe de Césarée: Histoire Ecclésiastique, Livres I-IV. Texte Grec, Traduction et Annotation, in *SC* 31 (Paris: Les Éditions du Cerf 1952).

—— , Eusèbe de Césarée: Histoire Ecclésiastique, Livre VII Texte Grec, Traduction et Annotation, in *SC* 41 (Paris: Les Éditions du Cerf 1955).

—— , Eusèbe de Césarée: Histoire Ecclésiastique, Livres VIII-X., et Les Martyrs en Palestine. Texte Grec, Traduction et Notes, in *SC* 55 (Paris: Les Éditions du Cerf 1958).

Botte B., Hippolyte de Rome: La Tradition Apostolique, in *SC* 11 (Paris: Les Éditions du Cerf 1968).

Colgrave B. and Myers R.A.B., *Bede Ecclesiastical History of the English People.*, (Oxford: Clarendon Press 1969).

Camelot P. Th., Ignace d'Antioche, Polycarpe de Smyrne, Lettres, Martyre de Polycarpe. Texte Grec, Introduction, traduction, et notes, in *SC* 10 (Paris: Les Éditions du Cerf 1950)

Connolly R. Hugh, *Didascalia Apostolorum: The Syriac Version Translated and accompanied by the Verona Latin Fragments*, (Oxford: Clarendon Press 1929).

Corpus Scriptorum Ecclesiasticorum Latinorum, (Wien: 1866-).

Dix G., *The Treatise on the Apostolic Tradition of St. Hippolytus of Rome*, Reissued with corrections, preface, and bibliography by H. Chadwick, (London: S.P.C.K. 1968).

Feldman L.H., *Josephus: Jewish Antiquities*, Loeb Classical Library, (Cambridge Massachusetts: Harvard University Press 1919).

Funk F.X., *Didascalia et Constitutiones Apostolorum*, (Turin: Bottega d'Erasmo 1979).

Hartel G., Cyprian. Opera omnia recensuit et commentario critico instruxit. 3 partes, in *CSEL* 2 and 3, (Wien: 1868-71).

Jaubert A., Clément de Rome. Épître aux Corinthiens. Introduction, Texte, Traduction, Notes, et Index, in *SC* 167 (Paris: Les Éditions du Cerf 1971).

Lighfoot J.B., *St. Paul's Epistle to the Philippians*. A revised text with introduction, notes, and dissertations. Fourth Ed., (London: MacMillan 1878).

Lightfoot J.B., *The Apostolic Fathers, Part 1 Clement of Rome;* Vols I and II, *Part 2 St. Ignatius and St. Polycarp,* Vols I and II Revised Texts with

218   SELECT BIBLIOGRAPHY

introductions, notes, dissertations and translations. Second Ed., (London: MacMillan 1889-90).
Migne J.-P. Patrologiae: *Cursus Completus.* Series 1 Graeca-Latina and Series 2 Latina, (Belgium: Brepols-Turnhout 1965-).
Monumenta Germaniae Historica. *Libelli de Lite.* Vols I-III. (Hanover: 1826-).
Reifferscheid A. and Wissowa G., Tertulliani Opera, in *CSEL* (Wien 1890).
Rousseau A. and Doutreleau L., Irénée de Lyon: Contre Les Hérésies, Livre II Tome II Texte et Traduction, in *SC* 294 (Paris: Les Éditions du Cerf 1982).
Rousseau A., with Hammerdinger B., Doutreleau L., and Mercier C., Irénée de Lyon: Contre Les Hérésies, Livre IV Tome I Introduction, Notes Justifications, Tables, Tome II Texte et Traduction, in *SC* 100, (Paris: Les Éditions du Cerf 1965).
Sagnard F., Irénée de Lyon: Contre Les Hérésies, Livre III. Texte Latin, Fragments Grecs, Introduction, Traduction et Notes, in *SC* 34 (Paris: Les Éditions du Cerf 1952).
Sources Chrétiennes, (Paris: Les Éditions du Cerf 1942-).
Thackeray H.St.J., *Josephus: The Jewish War,* Loeb classical Library, (Cambridge, Massachusetts: Harvard University Press). 1919).

2. *Dictionaries and Encyclopaedias*

Cross F.L. (Ed.), *The Oxford Dictionary of the Christian Church*, (London: Oxford University Press 1957).
Herbermann C.G. et.al. (Ed.), *The Catholic Encyclopaedia*, (New York: Encyclopedia Press 1912).
Hardon J.A. (Ed.), *A New Catholic Dictionary*, (New York: Doubleday 1980).
Kittel G. (ed.), *Theologisches Wörterbuch zum Neuen Testament; in Verbindung mit O. Bauernfeind, F. Baumgärtel, J. Behm*, (Stuttgart: Kohlhammer 1933-).
Kittel E.G. (Ed.), *Theological Dictionary of the New Testament*, tran G. Bromiley, (Grand Rapids, Michigan: Eerdmans 1959).
Lampe G.W. (Ed.), *A Patristic Greek Lexicon*, (Oxford: Clarendon Press 1961).
Rahner K. (Ed.), *Encyclopedia of Theology*, (London: Burns Oates 1975).
—— , *Theologische Realenzyklopädie*, (Berlin: Walter de Gruyter 1978–).

3. *Philosophical and Sociological Studies*

Aron R., *Main Currents in Sociological Thought*, (London: Penguin 1970) Vol.II.
Bambrough R., Universals and Family Resemblances, in *Proceedings of the Aristotelian Society*, 60 (1960-1), p. 207-222.
Berger P., and Luckman T., *The Social Construction of Reality*, (London: Penguin 1967).

——— , *A Rumor of Angels*, (London: Penguin 1971).

——— , *The Social Reality of Religion*, (London: Penguin 1973).

Bernstein B., Peters R.S., and Elvin L., Ritual in Education, in *Philosophical Transactions of the Royal Society of London*, Series B Vol. 251 No. 772 (1966.)

Bernstein B., Open School, Open Society?, in *New Society*, Sept. 14 (1967).

——— , On the Classification and Framing of Educational Knowledge, in M.F.D. Young, *Knowledge and Control*, (London: Collier MacMillan 1971).

Brent A., *Philosophical Foundations for the Curriculum*, (London: Allen and Unwin 1978).

——— , *Philosophy and Educational Foundations*, (London: Allen and Unwin 1983).

Chomsky N., *Aspects of the Theory of Syntax*, Massacheussets: M.I.T. Press 1965).

——— , *Language and Mind*, (New York: Harcourt, Bracc and Jovanovich 1968).

——— , *Problems of Knowledge and Freedom. Trinity College Cambridge. Bertrand Russell Memorial Lectures 1971*, (New York: Random 1971).

——— , *The Logical Structure of Linguistic Theory*, (Chicago: Chicago University Press 1975).

——— , *Reflections on Language*, (London: Pantheon 1976).

Durkheim E., *Les formes élementaires de la vie religieuse: le système totémique en Australie*, (Paris: Alcan 1912).

——— , *The Division of Labor in Society*, Trans. G. Simpson, (New York: MacMillan 1933).

Hudson W.D.A., *A Philosophical Approach to Religion*, (London: MacMillan 1974).

Kaplan D., and Manners R.A., *Culture Theory*, (New Jersey: Prentice-Hall 1972).

Katz J.J., *Semantic Theory*, (New York: Harper 1972).

Kroeber A.L., and Kluckhohn C., *Culture: A Critical Review of Concepts and Definitions*, (Cambridge Mass: Harvard University Press 1952).

Leach E., and Aycock D.A., *Structuralist Interpretation of Biblical Myth.*, (Cambridge: Cambridge University Press 1983).

Lévi-Strauss C., *Structural Anthropology*, (London: Allen Lane 1968).

Lewis I.M., *Social Anthropology in Perspective*, (London: Penguin 1976).

Lukes S., *Emile Durkheim: His Life and Work* , (London: Penguin 1973).

Quine W. van O., *Word and Object*, (Cambridge Mass.: MIT Press).

Sapir E., *Language: An Introduction to the Study of Speech*, (London: Hart-Davis McGibbon 1978).

Staniland H., *Universals*, (New York: Doubleday 1972).

Tylor E.B., *Primitive Culture*, (London: John Murray 1871).

220   SELECT BIBLIOGRAPHY

Vivelo F.R., *Cultural Anthropology Handbook*, (New York: McGraw Hill 1978).
Whorf B.L., *Language, Thought and Reality*, Select Writings of B.L. Whorf Ed. J.B. Caroll, Forward S. Chase, (Cambridge Massachussets: Harvard University Press 1956).
Wittgenstein L., *On Certainty*, (Oxford: Blackwell 1969).
——— , *Philosophical Investigations*, trans. G.E.M. Anscombe, (Oxford: Blackwell 1972).
Yudkin M., On Quine's contretemps of translation, in *Mind* 88 (1979), p. 93-96.

4. Historical and Theological Studies:Patristic and Pre-Reformation

Aland K., The Problem of Anonymity and Pseudonymity in Christian Literature of the First Two Centuries, in *JThS* n.s. 12 (1969), p. 39-49.
Ash J.L., The Decline of Ecstatic Prophecy in the Early Church, in *ThS*. 37 (1978), p. 227-252.
Bammel C. Hammond, Ignatian Problems, in *JThS* n.s. 33 (1982), p. 62-97.
Bammel E., Herkunft und Funktion der Traditionselemente in 1 Kor. 15, 1-11, in *ThZ* 11 (1955), p. 401-419.
Barnard L.W., *Studies in the Apostolic Fathers and their Background*, (Blackwell: Oxford 1966).
Barrett C.K., *The Gospel According to St. John*, (London: S.P.C.K 1958).
Bauer W., Rechtgläubigkeit und Ketzerei im ältesten Christentum, in *BZHT* 10, (Tübingen: Mohr 1964).
Benson R.L., The Bishop Elect: A Study in Medieval Ecclesiastical Office, (Princeton: Princeton University Press 1988)
Berthouoz R., Le Père, le Fils, et le Saint– Espirit d'après les lettres d'Ignace d'Antioche, in *FZPhTh* 18 (1971), p. 397-418.
Bethune-Baker J.F., *An Introduction to the Early History of Christian Doctrine to the Council of Chalcedon*, (London: Methuen 1954).
Beyer H.W., ΔΙΑΚΟΝΕΩ, art., in *TWNT*., p. 81-92.
Blum G.G., *Tradition und Sukzession: Studien zum Normbegriff des Apostolischen von Paulus bis Irenäus*, (Berlin: Lutherisches Verlagshaus 1962).
Böhmer H., Zur altrömischen Bischofsliste, in *ZNW* 7 (1906), p. 333-339.
Bommes K., Weizen Gottes, Untersuchungen zur Theologie des Martyrium's bei Ignatius von Antiochien, in *Theoph* 27 (Köln-Bonn: Hanstein 1976).
Borgen P., The Early Church and the Hellenistic Synagogue, in *StTh* 37 1 (1983), p. 55-78.
Brandon S.C.F., *Jesus and the Zealots*, (Manchester: University Press 1967).
Brent A., The Investiture Controversy– an Issue in Sacramental Theology? in *EThL* 63 1 (1987), p. 59-89.
——— , Pseudonymity and Charisma in the Ministry of the Early Church, in *Aug* 27 3 (1987), p. 347-376.

—— , History and Eschatological Mysticism in Ignatius of Antioch, in *EThL*, 65 4 (1989), p. 309-329.

—— , The Relations Between Ignatius and the *Didascalia*, in *SecCent* 8,3 (1991), p. 129-156.

—— , Ecumenical Reconciliation and Cultural Episcopates, in *AThR* 72 3 (1990), p. 255-279.

Brown M.P., *The Authentic Writings of Ignatius: A Study in Linguistic Critieria*, (Durham N.C.: Duke University 1963).

Brown R.E., *Priest and Bishop: Biblical Reflections,* (London: Geoffrey Chapman 1971).

—— , and Meier J.P., *Antioch and Rome*, (New York: Paulist Press 1983).

Burke P., The Monarchical Episcopate at the End of the First Century, in *ES* 7 (1970), p. 499-518.

Campenhausen H. von, Der Urchristliche Apostelbegriff, in *StTh* Vol. 1 Fasc. I-II (1947), p. 96-130.

—— , Die Nachfolge des Jacobus, in *ZKG* 63 (1950-52), p. 133-144.

—— , *Ecclesiastical Authority and Spiritual Power in the Church of the First Three Centuries*, (London: S.P.C.K. 1969).

Carlyle R.W., and A.J., *A History of Medieval Political Theory in the West*, (London: Blackwood 1928).

Caspar E., Die älteste römische Bischofsliste, in *SGK* 2 4 (Berlin: 1926).

Clifton Black II C., The Johannine Epistles and the Question of Early Catholicism, in *NT*. 28 2 (1986), p. 131-158.

Colson J. L'Évêque dans les Communautés Primitives. Tradition paulinienne et tradition johannique de l'épiscopat des origines à Saint Irénée, in *Unam Sanctam* 21 (1951).

—— , *Les Fonctions Ecclésiales aux deux premiers siècles*, (Paris: Desclée de Brouwer 1956).

—— , *L'Épiscopat Catholique, Collégialité, et Primauté dans les trois premiers siècles de l'Église*, (Paris: Les Éditions du Cerf 1970).

Congar Y., *Lay People in the Church*, (London: Geoffrey Chapman 1965).

—— , *L' Église de Saint Augustin à l'Époque Moderne*, (Paris: Les Éditions du Cerf 1970)

Corwin V., *St. Ignatius and Christianity in Antioch*, (Yale: Yale University Press 1960).

Craig W.L., The History of the Empty Tomb of Jesus, in *NTS* Vol. 31 1985), p. 39-67.

Dassmann E., Zur Entstehung des Monepiskopats, in *JbAC* 17 (1974), p. 27-39.

Dix G., *The Shape of the Liturgy*, (London: Adam and Charles Black 1945).

Dodd C.H., *The Fourth Gospel,* (Cambridge: Cambridge University Press 1958).

Elton G.R., *England under the Tudors*, (London: Methuen 1974).

Ehrhardt A.A.J., *The Apostolic Tradition in the First Two Centuries of the Church*, (London: Lutterworth 1953).

—— , Jewish and Christian Ordination, in *JEH*. 5 (1954), p. 125-138.

Fischer J., Bibliographic Note, in *ThRev* 2 77 (1981), p. 119-222.

Frend W.C.H., *Martyrdom and Persecution in the Early Church,* (Oxford: Blackwell 1965).

—— , *The Rise of Christianity*, (London: Darton, Longman & Todd 1984).

Funk F.X., *Die Apostolischen Konstitutionen: eine literar-historische Untersuchung*, (Frankfurt/Main: Minerva GmbH 1970).

—— , *Der Primat der römischen Kirche nach Ignatius und Irenaeus: Kirchengeschichtliche Abhandlungen und Untersuchungen*, 1.Bd, (Paderborn 1897).

Gore C., *The Church and the Ministry, New Ed. revised by C.H. Turner*, London: S.P.C.K. 1919).

Grant R.M., with Freedman D.N., *The Secret Sayings of Jesus,* (London: Fontana 1960).

—— , Hermeneutics and Tradition in Ignatius of Antioch, in *ArFil* 1-2 (1963), p. 183-201.

Halleux A. de, L'Église Catholique dans la lettre Ignacienne aux Smyrniotes, in *EThL* 58 (1982), p. 5-42.

Hamilton Thompson B., The Post-Reformation Episcopate in England, in K.E Kirk (ed.) *The Apostolic Ministry*, (London: Hodder & Stoughton 1946), p. 387-432.

Harnack A., Das Zeugnis des Ignatius über das ansehen der römischen Gemeinde, in *SPAW* VII (1896).

Harrison P.N., *Polycarp's Two Epistles to the Philippians*, (Cambridge: Cambridge University Press 1936).

Hatch E., *The Organisation of the Early Christian Churches*, (London: Rivington 1882).

Hemer C.J., The Letters to the Seven Churches of Asia in their Local Setting, in *JSNT.S* 11, (Sheffield: Department of Biblical Studies 1986).

Hengel H., Jacobus der Herrenbruder- der erste Papst? in *Glaube und Eschatologie, Festschrift für W.G. Kümmel zum 80 Geburtstag*, (Tübingen: J.C. Mohr 1985), p. 71-104.

Herbert A.G., *Apostle and Bishop: A Study of the Gospel, the Ministry, and the Church Community*, (London: Faber and Faber 1963)

Holtz T., Der Antiochienische Zwischenfall (Galater 2.11-14), in *NTS* 32 (1986), p. 344-361.

Hyldahl H., Hegesipps Hypomnemata, in *StTh* 14 (1960), p. 70-113.

Joly R., *Le Dossier d'Ignace d'Antioche*, (Université Libre de Bruxelles: Faculté de Philosophie et Lettres: LXIX 1978).

Kannengiesser C., Bulletin de Théologie Patristique: Ignace d'Antioche et Irénée de Lyon, in *RSR* 67 (1979), p. 599-623.

Kingsbury J.D., The Figure of St. Peter in Matthew's Gospel as a theological problem, in *JBL* 98 (1979), p. 67-83.

Kirk K.E., *The Apostolic Ministry*, (London: Hodder and Stoughton 1948).

Köster H., Geschichte und Kultus im Johannesevangelium und bei Ignatius, in *ZThK* 54 (1957), p. 56-9.

Körtner U.H., Papias von Hierapolis, in *FRLANT* 133 (Göttingen: Vandenhoek & Ruprecht 1983).

Koestler H., ΓΝΩΜΑΙ ΔΙΑΦΟΡΟΙ: the origin and nature of diversification in the history of the early church, in *HThR* 58 (1965), p. 290-306.

Kötting V.B., Zur Frage der "successio apostolica," in *Catholica* 27 (1973), p. 234-247.

Kretschmar G., Die Ordination im Frühen Christentum, in *FZThPh* 22 (1975), p.35-69.

Kümmel W.G., Das Urchristentum. II. Arbeiten zu Spezialproblemen. d. Ämter und Amtsverständnis, in *ThR* 2 (1987), p. 111-154.

Laechli S., The Drama of Replay, in *Searching into the Syntax of Things*, (Philadelphia: Fortress Press 1972), p. 69-72.

Lampe P., Review of Körtner's *Papias of Hierapolis* , in *JbAC* 29 (1986), p. 192-194.

——, Die stadtrömischen Christen in den ersten beiden Jahrhunderten, in *WUNT* 2 18 (Tübingen: Mohr 1989).

Larson E., Die Paulinischen Schriften als Quellen zur Geschichte des Urchristentums, in *StTh* 17 (1983), p. 33-53.

Lawler H.J., *Eusebiana*, (London: Oxford University Press 1912).

Layton B., The Date, Sources, and Transmission of the Didache, in *HThR* 61 (1968), p. 343-383.

Lemaire A., Les Ministères aux Origines de l'Église: Naissance de la triple hiérarchie: évêques, presbytres, diacres, in *LeDiv* 68 (Paris: Les Éditions du Cerf 1971).

Lohse E., *Die Ordination im Spätjudentum und im Neuen Testament*, (Göttingen: Vandenhoek and Ruprecht 1951).

McArthur A., The office of a Bishop in the Ignatian Epistles and in the Didascalia Apostolorum compared, in *StudPatr* 4 (Berlin 1961) *TU.* 79, p. 298-304.

McCue J.F., The Roman Primacy in the Second Century and the Problem of Development of Dogma in *ThS* 25 (1964), p. 828-834.

—— , Bishops, Presbyters, and Priests in Ignatius of Antioch, in *ThS* 28 (1967), 161-196.

Maurer C., Ignatius von Antiochien und das Johannesevangelium, *ATANT* 18 (Zürich: Zwingli 1949).

Meinhold P., *Studien zur Ignatius von Antiochien*, Veröffentlichungen des Instituts für europäische Geschichte, (Weisbaden: Steiner 1979).

Merrill E.T., *Essays in Early Church History*, (London: MacMillan 1924).

Metzger B.M., Literary Forgeries and Pseudonymous Pseudepigrapha, in *JBL* 91 1 (1972), p. 3-24.

Munck J., Presbyters and Disciples of the Lord in Papias, in *HThR* 52 (1959), p. 223-243.

Munier C., A–propos d'Ignace d'Antioche, in *RSR* 54 (1980), p. 55-73, and 55 (1981) p. 126-131.

Nautin P., L'évolution des ministères du IIe au IIIe siècle, in *Revue de droit canonique*, 23 (1973), p. 47-58.

Newman J.H., *The Development of Christian Doctrine*, (Westminster: Christian Classics 1968).

Norris F.W., Ignatius, Polycarp, and 1 Clement: Walter Bauer reconsidered, in *VCh* 30 (1976), p. 23-44.

Padberg R., Geordnete Liebe, Amt, Pneuma, und Kirchliche Einheit bei Ignatius von Antiochien, in *Unio Christianorum. Festschrift für Erzbischof Lorenz Jager*, (Paderborn: Bonifacius 1962), p. 201-217.

——, Vom gottesdienstlichen Leben in den Briefen des Ignatius von Antiochien in *ThG* 53 (1963) p. 337-347.

——, Das Amstverständnis der Ignatiusbriefe, in *ThG* 62 (1972), p. 47-55.

Paulsen H., *Studien zur Theologie des Ignatius von Antiochien*, (Göttingen: Vandenhoek & Ruprecht 1977).

Pelikan J., *The Emergence of the Catholic Tradition (100-600)*, (Chicago: University of Chicago Press 1971).

——, *The Spirit of Eastern Christendom*, (Chicago: University of Chicago Press 1971).

——, *The Growth of Medieval Theology*, (Chicago: University of Chicago Press 1971).

——, *Reformation of Church and Dogma*, (Chicago: University of Chicago Press 1971).

Pelland G., Le dossier des lettres d'Ignace d'Antioche. A propos d'un livre récent, in *SciEsprit* 32 3 (1980), p. 261-297.

Perler O., Ignatius von Antiochien und die römische Christengemeinde, in *FZPhTh* 22 (1944), p. 413-451.

——, Das vierte Makkabäerbuch, Ignatius von Antiochien, und die ältesten Martyrberichte, in *RivAC* 9 (1949), p. 47-72.

Preiss Th., La Mystique de l'imitation de Christ et de l'unité chez Ignace d'Antioche, in *RevHPhR* 18 (1938), p. 197-241.

Prestige G.L., *Fathers and Heretics. Six Studies in Dogmatic Faith with Prologue and Epilogue*, (London: MacMillan 1958).

Previté-Orton C.W., *The Shorter Cambridge Medieval History Vols I-II*, (Cambridge: Cambridge University Press 1952).

Prigent P., L'Hérésie Asiate et l'Église confessante de l'Apocalypse à Ignace, in *VCh* 31 (1977), p. 1-22.

Rengstorf K.H., ΑΠΟΣΤΟΛΟΣ, in *TWNT*.

Rhode J., Häresie und Schisma im ersten Clemensbrief und in den Ignatius-Briefen, in *NT* 10 (1968) p. 214-217.

Rist M., Pseudepigraphy and Early Christian Literature, in D.E. Aune(ed.) *Studies in the New Testament and Early Christian Literature*, (Leiden: Brill 1972).

Rius-Camps J., *The Four Authentic Letters of Ignatius the Martyr*, (Rome: Pontificium Institutum Orientalium Studiorum 1980).

Roloff J., Apostel/ Apostolat/ Apostolizität, in *Theologische Realenzyklopädie* Band III, (Berlin: Walter de Gruyter 1978).

Sanders J.C.J., Autour de la Didascalie, in *A Tribute to Arthur Vööbus ed. R.A. Fisher*, (Chicago: Lutheran School of Theology 1977), p. 47-54.

Satake A., Die Gemeindeordnung in der Johannesapokalypse, in *WMANT* 21, (Neukirchen: Neukirchener Verlag 1966).

Sausser E., Tritt der Bishof an die Stelle Christus? Zur Frage nach der Stellung des Bischofs in der Theologie des hl. Ignatios von Antiocheia, in *Festschrift für Franz Loidl, ed. Viktor Flieder*, (Vienna: Hollinck 1970), p. 325-39.

Schillebeeckx E., *Ministry: A Case for Change,* (London: 1981).

Schoedel W., Are the Letters of Ignatius of Antioch Authentic? in *RelStRev* 6 (1980), p. 261-297.

——— , *Ignatius of Antioch*, (Philadelphia: Fortress 1985).

——— , Polycarp's Witness to Ignatius of Antioch, in *VCh* 41 (1978), p. 97-106.

Schöllgen G., The Didache as Church Order, in *JbAC* 29 (1986), p. 5-26.

Schmitals W., Das Kirchliche Apostelamt. Eine Historische Untersuchung, in *FRLANT* N.F. 61, (Göttingen: Vandenhoeck & Ruprecht 1961).

Schürer E., *The History of the Jewish People in the Age of Jesus*. (Ed.) G. Vermes, F. Millar, and M. Black, (Edinburgh: T.& T. Clark 1979), Vols 1 and 2.

Schüssler Fiorenza E., *The Book of Revelation: Justice and Judgment* , (Philadelphia: Fortress Press 1985).

Schweizer E., Der Johanneische Kirchenbegriff, in *TU.* 73 (1959), p. 263-268.

Sieben H.J., Die Ignatianen als Briefe: Einige formkritische Bemerkungen, in *VCh* 32 (1978), p. 1-18.

Simonsen H., The Gospel Literature as a Source for the History of Primitive Christianity, in *StTh* 37 (1983), p. 3-16.

Smit Sibinga J., Ignatius and Matthew, in *NT* 8 (1966), p. 262-283.

Snyder G.R., The Historical Jesus in the Letters of Ignatius of Antioch, in *BR* 8 (1963), p.3-12.

Speyer W., Die literarische Fälschung im heidnischen und christlichen Altertum, in *HA* 1 2 (München: C.H. Beck Verlag 1971).

Staats R., Die Martyrbegründung des Romprimats bei Ignatius von Antiochien, in *ZThK* 73 (1976), p. 461-470.

Stauffer E., Zum Kalifat des Jacobus, in *ZRGG* 4 (1952), p. 193-214.

Strecker G., Die Anfänge der Johanneischen Schule, in *NTS..* Vol. 32 (1986), p. 31-47.

Streeter B.H., *The Primitive Church*, (London: MacMillan 1929).

Swartley W.M., The Imitatio Christi in the Ignatian Letters, in *VCh* 27 (1973), p. 81-103.

Swete H.B.(Ed.), *Essays in the Early Church and Ministry*, (London: MacMillan 1918).

Telfer W., *The Office of a Bishop*, (London: Darton, Longman and Todd 1962).

Thurian M., L'Organisation du Ministère dans l'Église Primitive selon Saint Ignace d'Antioche, *VC* , 21 1967, p. 26-38.

Trevett C., Prophecy and Anti-Episcopal Activity: A Third Error Combatted by Ignatius? in *JEH* 34 (1983), p. 165-171.

Turner C.H., The Early Episcopal Lists, in *JThS* 1 (1899-1900), p. 181-200, and 529-53.

—— , The Early Episcopal Lists, in *JThS* 18 (1916-17), p. 103-134.

Turner H.E.W., *The Pattern of Christian Truth,* (Oxford: Bampton Lectures 1954).

Vogt H.J., Ignatius von Antiochien über den Bischof und seine Gemeinde, in *ThQ* 158 (1978), p. 18-19.

Vööbus A., *Liturgical Traditions in the Didache*, (Stockholm: Etze 1968).

Walter J.W. von, Ignatius von Antiochien und die Entstehung des Frühkatholizismus, in *(W. Koepp ed.) Reinhold Seeberg Festschrift. Vol. 12. Zur Praxis des Christentums,* (Leipzig: Deichert 1929), p. 105-118.

Wehr L., Artznei der Unsterblichkeit : die Eucharistie bei Ignatius von Antiochien und im Johannesevangelium, in *NA* N.F. 18, (Münster: Aschendorf 1987).

Winling R., A propos de la Datation des Lettres d'Ignace d'Antioche, in *RSR* 54 (1980), p. 259-265.

Young F., *From Nicaea to Chalcedon*, (London: S.C.M. 1983).

Zernov N., *Eastern Christendom: A Study in the Origin and Development of the Eastern Orthodox Church*, (London:Weidenfeld and Nicolson 1963).

Zollitsch R., *Amt und Funktion des Priesters: Eine Untersuchung zum Ursprung und zur Gestalt des Presbyterats in den ersten zwei Jahrhunderten*, (Freiburg: Herder 1974).

Zuckschwerdt E., Der Naziraat des Herrenbruders Jakobus nach Hegesippus, in *ZNW* 68 (1977, p. 276-87.

5. Contemporary Reports, and modern and post Reformation historical and theological studies

Abbott W.M., and Gallagher J., *The Documents of Vatican II*, (London: Geoffrey Chapman 1966).

Anglican- Roman Catholic International Commission, *The Final Report.*, (London: S.P.C.K. & C.T.S. 1981).

Baptism, Eucharist and Ministry, *Faith and Order Paper No. 111*, (Geneva: World Council of Churches 1982).

Brent A., Newman's Conversion, the *Via Media*, and the Myth of the Romeward Movement, in *DR* 345 (1983), p. 261-80.

—— , Newman and Perrone: Irreconcilable Theses on Development, in *DR* 349 (1984), p. 276-89.

—— , Newman's Moral Conversion, in *DR* 355 (1986), p. 79-94.

—— , The Hermesian Dimension to the Newman-Perrone Dialogue, in *EThL* 61 1 (1985), p.73-99.

——, The Crisis of Authority in the Anglican Communion, in *Women Priests in Austalia, the Anglican Crisis*, (Ed.) D. Wetherell, (Melbourne: Spectrum 1987), p. 1-20.

Cary K.M., *The Historic Episcopate in the Fullness of the Church. Seven Essays by Priests of the Church of England*, (London: Dacre 1954).

Chupungco A.J., *Towards a Philipino Liturgy*, (Manila 1976).

Clark F., *The Eucharistic Sacrifice and the Reformation*, (Devon: Augustine Publishing 1980).

Couraiyer P.F., *A Dissertation on the Validity of the Ordinations of the English*, (Oxford: Parker 1844), originally published March 14, 1724.

Halliburton J., *The Authority of a Bishop*, (London:S.P.C.K 1987).

Hughes J.J., *Absolutely Null and Utterly Void: The Papal Condemnation of Anglican Orders: 1896*, (London: Sheed and Ward 1968).

—— , *Stewards of the Lord: A Reappraisal of Anglican Orders*, (London: Sheed and Ward 1970).

Inter-Anglican Theological and Doctrinal Commission, *For the Sake of the Kingdom*, (London:Anglican Consultative Council 1986).

Jewel J., Apologia Ecclesiae Anglicanae, in *The Works of John Jewel: The Third Portion*, (Cambridge:Parker Society 1848).

Lambeth Conference 1988, *The Truth Shall Make You Free: Reports, Resolutions, and Pastoral Letters from the Bishops*, (London: Anglican Consultative Council 1988).

Lash N., *His Presence in the World*, (London: Sheed and Ward 1968).

—— , *Change in Focus: A Study of Doctrinal Change and Continuity*, (London: Sheed and Ward 1973).

—— , and Rhymer J., *The Christian Priesthood. 9th Downside Symposium*, (London: Darton, Longman and Todd 1970).

Llandaff Bishop of (Ed.), *Bishops*, (London: Faith Press 1961).

Leo XIII and the Archbishops of England, *Anglican Orders. (Apostolicae Curae and Saepius Officio)*, (London: Church Historical Society: S.P.C.K. 1953).

Palmer W., *The Apostolical Jurisdiction and Succession of the Episcopacy in the British Churches Vindicated*, (London: Rivington 1840).

Rahner K., *Theological Investigations*, trans. D. Bourke, Vols I-X, (New York: Herder 1971).

Robinson Archbis. J., Rogers M., and others, *Ordination*, (Sydney: Anglican Information Office 1978).

Seasoltz R.K., *New Liturgy, New Laws*, (Minnesota: Liturgical Press 1980).

Schillebeeckx E., *Christ the Sacrament*, (London: Sheed and Ward 1963).

Sykes S.W., *The Integrity of Anglicanism*, (London: Mowbrays 1978).

—— , (Ed.), *Authority in the Anglican Communion*, (Toronto: Anglican Book Centre 1987).

Wetherell D. (Ed.), *Women Priests in Australia? The Anglican Crisis*, (Melbourne: Spectrum 1987).

Wiseman N., *A Letter on Catholic Unity addressed to the Earl of Shrewsbury*, (London: 1841).

INDEX

1. SOURCES

Apoc.
  1,10-11 106
  1,16 108
  1,6 112
  1,8 112
  1,20 108
  2,1 106
  2,7 70, 112
  2,8 106
  2,12 106
  2,14 113
  2,18 106
  2,20 108, 113
  3,1 106
  3,7 106
  3,14 106
  4,1 113
  4,4 70, 112, 167
  4,9 116
  5 116
  5,1 116
  5,6 114
  5,7 116
  5,8 70, 116
  5,11 114
  5,11-12 114
  5,13 114
  5,14 114
  6,9 70, 112, 167
  6,16-17 114
  7 114, 167
  7,11-14 70, 114, 167
  7,17 114
  8,3 70, 112, 167
  8,3-6 167
  9 114
  10 114
  11 114
  13,18 115
  14 114
  14,2 70
  15 114
  15,2 70
  17 114
  17,8 115
  19 114

  19,4 114
  19,7 114
  21,19 70, 112
  22,1-3 114
  22,2 70, 112

Athanasius

Gent.
  26 81

Augustine

Ep.
  49 173
  194,31 173

Narr. in Psa.
  95,1 174

De Pecc. Mer. et Rem.
  1,24 174

Basil of Caesarea

Ep.197 179

Basil of Seleucia

Vitae Thecl.
  1 81, 84

Bede

H.E.
  III,3 177
  III,22 177
  IV,3 177

Clement of Rome

Cor.
  inscr. 109, 122
  44,1,4-6 13

2. NAMES OF AUTHORS

3. GREEK WORDS AND PHRASES

4. SUBJECTS

STUDIES IN
CHRISTIAN MISSION

E.J. BRILL — P.O.B. 9000 — 2300 PA Leiden — The Netherlands

STUDIES IN
CHRISTIAN MISSION

E.J. BRILL — P.O.B. 9000 — 2300 PA Leiden — The Netherlands